PIONEERS OF LATINO MINISTRY

Pioneers of Latino Ministry

Claretians and the Evolving World
of Catholic America

Deborah E. Kanter

NEW YORK UNIVERSITY PRESS
New York

NEW YORK UNIVERSITY PRESS
New York
www.nyupress.org

© 2025 by New York University
All rights reserved

Please contact the Library of Congress for Cataloging-in-Publication data.

ISBN: 9781479832484 (hardback)
ISBN: 9781479832538 (library ebook)
ISBN: 9781479832521 (consumer ebook)

This book is printed on acid-free paper, and its binding materials are chosen for strength and durability. We strive to use environmentally responsible suppliers and materials to the greatest extent possible in publishing our books.

The manufacturer's authorized representative in the EU for product safety is Mare Nostrum Group B.V., Mauritskade 21D, 1091 GC Amsterdam, The Netherlands. Email: gpsr@mare-nostrum.co.uk.

Manufactured in the United States of America

10 9 8 7 6 5 4 3 2 1

Also available as an ebook

To the people who accompany and
to Dan who accompanies me

CONTENTS

List of Figures   ix

Foreword   xi
     ROSENDO URRABAZO CMF

Abbreviations   xiii

Introduction   1

1. Following the Mexicans: Farmworkers, *Mineros*, and *Traqueros*   21

2. Building Urban Parishes: *Refugios* and Spaces of
   Catholic Americanization   48

3. Communicating in Two Languages: Race and the Emergence
   of the US Province   76

4. Working in the Shadows of Empire: Missions in Panama
   and Guatemala   101

5. Re-Imagining Mission: Challenges and Opportunities in the
   Wake of Vatican II   130

Conclusion   161

Acknowledgments   175

*Appendix: Claretian-Administered Mission Churches
by County in South Central Texas, ca. 1903–20*   179

Note on Sources   181

Notes   185

Selected Bibliography   205

Index   213

About the Author   225

LIST OF FIGURES

Figure I.1 Lay pilgrims, Cordi-Marian sisters, and Claretian priests, Italy, May 1950. On the right, Fr. Severino Lopez   3

Figure I.2 Worldwide Claretian Missions, from 1952 commemorative album *Claretians in America*   12

Figure I.3 Claretian communities in the United States, 1952   15

Figure 1.1 Immaculate Heart of Mary Mission, Martindale, Texas, likely 1919   32

Figure 1.2 Immaculate Heart of Mary Mission and School, Martindale, Texas, 1925   33

Figure 1.3 Claretian houses and mission churches in South Central Texas counties, ca. 1903–20   35

Figure 2.1 Ushers, Immaculate Heart of Mary Church, San Antonio, 1934   55

Figure 2.2 Celebration following Fr. Robert Alvarado's first Mass at Immaculate Heart of Mary Church, San Antonio, 1939   56

Figure 2.3 Children in summer program with Fr. Thomas Matin, Perth Amboy, New Jersey, n.d.   68

Figure 3.1 Meeting of Provincial Chapter, 1935   81

Figure 3.2 Postcard, St. Jude Seminary, n.d.   88

Figure 3.3 St. Jude Seminary basketball team, 1950s   91

Figure 4.1 Panama: Claretian residences, ca. 1940   103

Figure 4.2 Bishop Joseph Preciado with children, Panama, 1935   104

Figure 4.3 Guatemala: Diocese of Izabal and Claretian missions, ca. 1970   115

Figure 4.4 Frs. Greg Zimmerman, Anthony Briskey, and Roger
Bartlett, Guatemala, 1966. Photo by Edward Lettau   117

Figure 4.5 Fr. Edmundo Andrés celebrating liturgy at an aldea,
Santo Tomás de Castilla, Guatemala, n.d.   127

Figure 5.1 Ordination invitation, 1978   131

Figure 5.2 Claretian Religious in the United States, 1902–2020   137

Figure 5.3 Vocation ad, *U.S. Catholic*, 1969   139

Figure 5.4 Henry Hererra drawing, n.d.   156

Figure 5.5 St. Anthony Mary Claret, St. John the Evangelist
Church, San Marcos, Texas   158

FOREWORD

ROSENDO URRABAZO CMF

The congregation of Missionaries Sons of the Immaculate Heart of Mary, more commonly known as Claretian Missionaries, came to the United States in 1902 from Mexico at the request of a Catholic bishop in south Texas. We are called Claretians after our founder, St. Anthony Mary Claret, who began the order in Spain in 1849. Deborah Kanter, an expert in the history of Mexican immigration to the United States, has written extensively on the role the Catholic Church played in attending to the needs of Spanish-speaking peoples already in the United States and the many who have come into this country since the establishment of a southern border.

Spanish-speaking missionaries were asked to come here because they knew this growing population's language, customs, and religion. This book offers a brief synopsis of the story of one of those groups of missionaries. Kanter paints the story with broad strokes of her pen, providing the social, cultural, and political backgrounds that existed at the turn of the last century and the subsequent decades as the Claretians navigated the complex and contradictory situations of the United States during this period. She also focuses on particular people and places to present vivid examples of the men who called themselves Claretians and the many people who worked with them in helping to integrate the dialogue of cultures taking place.

Virgil Elizondo described the culture clash between Spaniards and Natives of Mexico as "the painful birth of a new people." Kanter documents a similar emergence of a new American face that some call Mexican-Americans. We are part of that larger Latino/Hispanic group now known in the United States as Latinx. The hyphen is not a diminishment in identity but the proud proclamation that immigrants do not come here empty-handed; the languages, customs, and cultures of immigrant groups make America richer in its diversity.

Kanter does not offer an idealized portrait of the missionaries but, from the available evidence, portrays men of their times who did their best to accompany people on the move; men who, like the people they served, were searching for a place to call home. Together, they joined the many thousands of indigenous and Spanish-speaking peoples already here since the Spanish colonization. Documenting the story of the missionaries can only be done by also telling the story of the people they came to serve. We are all grateful to Deborah Kanter for writing this book and helping us see ourselves and this amazing story through her eyes.

Rosendo Urrabazo, CMF
Provincial Superior, Claretian Missionaries of the United States-Canada Province, 2014–23

ABBREVIATIONS

ARCHSA Catholic Archdiocese of San Antonio Archives

CMAC Claretian Missionaries Archives USA-Canada

IHM Immaculate Heart of Mary Church (San Antonio) Papers, in CMAC

OLF Our Lady of Fatima Church (Perth Amboy) Papers, in CMAC

OLG Our Lady of Guadalupe Church (Chicago) Papers, in CMAC

PAFPL Perth Amboy Free Public Library

PB *Bulletin of USA Province*, in CMAC

PB-E *Bulletin of East Province*, in CMAC

PB-W *Bulletin of West Province*, in CMAC

SJS St. Jude Seminary Papers, in CMAC

VSJ *Voice of St. Jude*, in CMAC

Introduction

The Claretian missionaries have kept the faith alive among the Spanish-speaking people whether it be in the wild fields of Texas, the dry deserts of Arizona, the uncultivated gardens of California or frozen plains of Illinois.
—*Claretians in America* (1952)

Dawn, Sunday, May 7, 1950, in Rome. Barely light in the Holy City. Carmen Hernández of Los Angeles, in her smartest suit and heels, made her way along the cobbled streets, in the company of her roommate Isabel Álvarez and a small group of American pilgrims. As their group fell into a steady stream of visitors heading to St. Peter's Square, her nerves gave way to excitement. She entered the massive square; amazed, she scanned the colonnades and the Egyptian obelisk at the center. St. Peter's Basilica loomed ahead. As the sun rose, Carmen took in the growing crowd around her: plenty of Italians, but also a surprising number of Spanish men and women speaking the lispy *castellano* familiar to her from the parish priests at home. Sisters in a wide range of habits, monks in dark robes, and priests in black cassocks, talked among themselves in German, French, and other unfamiliar languages. Soon her group merged with hundreds of Catholics from Washington, DC, led by their monsignor. Carmen's cluster felt a special claim on the day's main event: the canonization of Anthony Mary Claret, the Spanish priest and founder of the Claretian Missionaries. The Claretians, after all, were their pastors, confessors, shrine directors, baseball coaches, and more back home in Los Angeles, San Antonio, Chicago, and beyond.

Here in Rome, against all odds, humble Carmen found herself in this well-dressed, polyglot sea of the faithful—this was the Universal Church. Wait, was that Hollywood actress Irene Dunne? The doors opened and the river of Catholic people poured into the vast basilica. Hours later Pope Pius XII declared, "We decree and define as a saint and

we inscribe in the catalog of saints Blessed Antonio Maria Claret, or-
daining that, his memory be celebrated with devotion every year in the
universal Church." Finally, the Pope called out "Saint Anthony Claret,
pray for us!"[1]

As the Roman sun beat down that afternoon, the priests and brothers
of the Missionary Sons of the Immaculate Heart of Mary, or the Claretians, gathered for a group portrait on the steps of St. Peter's.* Some
five hundred Claretians gradually formed twenty rows. Mostly trained
in Spanish seminaries, the men now lived dispersed in Chile and Brazil,
Germany and Portugal, England and the United States. Long-lost classmates shouted greetings in Spanish, with more than a few in Catalan or
Basque (*euskerra*). Forty-seven-year-old Fr. Joaquin De Prada had not
seen these now middle-aged men since he left Spain for California as
a young man. Fully bilingual in English and Spanish, he had spent his
adulthood at Claretian-run parishes in southern California and Texas.
He currently directed the National Shrine of St. Jude: the patron saint
of impossible causes known to Catholics throughout the country. De
Prada's global confreres recognized the vigor of his adopted American
province (a geographic region), headed by a provincial superior appointed by the Claretian superior general in Rome. The US province
oversaw parishes in five states, a house of studies in Washington, DC,
and seminaries producing a steady crop of American Claretians. Two
of these, Fr. Louis Bossi, a vocation from San Antonio, and Fr. Severino
Lopez, from Chicago, squeezed into the rows of Spaniards for the photo.
Elena Flores, a young española from Córdoba, was pulled into one of the
pictures. Flores suffered from a partial paralysis of her body for years.
She prayed with a relic from Blessed Anthony Claret in 1948 and she was
cured, so providing the necessary second miracle to make the case for
Claret's sainthood. Dressed plainly in black, Flores beamed at the cam-
era, radiating her recovered health and joy at public recognition of St.
Claret. Her sturdy son grasped the hand of a healthy woman. The priests
and brothers gathered again that evening for a celebratory feast, presided by the bishops of La Paz, Bolivia, Spanish West Africa, Alicante,
Spain, and Darién, Panama: all Claretians.[2]

---

* Priests and brothers named throughout the book are all Claretian Missionaries, unless otherwise
designated. To avoid repetition, I have left out CMF, the letters that stand for *Cordis Mariae Filis*, or
Son of the Heart of Mary.

Figure 1.1 Lay pilgrims, Cordi-Marian sisters, and Claretian priests, Italy, May 1950. On the right, Fr. Severino Lopez. Source: Claretian Missionaries Archives USA-Canada.

With the canonization complete, the lay pilgrims and many of the Claretians toured Rome together. They filled buses that wound their way through the hill towns, stopping at Assisi and Florence. Fr. Lopez, the thirty-two-year-old son of Mexican immigrants, marveled at the sights. Aboard trains, he and the other Claretians crowded around a small table, enjoying wine, sandwiches, and tiny cups of coffee. During these traveling picnics, he took in the older Claretians' jokes and stories, told in a mix of Spanish and English. In front of the Hotel Santa Lucia, the pilgrims paused for a group portrait with their tour bus. Joined by three Cordi-Marian sisters and seven Claretians, the mostly female and middle-aged pilgrims proudly wore their medals, signaling their attendance at the Claret canonization. Lopez playfully posed atop the bus's front fender, while Fr. Patrick McPolin, age thirty-four, also an early vocation from Chicago, hung out the front door, sporting a pair of dark sunglasses. In Rome and elsewhere, McPolin carried a copy of *The Voice of St. Jude*, the monthly magazine published by the Claretians; with a designated photographer at the ready, he planned to create a "picture pilgrimage" for the tens of thousands of subscribers when he returned to Chicago.

The lay pilgrims had spent weeks with the Claretian guides. A week after the canonization, half the group departed for London and Ireland, with their travels including time to visit family there. The other pilgrims traveled to Lourdes, where their own Fr. De Prada celebrated a Mass at the miraculous grotto, replete with an array of crutches and braces, a testimony from the healed. This group continued into Spain, visiting sites associated with Claret, and even had a solemn audience with the *caudillo* Francisco Franco—no one smiled in those photos. Time spent in Spain provided the Spanish Claretians who missioned abroad a long-awaited opportunity to see friends and family.[3] The group then pushed on to Fátima in Portugal. The pilgrims acquired relics in the forms of holy cards, medals, crucifixes, and filigree brooches. The travelers would give these artifacts, one by one, to family, friends, and parishioners, spreading these popular devotions from Fátima, Lourdes, and especially of St. Anthony Claret. Many displayed their medals on a small home altar, remembering, for decades, that once-in-a-lifetime experience of witnessing the canonization.[4]

"Go on foot, like Jesus": Claret's Life and Legacy

Who was Claret? Why did the congregation that took his name find him so inspirational? Antonio María Claret (1807–70) was a priest from Catalonia, devoted to mission work, named archbishop of Santiago, Cuba, and then Confessor to the Queen of Spain. In 1849, he joined a few other priests "to whom God had communicated the same Spirit as my own" in creating a male religious order dedicated to mission work and Marian devotion, especially the Immaculate Heart of Mary. Claret believed that "the virtue an apostolic missionary needs most of all is love." He saw the Virgin Mary as "the primary exemplar of the love of God." His emphasis on the Immaculate Heart of Mary arose out of the confraternity so named in Paris in 1836. Claret transplanted the new devotion in Catalonia and Cuba.[5] He sailed to his post in Cuba in 1850, leaving the emerging congregation to others.[6] Myriad biographies of Claret exist in English, Spanish, and other languages, in addition to Claret's autobiography (drafted ca. 1861–62). A Spanish-made film *Esclavos y Reyes* (*Slaves and Kings*) brought Claret's life to movie screens in 2022. In these writings, facts, legend, myth, reinterpretations, and miraculous incidents commingle.

Certain words surface repeatedly in Claret's autobiography: prayer, obedience, publications, preaching, the Virgin Mary, poverty, generosity, abstinence, and (avoidance of) politics. Claret began his story winningly, with memories of his innocent, inherently devout childhood in his Catalan village, Sallent. He moved to Barcelona as a teen to enhance his contributions to the family's weaving business. There Claret encountered an urban, modernizing world full of temptations, conniving strangers, politics, and the "formidable giant of modern greed." Claret soon went from pursuit of a personal spiritual devotion to the commitment of priesthood, dedicated to helping save others for eternity, or *siempre*, a term that he fixated on as a boy. As a parish priest, he toyed with joining the Jesuits, whom he admired for their missionary aims and rigor. Claret felt bound to obey his superiors, the bishops, but eventually gained their approval to conduct missions within his diocese and nearby. As he stressed, "let missionaries understand from this that they should not go to any town . . . except under obedience."[7] Claret looked beyond parish boundaries with short-term missions to engage people with fiery preaching, hands-on teaching of catechism to children and adults, and holding retreats. His tactics drew from time-tested practices by Catholic Reformation priests, especially of missionary orders.

In a more modern method, Claret championed the potential of what he called "good books," or devotional publications. Early in my research in the Claretian Missionaries Archives (CMAC), I noticed two tall bookcases filled with hundreds of old books. The colors and leather bindings suggested these volumes dated back to the nineteenth century. I pulled out a small book, a bit larger than a deck of playing cards. The soft brown leather cover gave way to the title page: a collection of short moral writings (*opúsculos*) by *Reverendo* Antonio Claret, published in Barcelona in 1849. Miniatures of Jesus and Mary, angels, and female saints frame the page. At the center-bottom, a tiny, black-robed Fr. Claret ministers to children. These detailed scenes of piety and paternal guidance reflect the volume's contents: *Avisos útiles a varias clases.*[8] Claret directed his words to specific classes of readers: fathers, married women, widows, and children. He gently warned his nineteenth-century readers about the evils of dances, laziness, sensuality, and bad books (*malos libros*). In this exemplary good book, Claret addressed his readers conversationally, paternally, and with a strong dose of moralizing throughout. Several volumes of opuscules followed. He reportedly wrote 144 books. As the archive's crowded bookshelves show, Claret certainly had readers in his time.[9]

Claret's exemplary actions stood as a model for his confreres and other readers. Boys and girls, women and men, sinners and struggling Catholics all witnessed his commitment to a life of chosen poverty, generosity, and abstinence. Consider Claret's approach to transportation. In an era of expanding railroads, the missionary chose to walk wherever possible: "Go on foot, like Jesus, or with an ass."[10]

Claret lived, preached, and wrote through turbulent times. Struggles between anti-clerical, anti-monarchical actors and more traditional institutions rocked mid-nineteenth century Spain, and its colony, Cuba. As his aura grew as a holy man (enhanced by his reputed healing skills), churches overfilled when he preached; his missions moved into open plazas. While Claret repeatedly penned "not one word of politics escaped my lips," he could not escape the mounting antagonism toward the institutional church. Strangers physically attacked him fourteen times. In Cuba, a stranger swiped Archbishop Claret with a razor, from his left ear to his chin, leaving him covered in blood. After commending himself to the Virgin Mary, Claret recalled instant healing. In his autobiography's later chapters, he called out the era's "enemies": Protestantism and Communism.[11]

In 1869, the year before his death, Claret attended the First Vatican Council, where he impressed the American James Cardinal Gibbons (who supposedly declared, "There goes a true saint"). That same year, Claret's small congregation sent its first members overseas to the Americas, specifically to Chile. He prophesized, "more souls will be saved for Heaven under the skies of America than under that of Europe."[12]

Claret's words, example, and physical image lived on among the expanding Claretian congregation after his death in 1870. Just a handful of founding priests had an idealistic if vague vision of a new missionary order. In 1849, Fr. Claret prophetically told his confreres, "you will see. Yes, we are few, and God's power will shine."[13] The Claretians took a vow of poverty, lived in community together (but were not cloistered), regularly engaged in spiritual exercises, and devoted themselves to preaching in Claret's model, acting without the constraints of bishops and diocesan structures. They wore basic clerical garb, collar and cassock, but not visually distinctive compared to other orders such as the Franciscans. The small band established their first of many seminaries in Catalonia in 1861. They devoted themselves to training a cadre of missionaries with schools throughout Spain. By century's end, the Claretians ministered in seven countries with nearly 1,800 members. Claret's visage hung on the walls at Claretian seminaries and residences, first in Spain and then in South America, Africa, Mexico, and, after 1902, in the United States. Following his beatification in 1934, Blessed Antonio María Claret's likeness became the center of altars in Claretian-run parishes in a dozen countries. Priests and brothers gave away holy cards with his image; the verso bore a prayer in Spanish, English, Catalan, or the local language. This excerpt from the *Autobiography*'s English translation embodies the Claretians' charism:

> A son of the Immaculate Heart of Mary is one who is on fire with love of God, who spreads this fire wherever he goes, and who ardently desires and procures by all possible means to inflame the whole world with the fire of divine love. Nothing daunts him; he takes pleasure in privations, accepts all labors, embraces all sacrifices, cheerfully welcomes all calumnies, and rejoices in every torment. His only thoughts are how he can follow and imitate Jesus Christ in all his labors and sufferings, and how he can best procure the greater glory of God and the salvation of souls.[14]

For the Claretian seminarians in the United States, for Spanish priests and brothers far from home, Claret remained—and remains—a powerful example.

Fr. Michael Castillon, among others, embodied this legacy. Upon this Spanish-born priest's death in San Antonio in 1947, a fellow Claretian recalled his "avowed devotion to our Founder." In decades of ministry in Mexico and the United States, Castillon, "while not abandoning the old, wanted to follow our Father Founder's eminently modern bent, which aimed at saving souls by all means possible."[15] This veteran missionary would have rejoiced over Claret's canonization just a few years after his passing.

Making a Name for Claret and Claretian Missionaries

Few Americans had even heard of Claret or the Claretians when the first two missionaries arrived in the United States in 1902, barely able to communicate in English. The Claretian newcomers demonstrated energy and vision as they plunged into ministry to the poor, to immigrants, and particularly to the Mexican population. As that population moved to urban areas, they established parishes in Arizona, California, and Illinois and eventually across the country.

Indeed, the Claretians pioneered Latino ministry in the United States. Especially because they were native Spanish speakers, they became particularly involved with Latino communities, though they also ministered to other groups. When those first Claretians arrived in the United States, Spanish-speaking Catholics were barely recognized by the church. But today, Latinos make up about half of US Catholics. For this reason, the influence of the Claretians has been felt among the American Catholic population as a whole, given the high proportion of US Catholics who have been connected to the Claretians.

The Claretians have played a significant role in the development of Catholicism in the United States, establishing seminaries, developing popular Catholic magazines, and fostering a now widespread devotion to St. Jude. While several religious congregations today offer culturally sensitive ministries with Spanish speakers and their families, the Claretians were first, and on a near-national level. The Spanish-speaking Claretians were able to nurture developing communities when local dioceses and other religious orders could not. They cultivated respect and dignity for Latino people in regions where the wider society marginalized them. Because they encouraged education and leadership within their parishes, a significant number of Latinos emerged from these parishes to lead and contribute to the shaping of US Catholic life as priests, female religious, deacons, and lay leaders.

Beyond churchwalls, Claretian missionaries have advocated for the rights of immigrants, workers, and the poor. For example, Cesar Chavez and the United Farm Workers (UFW) organized out of a Claretian church basement in East Los Angeles. In cities across the country they have defended neighborhoods in the face of deindustrialization, urban renewal, and depopulation. This book makes the case that understanding the Claretians is important to understanding Latino Catholicism and Latino Catholic life, as well as the history of American Catholicism more broadly.

Catholics far beyond Claretian parishes came to know Claret's name and story over time. The congregation promoted his exemplary life to English speakers especially after his beatification in 1934. In 1944, Fr. Louis Moore translated Claret's autobiography to English; the Claretians soon published it. Now their founder's life story was readily accessible to American seminarians who otherwise struggled through Spanish grammars. The *Autobiography* was a ready-made gift for bishops and cardinals who might hasten the canonization cause when the time was right. Catholic historian and poet Daniel Sargent certainly read the translated *Autobiography* before writing his book, *The Assignments of Antonio Claret* (1948).[16] As the Catholic Book Club selection for January 1949, thousands of subscribers received the laudatory biography of Claret in the mail that month. (For context, the book club selected books by Thomas Merton, Willa Cather, and Graham Greene in 1948. Selections in 1950 included Fulton Sheen and Von Trapp.) Catholic libraries across North America acquired Sargent's biography. "The faithful often see in their holy heroes what they want to see about themselves," writes Kathleen Sprows Cummings in her thoughtful take on the campaign for American saints.[17] In Sargent's telling, Communists constantly attempted to undermine Claret. This view resonated with many readers in the Cold War era. After the canonization, the Claretians dedicated their newest parish to St. Anthony Claret, making the name familiar to people, Mexican and others, in Fresno, California.

Most Claretians in the United States did not go to Rome, busy as they were administering parishes and running seminaries. They, and the tens of thousands of laypeople associated with them, experienced Claret's canonization in a variety of ways. Their parishioners took part in celebratory Masses, often graced by the local bishop; they decorated the new saint's altar. At home many people read about Claret in the Claretian magazines, seated at kitchen tables or in the living room.

A wider swath of Americans learned about the new saint on the radio. On the eve of the canonization, Saturday, May 6, people tuned their radio dials to the local NBC affiliate for a star-studded tribute to St. Anthony Claret. Listeners first heard bells ringing and organ music, then a resounding introduction: "The Claretian Missionary Fathers, in cooperation with the National Broadcasting Company, bring you a program commemorating the canonization tomorrow of their founder, Anthony Claret." The half-hour program featured well-regarded actors, popular singers, Catholic leaders from both coasts, as well as the Dominguez Seminary Choir. Bishop Timothy Manning of Los Angeles, with a lightly Irish-inflected tongue, reverentially outlined Claret's life. Actor Pat O'Brien delivered Cardinal Francis Spellman's lengthy tribute to Claret in a poem, "God's Wine." The New York cardinal exalted Claret, ending with "So heaven's Queen smiled down upon Claret. And whispered to the Christ, 'Here is indeed, My son, your richest wine!'" Young Hollywood stars Ricardo Montalbán, June Haber, and Roddy McDowell each retold a dramatic episode from Claret's life. Veteran stage and screen actor Pedro De Cordoba transported listeners to the jubilant scene soon to unfold in Rome. "The bells of the Vatican Basilica give the signal and bells of all the churches in Rome announce the glad news— they carry the news over the hills . . . over the whole earth!" With a thespian flourish, De Cordoba declared, "Saint Anthony Claret! Saint Anthony Claret!" The organ swelled and brought the program to a triumphant finish. This radio broadcast marked the Claretians' boldest effort to publicize their founder and their congregation's presence in the United States.[18]

La Esperanza, the Claretians' Spanish-language weekly paper, also drew attention to the new saint. The paper featured Claret's biography in weekly installments over months. We can glimpse some popular devotion to the new saint in the published endorsements of Claret's intercession. Readers learned how Señora Eusebia H. Rocha, of Maxwell, Texas, found herself with an untreatable illness. Yet when she held a Claret relic, she was miraculously cured. Carmen Hernández, our intrepid pilgrim, had so wanted to make this trip, but unable to raise the funds, "she fervently entrusted herself to Saint Anthony Mary Claret, who granted her a true miracle, being able to attend the canonization in Rome." Señora Irene de Sotelo, of Los Angeles, worried about her three unemployed children. She took part in a novena for the new saint and "as if by miracle all three found jobs at the same time." Spanish-speaking subscribers to *La Esperanza*, took in these testimonies of Claret's miraculous powers for his devotees, alongside more familiar testimonials about the Virgin of Guadalupe and the Virgin of San Juan de los Lagos.[19] The stores that sold religious articles in some Claretian parishes, for example La Placita in Los Angeles, sold small Claret relics.

The events surrounding the canonization spotlight the Claretians at their prime—a vigorous, growing congregation that served Latino Catholics, but also reached a wider Catholic America in a variety of ministries. The event likewise highlights the Claretians' Spanish roots and their increasingly international composition, including a growing number of American-born members, including Mexican American clergy. The Claretians' celebration of the new saint integrated the diverse laity to whom they ministered in the United States. Carmen Hernández, likely a parishioner and barrio dweller of modest means, found a place alongside the Claretians. Back in the US, the Claretians constantly interacted with the laity, learning ways both American and Mexican.

In 1952, the Claretians celebrated their golden jubilee: fifty years of Claretian Missionaries in the United States. The province began more as an accident than a plan. Entering Texas in 1902 as itinerant missioners, they soon accepted the call to administer a single parish, San Fernando Cathedral in San Antonio. At the time the United States still held its status as a Vatican-designated "mission country." Even when the designation was withdrawn in 1908, bishops with growing Latin American flocks would beckon the Spanish missionaries for decades.[20] In 1920, Bishop Henry Granjon of Tucson implored, "You speak the language of these poor people. Come and preach to them."[21] When the US province was established in 1922, the Claretians claimed nine houses, or communities. In 1952, the Claretians proudly counted twenty-six houses across the country, where three hundred members lived and worked. They had come a long way in five decades.

The golden jubilee left a remarkable time capsule: a two-hundred-page souvenir book, *Claretians in America 1902–1952*. The gold-tone cover was emblazoned with the Claretians' coat of arms, harking back to Claret and before, to medieval Spain's fight for Christianity. The Claretian editors assembled the volume entirely in English, thus firmly planting the Claretians in an American present and future. (The US *Provincial Bulletin* still contained many submissions in Spanish at that time.) Bishops nationwide, from Gallup to Joliet, penned tribute letters. ("Here in Chicago they have been a mighty help.") The editors

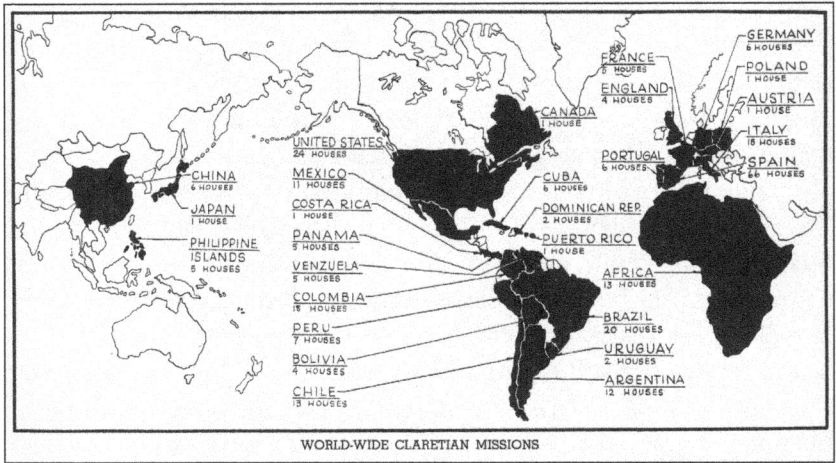

WORLD-WIDE CLARETIAN MISSIONS

Figure 1.2 Worldwide Claretian Missions, from the 1952 commemorative album *Claretians in America*. Source: Claretian Missionaries Archives USA-Canada.

triumphantly cataloged accomplishments in this country; abundant black and white photos illustrated their achievements. Due to the Claretians' efforts, a hundred churches had been erected—beginning with "Pioneer Work" in Texas to barrios in Chicago and Los Angeles (not counting dozens overseas). With strong promotion of devotion to St. Jude, their ministry reached tens of thousands, from Chicago's police officers to pious women across the Midwest and Northeast. The American flag flew at the entrance to Claretian seminaries in California and Illinois "to inspire the best American traditions." There young men trained for the priesthood, many of whom hoped to serve in the Claretians' own missions in Panama, Japan, and the Philippines. Priests became historians by preserving the historic missions at San Gabriel and San Fernando. Claretians followed Claret's model by creating American publications, in English and in Spanish, to further their apostolate wherever they could. Radio broadcasts in Spanish and English drew listeners in Texas, Chicago, and California. In time they would add pamphlets, cassette tapes, and podcasts to their ministry. Priests and brothers promoted devotion to the Immaculate Heart of Mary with lovely images, archconfraternities, and novenas wherever they ministered. The Claretians impacted a tremendous number of people in the United States at mid-century. *Claretians in America* must have impressed the local bishops, prospective donors, civic leaders, and Claretian leadership in Rome.

A map of worldwide Claretian missions, ranging from South America, Europe, the Philippines, and Africa, demonstrates the group's rapid rise and expansion in the United States. Spain, the congregation's birthplace, maintained sixty-six houses. The United States, in second place numerically, had twenty-four houses: an impressive number given the American province's short history.

Telling the Claretians' Story Today

Impressive though it was, the 1952 commemorative book *Claretians in America* neglected a crucial piece of their rise: the role of lay men and women in building, sometimes literally, Claretian parishes, seminaries, and missions.[22] Historian James O'Toole invites us to reimagine US Catholic history "as a story of its people—the Faithful, the laity—rather than its leaders and institutions."[23] This book puts the Claretian Missionaries and Latino laity, both understudied, into the same frame. In contrast to most histories of Catholic religious, I bring laypeople to the fore where relevant. The Claretians were intimately linked to the Mexican and other Latino people they served. They carried out missions and created parishes in marginalized communities whose histories deserve telling. Claretian sources offer windows into Latino life in many places: from Arizona mines to Chicago's steel barrio, from Oregon farms to New Jersey's factory towns.

I argue that laypeople and Claretians worked together to foster strong foundations, identities, and voices for Latino Catholics. The Claretians' accompaniment of Hispanic Catholics stands out as a continuity in more than 120 years of work in the United States. That said, since their arrival, a subset of Claretians proved uneasy with their mission's concentration on Hispanic ministry. Too often individual Claretians held notions of racial difference and hierarchy (for example, white/European/Spaniard versus mixed race/indigenous/Mexican) that fueled a prolonged, fundamental ambivalence about the congregation's purpose in the United States. Some priests picked up these understandings of race during their time working in Mexico. Others arriving from Spain sought to align themselves with white American Catholics, so taking on judgmental attitudes about the *católicos* they served. The majority of Claretians, however, demonstrated a fundamental sense of empathy and connection with their Latino flock.

The Claretians' efforts embody the many meanings of "mission": from preaching in a storefront chapel or a railroad camp, building multilayered parishes for adults and children, strengthening Catholic life in disrupted countries, and speaking out for farmworkers and undocumented immigrants. When the Claretians arrived, Spanish speakers constituted a small, often unrecognized—and frequently maligned—part of Catholic America. Today, as noted earlier, Latinos constitute half of US Catholics. The Claretian Missionaries pioneered Latino ministry across the United States, with vibrant parishes from Los Angeles to New Jersey, from San Antonio to Chicago. With their Spanish language skills and familiarity with Latin American faith, devotion, and needs, Claretians proved essential to the rise of Latino Catholicism.

This book is the first scholarly treatment of the Claretian Missionaries in the United States. Until now, the Claretians have received passing treatment by a few historians of religion, including myself. These works have focused on a specific location, devotion, or individual.[24] The Claretians themselves attempted a book-length history in the mid-twentieth century, but a narrative history of the US province is long overdue.

Telling the Claretian story offers an opportunity to explore the energetic, evolving world of Catholic America in a way that centers Latinos. Only a few published works focus on the history of Latinos and the Catholic Church.[25] This book offers a kaleidoscopic view as the Claretians encountered movie stars and Chicago police officers, collaborated with exiled Mexican sisters and American bishops, and nurtured devotion to St. Jude as well as athletics for Mexican American youth. Crucially, the once foreign Claretians educated men—Latino and Euro-American—to form American-reared Claretian missionaries ready to serve the continuous arrival of Latin Americans to churches here.

Claret's canonization in 1950 and attendant celebrations showcased the Claretians at their apogee in the United States, as they staffed dozens of mostly Latino parishes throughout the country and trained hundreds of young men at seminaries and novitiates. The canonization generated a bonanza of sources about the Claretians and the people affiliated with them.

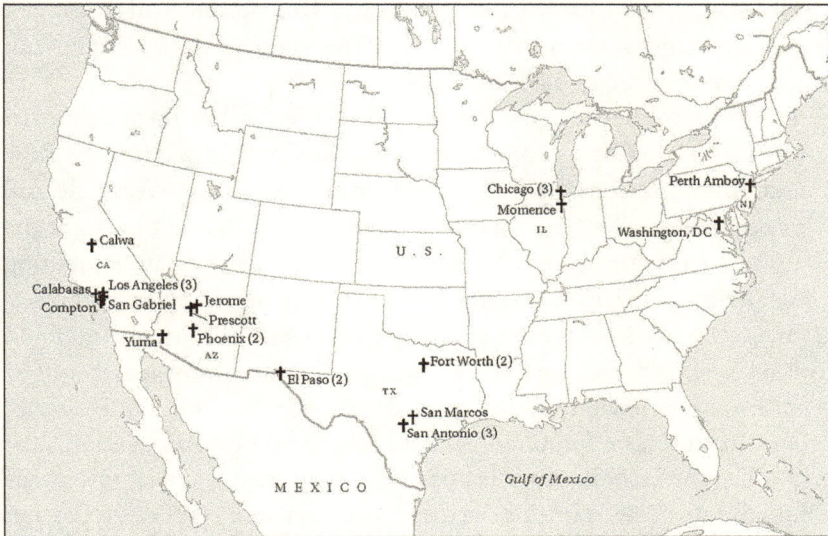

Figure 1.3 Claretian communities in the United States, 1952. The province also maintained communities in the Philippines (five), Panama (eight), and one each in England, Japan, and Canada. Map by Molly O'Halloran.

Chapter 1 charts the Claretians' first weeks and years in the United States as they, themselves immigrants, followed Mexican immigrants as they sought work and created communities. Many Spanish-born priests and brothers first served in Mexico prior to arrival. Here they attended to underserved communities, from isolated ranches to impoverished barrios. As Spanish speakers familiar with Latin American faith, devotion, and needs, the Claretians were ready for Latino ministry. This chapter explores the religious life of Mexican immigrants and Mexican Americans in an array of locales: the cotton fields of Texas, the mines in Arizona, the railroad yards in Kansas, and a munitions plant in Tennessee. The Claretian Missionaries and the Mexican people found common ground in the Catholic faith and rituals. Collaborating with Mexican laity, the missionaries established many dozens of missions and formal parishes throughout the Southwest by the 1920s. The early twentieth century proved a challenging time for Catholic missionary work. In an era of anti-Catholic and anti-Mexican attitudes and actions in the Southwest, the Claretians persisted in the face of Anglo hostilities. The itinerancy of this period, which aligned with Claret's missionary drive, would wane as the Claretians grew into an unexpected role as parish priests.

As Mexicans settled into cities, bishops requested these Spanish-speaking missionaries for their dioceses. Chapter 2 explores how Claretian-administered parishes arose in San Antonio's West Side and Chicago before 1930. A growing Puerto Rican settlement brought the Claretians to Perth Amboy, New Jersey, where they oversaw something new: a truly pan-Latino parish of people from several Caribbean nations. Newcomers from Mexico and the Spanish Caribbean sought and found *refugio* in these parishes, but further gained respectability as members of these US Catholic parishes. These parishes became sites of refuge for immigrant adults—with homilies and novenas in Spanish—and spaces of Catholic Americanization—with their scout troops, parochial schools, Holy Name Society, sports teams, and Halloween parties. Claretian parishes served as a glue that connected immigrant parents and their US-reared children. Building urban parishes offered opportunities for lay leadership and these refuge-parishes became home for multiple generations in the United States.

Chapter 3 shows how the Claretians communicated in two languages to create a wide support network and to foment devotions among Latino and Anglo Catholics. While the Spanish language was essential in the Claretians' work, the early Spanish-born leaders also learned English, sought American citizenship, and established connection with larger Catholic networks in their new country in order to best advocate for the Mexican laity. The Claretians' linguistic and cultural savvy proved indispensable as they pioneered Latino ministry across the nation.

Building support among English-speaking Catholics had unanticipated results, as emerges in the story of the Claretian-sponsored St. Jude devotion. Mostly Euro-American pilgrims made their way by train and bus to "St. Jude's" (based in South Chicago's Our Lady of Guadalupe Church). Others mailed in prayers and donations as a national following arose. Chicago's Catholic-dominated police department organized a fraternal and devotional St. Jude Police League. These Claretian-aligned police officers funded a seminary near Chicago that recruited mainly Euro-American youth to become future Claretians. The seminary recruited boys by offering a future as *missionary* priests, in far-off lands like Panama and China. The ties to Spanish-speaking ministry in the United States remained hidden in seeking students. After 1950, the Claretians were no longer a markedly Spanish community, but a mostly American group of religious including many Mexican American clergy. Their seminaries, however, did not stress Spanish language and even undermined its use among native speakers. The province long harbored ambivalence about its mission: whether to concentrate on Hispanic ministry or to reach whiter, wealthier Catholics. Most Claretians, however, demonstrated a fundamental sense of empathy as they accompanied their Latino flock.

Chapter 4 places missionary efforts in Central America in the context of imperialist projects, the Cold War, genocide, and Vatican II sensibilities. Working in the shadows of empire, the Claretians established missions in Panama (1927) and Guatemala (1966). In both places they endured grueling travel to far-flung communities to celebrate baptisms in churches with thatch roofs and to bless school buildings. The Panama missions embodied traditional, hierarchical Catholic projects in lands deemed exotic. Most Claretians in Panama felt a deep discomfort with the targets of their labor: native people. Presentations in the United States about Panama attracted young seminarians to seek foreign mission work. In the late 1950s the Pope challenged Catholics with a "Call to Assist Latin America," followed by Vatican II's exhortations for *aggiornamento* (updating). In 1966, the US Claretians established missions in eastern Guatemala, including among indigenous and Afro-Garifuna people. The Claretian priests and brothers worked in pastoral teams, closely with nuns, in development work such as fishing co-ops and medical clinics. Through the worst years of government violence against indigenous people (1978–85), they remained in Guatemala continuing to build capacity in poor, rural communities. The missionaries demonstrated an overall willingness to experiment with the possibilities of Catholic life and to foreground social justice. The liberationist approaches employed in Guatemala would in time influence the Claretians' ministry in the United States.

Chapter 5 considers how the Claretians reimagined mission in response to the internal and external challenges in the Vatican II era (1962–65) through the 1980s. Both the Chicano movement and Vatican II influenced their work. With their long-standing dedication to the poor and the immigrant, Claretian attitudes presaged the changes that reformed the Catholic Church. The era brought about much more than Vatican II–inspired theological debates. Urban renewal and highway construction decimated some long established parish neighborhoods. Rapid changes everywhere challenged the Claretians and they struggled to find their path. The ferment forced new ways of thinking and stimulated experimentation, renewal, and new ways of being Church, while also continuing their association with Latino Catholics.

The Claretians were at the height of their membership in the mid-1960s, with about two hundred priests and brothers. They soon faced a concerning drop in prospective and current members. The Claretians overhauled their seminary training to bring future priests into regular contact with the wider world. They entered campus ministry at secular, state universities. They developed experimental projects, including team ministry and community development programs. The Chicano movement pushed the Claretians to engage in more explicit discussions about Latino ministry and colored their apostolate. A team planted itself in Oregon to work with farmworkers from Mexico. In Los Angeles and Chicago, Claretian priests publicly denounced restrictive immigration policies.

The conclusion highlights the landscapes and cultures of present-day Claretian missions while looking to the future. It explores Claretian legacies through my visits to former and current Claretian-administered parishes in 2022–24. I enjoyed dining at parish-wide meals in parking lots and church halls. I visited with retired priests at the Provincial House in Oak Park and twenty-something seminarians in Chicago. I watched livestreamed funeral Masses from Guatemala and Our Lady of Fatima in New Jersey. I paid my respects at Claretian graves in San Antonio's San Fernando Cemetery #2 and at San Gabriel Mission. This crazy quilt of encounters taught me that while Claret may stand forgotten in a choir loft, the Claretians' sustained mission often left a vigorous legacy. When the Claretians arrived, Spanish speakers constituted a small and often unrecognized part of Catholic America. The Latino population has grown steadily in the past decades and today comprises about half of the US Catholic laity. In many ways, the Claretians have circled back to their original mission: their accompaniment with Hispanic Catholics.

Looking forward, the conclusion considers some challenges that the province faces. The Claretians need greater transparency as they respond to accusations of clergy sexual abuse of minors. Finally, the inherently global nature of the Claretian Missionaries means that the US province draws widely for its membership, including men from India, Africa, Vietnam, as well as Latin America. This linguistic and cultural diversity brings gifts and challenges as the Claretians learn to strengthen their intercultural community.

* * *

The Claretians understood the historic nature of their foundations in this country, but they tended to record their history in bits and pieces. Members logged daily activities in handwritten *crónicas*, pastors periodically shared the history of their parishes in the *Provincial Bulletin* (and with the global *Anales*). They hired photographers to document major events and improvements for the press, both secular and Catholic. The men wrote each other Christmas letters and slipped snapshots from their current posting inside the envelopes. Some held on to clippings about a seminary mate's ordination and, decades later, a prayer card from his funeral.

In the process of preserving things big or small, Claretians created puzzle pieces of an astonishing history, much of which has made its way to the archive. But the pieces lay scattered. In writing this book, I have fit the pieces together to tell a history of the Claretians' ministry, evolution, and influence in this country through our times. Wherever the documentation exists, I enlarge the puzzle by integrating the stories and actions of laypeople. The Claretians worked in over one hundred places in the United States, of which some thirty were longtime Claretian parishes. From the start I understood I couldn't cover it all. This book is neither an annotated list nor an encyclopedia. With few exceptions, I focus on Latino-majority parishes.

As I read through historic reports, sometimes a direct message written to a future historian jumps out. Fr. Joseph Berengueras, for example, understood the historic value of these documents. Reflecting on a new mission in New Jersey in 1948, he wrote in Spanish, "the future historian will dedicate necessary space to the new foundation's ample documentation."[26] With this book, the future has arrived.

1

Following the Mexicans

Farmworkers, Mineros, *and* Traqueros

*Nadie vió la importancia para la Congregación de tener casas
en los Estados Unidos.*
No one saw the importance for the Congregation of having
houses in the United States.
—Fr. Joseph Berengueras (ca. 1947)

In their first twenty years in the United States, the Claretians followed
the Mexican population and carried out many hundreds of missions and
inaugurated parishes throughout the Southwest and along the railway
tracks to northern states. With previous experience as missionaries in
Mexico, the Claretians were familiar with Mexican people, their culture,
and ways of speaking.

When the congregation arrived in 1902, the United States was still a
"mission country."[1] The Vatican withdrew that status in 1908 just years
before the great influx of Mexican people would increase the need for
Spanish-speaking clergy in many new regions. Bishops invited missionaries to bolster small Spanish-speaking communities without a priest
or regular access to the sacraments. The Claretians boarded trains for
Texas counties dominated by cotton farms, to Arizona mining camps, to
villages of trackworkers in the shadow of a Kansas roundhouse, and to
the company housing of munitions workers in Tennessee. They arrived
in unfamiliar locales to accompany a Mexican people who were generally devout and kept up religious practices in their daily routines, even
without access to a priest who spoke their language.[2] Where they were
needed, the Claretians went. I argue here that the Claretians and Mexican
people often found common ground in their Catholic faith and rituals.

Following the Mexicans into the nooks and crannies of the American
landscape required that the Claretians exhibit humility, self-sacrifice, and

persistence. In this pioneering era (ca. 1902–25) the Claretians all hailed from Spain. They were themselves mostly involuntary migrants, far from home and unlikely to return there. Each *claretiano* in the United States, in addition to their intended work to missionize to Spanish-speaking people, struggled to learn fluent English. They had to acculturate to American ways, including the mores of lived race in the United States. The four cases here allow a glimpse at the regional nuances of racial difference for Mexican-descent people in the early twentieth century.

Before Texas: Claretian Missionaries in Mexico

Mexico was the jumping off spot for the emerging Claretian missions in the United States. Before 1920 nearly every Claretian, born and educated in Spain, first worked in Mexico. The possibility of a Claretian presence in Mexico began in Barcelona. Mexican cleric Antonio Plancarte y Labastida chanced upon the Claretian bookstore while visiting there in 1883. The Claretians impressed Plancarte, nephew to the archbishop of Mexico, and he soon invited the missionaries to work in his home country. A Claretian leader sailed to Mexico to scout its potential for a new foreign outpost, expanding on overseas missions in Equatorial Guinea and Chile. Mexico offered a good challenge, it was determined, with its "faith as robust as oak trees," if hampered by "poor circumstances for religion." In 1884, the Spanish congregation established its first residence in Toluca, soon opening el Colegio Hispano-Mexicano, a boys' school (in operation 1885–1914). The early association with the influential and connected Fr. Plancarte gave the Claretians a strong start. In the next two decades, they took over two Mexico City parishes, as well as parishes in Guanajuato, León, Monterrey, Orizaba, and Puebla, all before Texas.[3]

In Mexican cities the Claretians administered parishes, established schools, taught catechism, and also developed a ministry to the deaf in the capital. They cultivated connections with middle-class Catholics, including some fellow immigrants from Spain. These "better sort" (*gente decente* as they self-identified in Mexico), for example, gladly provided the white dresses and sailor suits for poor children celebrating their first Holy Communion. While the Claretians avoided explicit political stands, they labored during the highly charged Porfiriato (1876–1910), the era named for Porfirio Díaz, Mexico's long-standing president and de facto dictator. Díaz pushed the republic toward a vision of progress that privileged foreign businesses and large landowners: both groups that destabilized the poor and pushed people out of subsistence farming and toward wage work. The Claretians worked with the poor, but also developed warm ties with wealthy landowners. The latter offered their haciendas to the Spanish missionaries for provincial retreats and meetings.

The Claretians fanned out from these urban foundations into the Mexican countryside for periodic missions in ranches, haciendas, mining towns, and indigenous villages. The rural landscape was "everywhere dotted with roadside crosses, church towers, and village sanctuaries." Nearly all people were Catholic, but that varied in terms of practice. As historian Matthew Butler describes it, people and entire villages were "more or less committed to the public observance of their religion, and attached greater or lesser importance to the roles of Catholic priests." Many remote villages saw a visiting priest just a few times a year.[4]

The Claretians crossed the republic in every direction, mostly by train, but often on horseback or wagon on slow and arduous journeys. Beneath an unrelenting sun, the priests' black cassocks became a form of mortification. They scaled pine-covered mountains on narrow trails, uneasily peering into deep abysses. In tropical Veracruz, the missionaries crossed the same river thirty-three times in hours to reach their destination. They kept an eye out for the *mahuaquite*, a feared venomous snake. When describing these journeys for their brethren in Spain, they stressed the travails and sacrifices of mission work in the New World.[5]

In early 1902, the year the first Claretians went to the United States, their confreres carried out challenging missions of different types in Mexico. The Claretians in Guanajuato boarded a train, heading three hundred kilometers north for a multi-day mission in the mining city of Zacatecas. Before arrival, a train wreck closed the line and jeopardized their plans. The missionaries made the rest of the journey on "mules (*borricos*) like Jesus Christ entering Jerusalem." The local liberal newspapers mocked their arrival, saying it was akin to the onset of the plague. These diatribes did not stop people from attending the missions to hear the visiting preachers. The rose-colored cathedral filled every day. The papers dispatched reporters to the mission services, hoping to find clerical missteps and excesses. In a tense situation, the missions won. The

Claretians boasted that thirty thousand people took communion during their Zacatecas stay.[6]

That same spring Frs. José Rementeria (1872–1916) and Jerónimo Pomés (1875–1928) took on a Lenten mission at the Hacienda del Lobo in Querétaro. The centuries-old estate, tucked away in the mountains, was home to five thousand inhabitants, including many indigenous people. The missionaries urged people to confess and take communion before Holy Week. After the final night's sermon, Rementeria dismissed the women and locked the church door. Inside he oversaw the intonation of the *Miserere*: "Have mercy on me, God, in your kindness . . . cleanse me from my sin."[7] The men, in turn, begged for God's mercy. They took off their shirts and whipped their bare backs. Pomés noted with satisfaction as blood dripped and darkened the sanctuary floor. Leaving the church, the flagellants formed a line and processed to their modest homes, their melancholy voices penetrating the darkness. The missionaries had accomplished their goal; the entire community at Hacienda del Lobo had confessed. With purified consciences, 4,900 people took communion. Crowning this Lenten observance, at midnight the Claretians led a pilgrimage to the Santuario de Nuestra Señora de Dolores de Soriano. In orderly fashion, the hacienda's men and women made their way through the dark; led by the missionaries, they chanted the rosary and "beautiful verses to Jesus and Mary." After traveling some twelve miles, before daylight, the procession arrived. People dropped to their knees and entered the sanctuary, sobbing as they humbly crawled toward the altar. Pomés, moved by the experience, effused "I couldn't contain myself—I cried like a child." Rementeria then celebrated Mass at which 1,500 people took communion.[8] The Claretians and Mexican people apparently shared faith and rituals. Frs. Rementeria and Pomés may not have known of the local devotion to Nuestra Señora de Dolores de Soriano, but as they were pledged to the Immaculate Heart of Mary, they appreciated robust demonstrations of devotion to Mary. The Claretians' early work in Mexico seems unfaltering.

But their trust in Mexican people did falter at times. Some Claretian reports conveyed ethnocentrism and condescension, especially regarding rural people. One priest commented that the country people who come to confess were "very rude and repugnant to the eye and sense of smell.[9] Fr. Camilo Torrente (1870–1946) had only been in Mexico for a few weeks when his superior in Puebla sent him to preach in the outlying town of Atlixco. Arriving by train, the priest stepped onto the platform as darkness fell. Nervously, he followed an indigenous guide up into the hills, dogs barking. Upon arriving at the rectory for the night, he was welcomed with a mug of pulque. Certain it was milk, Torrente took a sip and spit out the alcoholic brew in confusion and disgust. A servant brought him a dinner of turkey with mole, but the Spaniard found it too spicy. Decades later he recalled the awkward meal in terms of "my tenderness of mouth and lack of experience." When his mission was complete, Torrente gladly departed Atlixco, eager to return to the Claretian house in the city of Puebla. The pleasant residence, with its Andalusian patio, birds, and flowers, offered a familiar refuge in the often-daunting Mexican terrain. Living there with other Spanish Claretians, Torrente mused, "I felt at home, I had a family, the same faith with the same ambitions and ideals." Being a missionary in the city seemed possible; Torrente declared enthusiastically "If this is Mexico, long live Mexico."[10]

Mexico was the mother province of the US Claretians until 1922. Most Claretian pioneers first lived and labored in Mexico for years before an assignment (or exile in 1914) sent them to Texas or Arizona. The Spanish-born and -educated Claretians became familiar with Mexican people: their speech and customs, their living conditions and expressions of faith. Torrente notably picked up *mexicanismos*, local ways of speech, from time spent in Puebla, Mexico City, and during backbreaking missions in Guerrero. There indigenous guides urged him up mountain paths, repeating the soon familiar phrase, *arribita Padrecito*.

Some Claretians adopted the racialized, often contradictory denigration of native peoples. For example, "The *indio* is naturally religious, but mixed with many superstitions, also lazy and weak." In 1908 one Claretian unhappily asserted, "the copper race (*raza cobriza*) of Mexico respects the clergy, but is nearly impossible to educate in Christian piety."[11] Many of their Mexican peers held the same views during the Porfiriato. While the Claretians generally empathized with Mexican people in the United States, some individuals persisted with these classist and racist perspectives as they ministered in this country.

Work in Mexico immersed the Claretians in the highs and lows of Mexican Catholicism. While ever devoted to the Immaculate Heart of Mary, the Spaniards came to appreciate the Mexican people's love of Our

Lady of Guadalupe. When several Claretians safely arrived after a hazardous Atlantic voyage, on their second day in the capital they hastened to "the famous Sanctuary of Guadalupe to give thanks to our Mother who twice saved us from shipwreck."[12] At times they assisted other priests with the December 12 celebration at Tepeyac.

The Claretians regularly battled the vocal anti-clerical movement, which would gain strength with the outbreak of the Mexican Revolution (1910–17). Protestant efforts in Mexico concerned them. The country was rife with Protestants ("infestada de protestantes"), they asserted with alarm, and they devised ways to counter them, such as publishing the Catholic magazine *La Esperanza*.[13] The fiery missions in the cities and mining outposts were a tried-and-true method to bolster people who were Catholics by birth, if irregular in their churchgoing and sacramental practices. Giving away devotional items always proved popular. The Claretians reported on the "fruitful missions in the *tierra caliente* where thanks to four thousand scapulars of the miraculous and very gentle Heart of Mary, we saw amazing marvels of grace." They handed out many colored prints and holy cards with the "same enchanting Heart." Bishops across Mexico recognized the Claretians' multifaceted work and invited them to establish new houses in their dioceses. The Mexican province announced with pleasure that "A Mexican bishop who wants the Claretian Missionaries, as much or more than the Jesuits, wants the Claretians not to exclude any ministry, but to use any means to influence society. We do—our regulations allow us to teach as well to preach."[14] The Mexican bishops' esteem affirmed the Claretians' efforts.

The years of service in Mexico proved invaluable when Claretians faced related challenges north of the border. Porfirian plans for modernization, in the forms of foreign business penetration, large-scale commercial agriculture, and railroads, steadily pushed people out of subsistence farming and traditional communities. Mexico's uprooted people moved for work in the republic. Increasingly these same people tried their fortunes in the fields, railroads, mines, and factories *al norte*. The Claretians followed them north to the United States in hopes of meeting their spiritual needs. Dozens of one-time "Mexican" Claretians grew old in the United States, buried in Catholic cemeteries in California, Illinois, and Texas.

Texas 1902: First Steps

Peter Verdaguer, the bishop of Brownsville, invited the Claretians to send Spanish-speaking missionaries from Mexico to Texas. Verdaguer was a Catalan like their founder, Fr. Anthony Claret. For this assignment the Mexican provincial tapped Fr. Mariano Luisilla, a forty-one-year-old Spaniard who had long served in Mexico and was a powerful preacher. Fr. Camilo Torrente would partner with him. At age thirty-two, he had spent little time in Mexico, but his intrepid spirit stood out. Before leaving Mexico City, Luisilla and Torrente attempted to learn English. The lessons overwhelmed Luisilla, who believed the Texas mission would be futile. He begged off studying English. To encourage him, Torrente countered with the refrain (which he attributed to *Don Quijote*): "Whoever waits, despairs; he who despairs does not reach his goal: what shall one do?" In 1902, the ill-prepared priests traveled north to carry out missions in Corpus Christi on Ash Wednesday. Verdaguer, who had heard Claret preach many decades earlier in Catalonia, expected the Claretians to execute something phenomenal. He cautioned the Claretians not to expect the splendors of Mexico and its churches since "the Church of Texas is one of poverty, hard work and suffering."[15] The bishop's warning of the poor state of the Catholic Church and rough work in Texas proved fair.

Fr. Torrente, an avid storyteller, is our source for these earliest missions in which South Texas stands in as the Claretians' Plymouth Rock. The first mission in Corpus Christi was poorly received. Torrente admitted "it didn't go down well with the Mexicans." Hoping to improve attendance, the missionaries announced that the next evening's mission would follow the style of Mexico City, with chanting the rosary, examination of conscience, songs from "the land of Guadalupe," and a sermon. On the dusty streets of Corpus, they overheard a man say to a pal, "This is going to be serious" ("Amigo, esto va en serio"). A half hour before the service, people filled the church. The "men's coarse voices" dominated the rosary and the singing. Luisilla delivered his sermon with "clear, potent and tranquil words that captivated all." At the service's end, everyone knelt before the Christ image, performing acts of repentance and pain for their sins. Some people left the church sobbing. The powerful scene repeated on succeeding nights in Corpus: Three hundred men confessed, two thousand people took communion. The parish priest thanked the missionaries, adding, "this is a miracle."[16] For the next two months, Torrente and Luisilla crisscrossed southeastern Texas, usually separately to cover more territory. Ethnic Mexicans began to call Fr. Luisilla "padrecito santo," expressing respect and affection.

Torrente delighted in sharing tales of his own challenges and deprivations as an itinerant missionary in Texas. In Aransas Pass on the Gulf, Torrente found an abandoned chapel and few people. He slept in the sacristy and got by, eating just tortillas and peanuts. He gathered a small group of Mexicans on the beach six times to impart basic lessons. Only ten people confessed. When a local priest asked if he needed a cook, the Spaniard declined. No, he would make do with raw eggs and a box of crackers. He met open hostilities in some places. Troublemakers in Hebbronville strung together empty cans. As Torrente began his sermon, the youth dragged the banging cans near the church. When he complained to the local pastor, the man shrugged, commenting, "they are capable of burning us alive along with the church."[17] Few priests in Texas spoke Spanish, which tested the missionary pair but truly limited the Mexican Catholics. I believe the Claretians exaggerated the dearth of local clergy able to speak Spanish (they ignored the Oblate priests) to make a case for the necessity of their work.[18] Essentially they argued that a prolonged Claretian mission, perhaps even parish administration, would reach these underserved Catholics.

In Texas cities, local bishops and hordes of laypeople welcomed Luisilla and Torrente, eager to take part in their missions. At Laredo, a crowd awaited them as their train came into the station. Torrente noted that thieves often sneak up on new arrivals. Smiling, he added, that day Laredo saw the arrival of "two thieves . . . of souls." After a highly successful Holy Week mission, Mexicans implored the Claretians to extend their stay in Laredo. Meanwhile Bishop John Forest of San Antonio, the state's largest city, invited the pair to hold a mission in the cathedral. A thousand voices joined in hymns of repentance.[19] Again, people begged them to stay. But the missionaries moved on, keeping promises to the Mexican people who awaited them in Los Angeles. San Antonio clergy bade them farewell as they boarded the westbound Sunset Limited. The bishop urged them to return to San Antonio. When their train stopped in El Paso, Fr. Andres Resa joined them after traveling north from Mexico. In California, the Claretian trio would carry out a nonstop schedule of visiting missions for Mexican people. Mere visitors in 1902, the three certainly could not foresee "the importance for the Congregation of having Houses in the United States."[20] Nor could they imagine how the Claretians would stabilize and nurture Spanish-speaking Catholic communities across this unfamiliar country.

Creating *Refugios* in the Small Places of Texas

The itinerant Claretians so impressed Bishop Forest that he invited the congregation to minister on a permanent basis in San Antonio. Starting at San Fernando Cathedral in 1902, the Claretians established a continuous presence and began over a century of ministry in neglected corners of the diocese. Historian Gilberto Hinojosa points out the Catholic Church attempted to meet Mexicans needs, but in practice focused more on institution building and serving Euro-American Catholics. And so, the diocese welcomed religious orders to take on ministry with Mexican people. The Claretians were one of several orders dedicated to this work in Texas.[21] The active presence of Protestants often motivated Catholic actions.

The initial Claretian trio soon reported to their confreres in Mexico, "The Mexicans have received us like rains in May." Speaking Spanish was essential to their welcome. Alluding to Jesus's successes, the Claretians confidently declared about San Antonio, "Here we have our ripening grain."[22] They often ministered to populations that included Tejanos and ongoing arrivals from Mexico, but seldom distinguished between the groups. About ethnic Mexicans in this era, historian Omar Valerio-Jiménez notes that "ambiguity and fluidity would remain cornerstones in the region's ethnic mortar into the twenty-first century."[23]

Outside of San Antonio, Catholic missionaries faced pervasive anti-Catholic and anti-Mexican attitudes in early twentieth-century Texas. Anglo Texans maintained a strong belief in Mexican inferiority and supported stark Jim Crow segregation. As one Anglo shared in that era: "Say 'Mr.' or 'Mrs.' to the Mexicans? No siree!!"[24] The constant threat of violence to ethnic Mexicans loomed, with extrajudicial murders on the rise from 1910 to 1920.[25] Arsonists torched new churches time and time again in rural communities. Yet the Claretians persisted in the face of

Anglo hostilities. They learned English and created connections with larger Catholic networks in their new country in order to best advocate for the Mexican laity. In a hostile and uncertain time, these Claretian-initiated religious communities provided crucial *refugios* and respectability for Mexican immigrants and US-born Mexicans. Refuge was sorely needed in rural Texas.

In 1906, a young Claretian team arrived in San Marcos, a heavily Anglo and Protestant town, to administer the small parish Our Lady of Guadalupe.[26] The Claretians labeled this challenging place *la Roma Protestante*, referring to the dominance of evangelical churches and colleges. On Easter Sunday 1915, a fire destroyed the church and the priests' residence. Notably that year saw a spike in extralegal violence against Mexicans—endemic in the first decades of the century in south Texas.[27] The Claretians did not dwell on the likely arson, but pushed ahead to build a new brick house and church (at a cost of $22,000). In December 1915, San Antonio's bishop and two archbishops from Mexico blessed the new church, with its new name St. John the Evangelist Church.[28]

From San Marcos, the Claretians fashioned a grueling circuit of weekly visits to the much smaller towns of Kyle, Uhland, and Martindale. None of these towns had a Catholic church in 1900. Aging priests later recalled, "The trips were long, tiresome. We had no automobile and no highway existed." They traveled by train when possible, if not by horse, or simply walking.[29] Cotton fields dominated the area and employed most Tejano families and an increasing number of arrivals from Mexico. Mexicanos and Anglos lived separately from one another.[30] While the segregated schools have vanished, the separate cemeteries still dot the area.

In Martindale the Spanish-born priests encountered an avid, devout population of ethnic Mexicans: *un pueblo católico de corazón*. Early twentieth-century Martindale had about five hundred residents.[31] The Claretians built a wooden frame church by 1908, largely paid for by local Mexican Catholics. The boxlike structure had little aesthetic appeal, but was overfilled on feast days. Local residents raised $525 to open a Catholic school.[32] Two teachers (*maestras*) taught some sixty pupils from December to May, but most of the year, the children worked in the cotton fields. The visiting priest often stayed overnight in the sacristy. One such night in March 1916, heavy smoke woke Fr. José Carulla. He rang the alarm, but no one came for fifteen minutes. Aided by winds, fire destroyed everything, from parish registers to the Stations of the Cross, leaving just nails and ash. The Claretian priests surmised that a criminal hand set the fire, possibly a "renegade Mexican, furious to witness the multitudes of people who gathered there on Sundays." The Mexican laity, for their part, suspected a Protestant arsonist.[33]

Facing messages of hate toward Mexicans and Catholics, the Claretians persisted in Martindale. With ash in the air, they collected the insurance money and found places to use as makeshift churches. (Some Mexican laypeople walked to church in San Marcos, eight miles away.) The Claretians quickly built a new church. They secured funds from the diocese and the Chicago-based Catholic Extension Society. Founded in 1905, Extension aimed to fund rural missions in dioceses that lacked infrastructure and local funds.[34] They hired an architect and construction team. While Catholics in Kyle and Uhland made do with wooden structures, the Claretians and laypeople reasoned that Martindale deserved a brick church. The community opted for arched windows, which meant raising walls three feet and cost more to build. But the Claretians defended the additional expense because the church "would gain more in appearance. The people are helping." One hundred Mexicans each pledged $10; many men volunteered to make the concrete blocks. Completed within six months, the new Immaculate Heart of Mary Church was larger and solidly made from brick and concrete; in 1919, a tower was added. By raising a bigger, more secure church for their Mexican parishioners, the Claretians communicated perseverance to Protestant neighbors. Mexican Catholics saw certitude and protection in a precarious era in Texas. As commemorated in 1987, "the people from miles around once more had a place of their own in which they could worship."[35]

A photographer captured Martindale's *católicos* in front of their new church. These people had readied themselves in tucked away ranchos and *jacales* (huts) for church—instead of a day in the cotton fields. Without running water or electricity, the men donned white shirts, a few wore ties, and combed their hair; the girls and women put on their Sunday dresses. Older women kept their hair in braids and covered with a shawl. Members of the Daughter of Mary sodality (*Hijas de María*) wore all white. Planted on the wide pathway to their church, a female

Figure 1.1 Immaculate Heart of Mary Mission, Martindale, Texas, likely 1919. Source: Claretian Missionaries Archives USA-Canada.

parishioner in contemporary dress carried the banner (*estandarte*) of the Immaculate Heart of Mary—the patron of their church (and of the Claretian congregation). With their new church behind them, this Mexican and Catholic community had an anchor in rural Texas.

Inside, wooden pews filled the modest sanctuary. The main altar was unassuming, but was easily decorated for May, Mary's month, or in December for the *fiestas guadalupanas*. Simple Stations of the Cross lined the sanctuary walls; additional altars and images found a place around the church. On certain Sundays the banners of different lay societies held pride of place alongside the main altar. Electric lights—and crucially a fan—hung from the ceiling, though the tall windows provided plenty of light for daytime devotions. A visitor from Zacatecas or San Antonio would find the interior quaint and small. But in Martindale, the *iglesia* was undoubtedly the largest building for Mexican people to gather.[36]

In 1917, the new church in tiny Martindale served five hundred Mexican families or 2,600 souls. The Claretians recorded no non-Mexican Catholics. They baptized 215 babies, and twenty-six couples married there; mourners came for twenty-seven funeral Masses. Sacramental statistics and sodality memberships at Immaculate Heart of Mary were exceedingly high compared to the parish center at San Marcos (with ten times Martindale's population).[37]

Beyond a place to pray and celebrate the sacraments, this church became so much more to ethnic Mexicans, including many recently arrived from Mexico. Fr. Inocencio Martín (1874–1940) visited Martindale each week from San Marcos, often staying for several days. A middle-aged Spaniard with more than a decade of ministry in Mexico and several years in rural Texas, Martín and his flock clicked. Immaculate Heart of Mary hosted diverse activities. One May Sunday in 1920 the community hosted a fundraising *jamaica* that attracted area Mexicans with an ice cream stand (*puesto de Ice Cream*), sweets, sodas, a fish pond, and games of Mexican bingo (*lotería*). The well-attended fair stayed open until 10 pm.

The next Saturday, twenty-nine children took their year-end exams, witnessed by some community members (Fr. Martín noted that most people could not attend due to their work in the fields). On Sunday afternoon after the rosary, however, a good crowd, including some forty children, attended the school party. The event featured recitations of poetry, musical interludes, and a "dialogue between a Catholic and a

Figure 1.2 Immaculate Heart of Mary Mission and School, Martindale, Texas, 1925. Fr. Inocencio Martín (center) and teachers. Source: Claretian Missionaries Archives USA-Canada.

Protestant which was lovely," according to the priest. The teacher, señorita Rosana Martínez, read a speech about the necessity of education.
Finally, Fr. Martín thanked the teacher, children, and parents, urging
all to promote the love of learning. He gave out prizes, saints' cards, and
candy. Despite a sudden cloudburst, many enjoyed the ice cream stand,
sodas, lotería, and coffee until 8 pm, "so ending the nice celebration."[38]

In addition to weekly Mass and rosaries, people came to Martindale
to march in religious processions; some took part as *danzantes* (suggesting dance in indigenous style). The fall devotions drew few people as
work in the cotton harvest restricted trips to church. The year ended on
a better note. On December 26, families gathered at the church to chant
the rosary. Parents and other adults enjoyed watching as boys and girls,
separately, broke the swaying piñatas, and candies, baked goods, dried
and fresh fruit showered the children.[39]

In preparation for Immaculate Heart of Mary's re-dedication in 1987,
people recalled how their elders had regularly walked to their "second
home." For the special Lenten missions held in the evenings, "everyone
walked to the church, direct from the fields, and were there until 10 pm."
During Holy Week, many simply stayed on the church grounds, cooking
and sleeping under the open sky. Padre Inocencio "would walk to Martindale from San Marcos every Friday and would return on Mondays.
He kept this up for quite a while until a man who delivered bread to
Martindale begin [sic] to give him a ride."[40] Fellow Claretians dubbed
Inocencio Martín as "the Great Missionary of small places" (*el Gran Misionero de los sitios pequeños*).[41] Martindale was certainly one of those
small places. With a brick and mortar church and a parish school, the
mexicanos there had a special space to nourish a Catholic community
and to dream of a life beyond the fields.[42]

Overalls-clad farmworkers and barefoot children, Tejanos and Mexican immigrants, spread across Texas seeking better working conditions
and greater security for their families. The Claretians followed them to
dozens of farming towns, including Lockhart, Seguin, and Cotulla—
where Lyndon B. Johnson taught at the "little Welhausen Mexican
School" in 1928.[43] In dusty Model Ts or on horseback, the missionaries
ventured to settlements that had no name or ranchos that, in time, disappeared from the maps, such as El Picoso, La Mota Seca, or Rancho de
los Vázquez. They said Mass, baptized children, celebrated marriages,

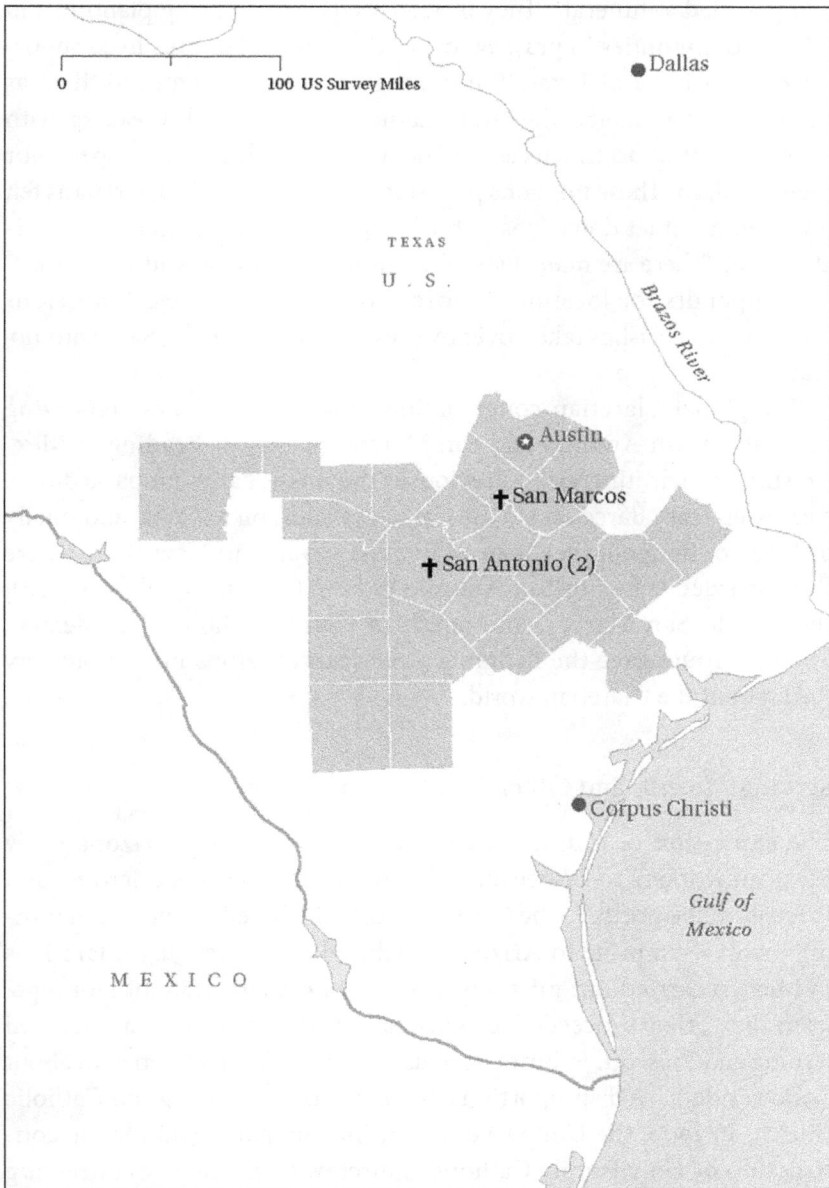

Figure 1.3 Claretian houses and mission churches in South Central Texas counties, ca. 1903–20. The Claretians also administered mission churches from their houses in El Paso, Ft. Worth, and Sweetwater. Sources: *PB*, March 1947; *Claretians in America*, 62. Map by Molly O'Halloran.

and presided at funerals. They blessed seeds before spring planting and joined communities in praying for rain.[44] Ethnic Mexicans lived subordinate lives in rural Texas. The visiting Claretians recognized them as more than farmhands. They were Catholics and Spanish speakers, with proper devotion to the deceased and a desire to improve prospects for their children. These missions persisted for decades as the Claretians felt they could not let down "los pobres mejicanos." One Claretian chronicler noted "there are many lists of missions—we tire of reading them."[45] (See appendix for locations.) Dozens of these once-a-week missions evolved into parishes taken over by the dioceses of Austin, San Antonio, and Dallas.

The global Claretian congregation took notice of these emerging outposts in San Antonio and San Marcos. Spaniards heading to Mexico shifted their itineraries. Previously, the missionaries embarked on a steamship from Barcelona to the Canary Islands, on to Cuba, and finally to Mexico. By 1909, they instead booked voyages to New York, where they boarded trains to San Antonio (where they inevitably stopped), then on to San Marcos, and south to Claretian houses in Mexico. The new route gave the fledgling American missions more notoriety throughout the Claretian world.

Serving *Mineros* and Other Catholics in Arizona

The expansion of mining in early twentieth-century-Arizona drew Mexican workers to Bisbee and Morenci in the south and Jerome and Prescott in the north.[46] The Claretians' orbit included the northern mining towns even prior to Arizona statehood (1912). In 1903, Claretians in Mexico carried out missions in the far northern state of Durango; from there, they proceeded to Arizona for brief missions that included Jerome and Prescott. Jerome was a fast-growing mining town with about 2,900 residents, a disproportionately male population, and no Catholic church. In 1909, the United Verde mining company paid for the construction of Holy Family Catholic Church with the hope of attracting European Catholic miners and their families.

The Claretians arrived at Holy Family through a strange twist of events in Europe, Mexico, and Jerome. Bishop Henry Granjon, a Frenchman, staffed the diocese of Tucson with French priests. When the Great War began, these priests—including Jerome's—were called back to France to serve as army chaplains. Aware of Jerome's increasing Spanish-speaking population, Granjon turned to the Claretians to administer Holy Family parish in 1914. The bishop made it clear that Jerome required clergy who could speak both English and Spanish. Meanwhile in Mexico, the staunchly anti-clerical politician Venustiano Carranza came to power in 1914 and unleashed the desecration of churches and the imprisonment of priests; the governor of Michoacán expelled foreign clergy and the archbishop.[47] Thirty Claretian clergy fled Mexico that summer with most arriving in San Antonio, beyond capacity of their residence. That fall the numbers rose to seventy priests and twenty-two brothers from Mexico who found themselves in Texas and California.[48] With excess manpower for the foreseeable future, the provincial gladly accepted invitations to staff parishes and missions in Jerome and Prescott, Arizona, and Dodge City, Kansas in 1914–15.[49] He assigned Fr. Camilo Torrente (whose English had improved greatly in the past decade) and Fr. Domingo Romeo to Jerome. The duo boarded a westbound train in San Antonio for their new mission. It took days to reach Jerome, which was off the beaten path. It required switching train lines several times, but the priests made the most of the pauses to say Mass in El Paso and Albuquerque.

Arriving in Jerome, Torrente found "a miniature of the city of Guanajuato, tucked into the mountains," graced with a beautiful valley where the Verde River flows. He did not mention the yellow haze and acrid sulfur smell that wafted into town from the smelter several miles away. Nor did he comment on the mountainsides denuded of trees and the absence of birds.[50] The priests initially had to take rooms in a hotel (which occupied the church's bottom floor). Living in community proved impossible, not to mention facing regular "indecencies" at the hotel. The parish itself presented challenges. As Torrente explained to his provincial, "This mission is sui generis, requiring a wealth of apostolic spirit." The parish was pretty well organized for the churchgoing Anglos. But as the Claretians would reflect at mid-century, the Mexicans lived "submerged in a terrible apathy."[51] It took time for the new priests to understand the hardships Mexican miners and their families endured.

Roberto Rabago, a miner's son, recalls that Mexican miners, regardless of birthplace, earned less for the same work and did more dangerous tasks, always below ground. Few would speak up about this basic inequality, as "a person fired from Jerome would not be able to find employment in any other mine in Arizona." Jerome was not strictly segregated, but most Mexicans lived clustered in "unpainted, weathered, wooden houses that balanced on long stilts supporting the downhill side of the houses."[52] A fire rendered one thousand people homeless in 1918. Mexican residents generally lived without access to running water and electricity. Women labored to wash clothing, carrying buckets of water to heat over a wood-burning fire. They fed their families and boarders a simple menu, with little variation. The aromas of frijoles, fried potatoes, and wheat tortillas combined with wood smoke and sulphur.

The mineros' children learned the unspoken rules of exclusion in their hometown. The schools were not explicitly segregated, though the school serving the Gulch barrio was in essence a Mexican school. Teachers renamed children, from Roberto into Robert, Conchita into Connie. At lunch they sat at their desks and furtively nibbled on the potatoes or beans wrapped in a tortilla, hidden in a paper sack. Their Anglo classmates, whose fathers earned a bit more, spread out their sandwiches on their desktops. Mexican kids understood that the public library wasn't for their use. The Young Women's Christian Association (YWCA) opened two facilities for the town's girls and ladies: the Blue Triangle for Americans and the International Institute for girls of "foreign nationality."[53] An Americanization School opened in 1925 that aimed to "make the population more homogeneous by having nothing but English spoken in the town within five years." Many adults held on to Spanish. A Spanish-language newspaper, *Don Quijote*, was published in Jerome from 1925 to 1927. Upon its demise, the town paper began to include pages in Spanish.[54]

Mexicans tiptoed around Anglo privileges in Jerome, including at the church. Even with the arrival of Spanish-speaking clergy, Mexican Catholics had to be coaxed to step into Holy Family. And coax the Claretians did. They encouraged Jerome's Mexican people to form lay societies and to enhance devotions. In addition to the guadalupanas, the Claretians inaugurated the Archconfraternity of the Immaculate Heart of Mary, as Fr. Claret had done decades before in Catalonia. The priests and lay leaders distributed holy cards of the Immaculate Heart and encouraged laypeople to wear the scapular. Many people attended the opening Mass on December 9, 1917, mostly Mexicans "drawn to the enchantments of this sweet Heart." Soon the church held a triduum for the Virgin of Guadalupe. The parish established the Apostolate of Prayer. With an increase in piety and Mass attendance, the Claretians believed their efforts were paying off.[55] But ministry in a mining town also frustrated them. Lay societies formed, but attendance proved irregular as members often worked, even on Sundays. Despite the frustrations, the Claretians made the best of it. As one priest reported, "we do what we can to win over all to God, speaking now in English, now in Spanish, now in both languages, as needed."[56]

The Claretians could not help but notice the tense politics of the miners and competing unions. Amidst the high demand for copper during World War I, the miners sought better pay and working conditions. Three unions competed for the loyalty of Mexican miners: the Mine Mill and Smelter Workers, the IWW (or Wobblies), and the Liga Protectora Latina. Two strikes gripped Jerome in 1917. During one strike, local officials rounded up sixty suspected Wobbly leaders and attempted to deport them out of state to California. At one point that year, three hundred mexicanos broke the picket line. This fact added to the growing racial tensions in Jerome. As the strikebreakers walked to the mines one morning, they passed Holy Family. Shots rang out; one bullet went through a church window during communion.[57]

As Jerome grew in the 1920s, so did its Mexican population. In 1920 Jerome had four thousand residents. By 1930 it counted 4,900 people, with Mexicans comprising about 60 percent of the population. In 1928, the United Verde Company opened a new, separate swimming pool for Mexican miners and their families, reserving the older pool for "Americans." The parish never opened its own school, but the Claretians organized catechism classes at the public schools, with the teachers' cooperation. The parish ran night classes in which adults could learn English (possibly influenced by the town's Americanization School), but here the youth could also study Spanish.[58]

Thirty-five miles from Jerome, the Claretians agreed to take over Sacred Heart parish in Prescott in 1915 (where they remained until 2024).[59] Fr. James Tort (1885–1955), one of the exiles from revolutionary Mexico, arrived in Prescott in 1921. He found a nicely appointed red brick church, but Mexican people would not visit Sacred Heart Church. Rather, they attended the modest, wooden chapel they called *la capilla de Guadalupe*.

Tort left the Claretians' comfortable rectory and went door to door in Prescott's barrio, introducing himself to a great many Mexican families. None of them, he reported, kept up with their sacramental obligations "as God commands." Tort sought land on which a church could be raised for them. News spread across Prescott about that "bold Spanish priest who wanted to erect another church for the Mexicans." Tort led an open-air rosary in the Mexican section. The next day he held the rosary in a Mexican home, with room for fifty people. When the house overfilled, Tort moved the rosary into the street. With elegies to St. Joseph and the Virgin of Guadalupe, he drew a crowd. Taking things up a notch, Tort stole a familiar *Niño Jesus* (possibly from Sacred Heart). He vowed to hold on to the beloved statue until land for the Mexican church was acquired. Soon after, a resident named Mrs. Doyle donated two lots. The new Mexican chapel was quickly built. The Claretians noted with satisfaction that a nearby Pentecostal chapel—described as noisy (*muy alborotado*)—soon disappeared. Tort's bold action in favor of Mexicans and a vital ability to create alliances with Anglo Catholics (here, Mrs. Boyle) would repeat in subsequent ministries in Chicago and New Jersey. Tort's daring advocacy for a better chapel for Prescott's Mexicans should be remembered. At the same time, he capitulated to the parish's ethnic segregation.

Back in Jerome the Claretians also tolerated ethnic division. Catholics of all stripes shared the single church building, but they settled into de facto segregation. Holy Family's children experienced an ethnically segregated parish. The Mexican children attended catechism classes on one day, while the "English speaking" children went on a different day. Each June the parish held separate first Holy Communion services. The first week, some fifteen American children made their first Holy Communion, with a celebratory breakfast put on by the women of the Altar Society. A week later the sanctuary filled when sixty Mexican children made their first Holy Communion. They enjoyed their festive breakfast on the rectory porch. The children relished a day out that month. One week the priest and señorita Lina took all the American catechism boys and girls for a picnic beyond Jerome. Six days later the Mexican boys enjoyed the same outing, including the delights of the river. The following week the Mexican girls enjoyed, separately, their picnic. Notably, the May crowning featured both Mexican and American girls, beautifully dressed in white: with an impeccable chorus, it was a "most lovely act of love for Mary." But the parish held separate Christmas parties for Mexican children and those in the English-language catechism classes.[60] The Claretians' capitulation to a racially divided parish is noteworthy given that Mexicans comprised the majority of Jerome's Catholics. The dominant, racial status quo in Arizona clearly influenced the priests' practices.

The onset of the Great Depression meant a declining demand for copper, and full-time employment shrunk in Jerome. During "la Creeses" a dedicated group of Mexicans regularly carried out fundraisers for the parish. In the summer of 1933, for example, two *señoras* organized a "very Mexican supper," which drew many diners and garnered good profits given the Depression's pall. Fr. Honorato Elorz started a Mexican men's club; they in turn hosted a dance open to the entire Mexican community. The popular Santa Cecilia Club, with nearly one hundred musically inclined young members, planned a fundraising dance. The well-attended function became a near-monthly event in 1930s Jerome. The Claretian priests partnered with the laity in the public celebration of Mexican independence on September 16, 1933. A Claretian noted that the Mexican people celebrated independence in Jerome with "great decency and to the satisfaction of all." Speeches greatly praised "our Spain, a rare thing . . . given so many Mexicans are rustic and simply parrots."[61] The priest's praise had quickly turned to a disdainful othering.

On December 12, 1939, Holy Family celebrated a dawn Mass for Our Lady of Guadalupe, and celebrated another one later that morning. People, their children in tow, sang *las mañanitas*. That night, after the novena, the Mexican faithful took part in a well-attended procession outside the church, with candles aglow and many children dressed as *indios*, in homage to Juan Diego. The Mexican Catholic community, supported by their priests, surprised their neighbors in Jerome with this novel celebration.

Given Jerome's geographic isolation, the ups and downs of the copper mining industry, and the degree of unease between Euro-Americans and ethnic Mexicans, Holy Family parish was a tough mission. Jerome's population reached its peak in 1930, declining in subsequent decades. The mines closed in 1953, the population plummeted, and Jerome became a shadow of itself. The Claretians administered Holy Family until 1979, returning it to the diocese following the death of longtime resident

Fr. John Atucha (1901–1979). The church is closed, but a Claret statue appears in many visitors' photographs online. Jerome bills itself to visitors as the "Wickedest Town in the West," playing up its rough-and-tumble days and reputedly haunted abandoned buildings and mines. The fact that Jerome had a Mexican-majority population for decades is, sadly, lost in this popular presentation of local history.

In the Railyards of Kansas

For the many thousands of Mexican railway workers, who called themselves *traqueros*, the only steady aspect of their lives was moving with the job.[62] A challenging mission for sure, Claretian missionaries tended to the spiritual needs of railway workers in yards and boxcar camps in several states. Dodge City, Kansas, had an important Santa Fe railyard that employed many men from Mexico. The extensive yards gave rise to a "Mexican Village" or a *colonia mexicana*. In the *yarda*, workers and their families raised simple homes, made from railway ties or sod. Visitors always noticed the homes' cleanliness, in defiance of the soot and lack of running water, as well as "their array of pasteboard saints and blessed candles."[63] To cope with modest salaries and growing families, mexicanos also tended vegetable gardens and animals. Children hung around the tracks, hoping a Santa Fe worker might toss them chunks of ice, or that an empty box car would contain wheat to bring home to feed the chickens. When possible, women washed clothing in the hot water that ran off the roundhouse. Not an intentionally segregated community, the Santa Fe Railroad's offer of land for housing appealed to newly arrived Mexican people. This noisy, makeshift place held constant and inherent dangers, including accidents on the tracks, a high infant mortality rate, and fatal disease. Mexican Village residents nevertheless created a tight-knit community.[64]

In the fall of 1913, San Antonio–based Fr. Rafael Serrano (1871–1946) gave a week-long mission in Dodge City, home then to some four thousand people. Arriving at the depot, he easily made his way to the Mexican Village. The colonia did not yet have a chapel. Instead, Mexican Catholics walked a mile to Sacred Heart Church every evening to take part in services at which they recited the rosary and sang hymns. With a decade of missionary experience in Mexico, Serrano connected easily with this community. He reported to his superior, "you can't imagine the great pleasure it gives these good people to hear me . . . a long time has passed for many without hearing Spanish." The visiting Claretian prepared young people for their first Holy Communion. Families, compadres, and neighbors gathered to celebrate the boys in their white suits and girls in their white dresses and veils. Assignment completed, Serrano left Dodge City and carried out similar missions in the area.[65]

In early 1914, Fr. Serrano served as a chaplain on the St. Peter Chapel Car, a long railway car outfitted as a worship space, under the auspices of the Catholic Extension Society. Aboard the Chapel Car, Serrano toured the Diocese of Wichita, carrying out missions for Mexicans in isolated places such as Pratt and Arkansas City. The Chapel Car headed to Woodward, Oklahoma, only to find that the Mexicans had all decamped to Texas. The Chapel Car then returned to Kansas, where Serrano ministered to small groups of Mexicans. Serrano's roving mission work in the Great Plains was positively received.[66]

In 1915, Fr. John Handly CSP (Paulist Father) and the local bishop invited the Claretians to establish a residence in Dodge City. Handly had witnessed the Claretians' work on a visit to rural Texas. Eager to take their work north, the Claretians agreed to a year in Dodge City with the hope of gaining a parish of their own in that "important railroad city." Fr. Arturo Vallvé (1878–1959), in tandem with Fr. Antimio Gete Nebreda (1882–1969) and a brother, headed north. They found a simple, wooden building in the yard for their use. Fr. Handly had it built a year earlier as a school for the traqueros' children, but it also served as a chapel for Mexican Catholics. At first, things seemed promising to the newly arrived priests. Daily Mass drew about sixty people. The faithful collected funds to purchase a picture of the Virgin of Guadalupe. Handly arranged for an English tutor for the Spaniards. A dogged fundraiser, Handly saw to the construction of a pleasant nine-room residence for the Claretian community. From the second-floor porch, the new priests looked right into the Village and the larger yards. The Claretians taught religion in the school, leaving other subjects to an Anglo lay woman teacher. The school pleased Bishop John Hennessy; he brought baskets of fruit and candy for the Mexican pupils when he visited from Wichita.[67]

The Claretians' prospects soon dimmed in Dodge City. Handly, their host, soured on them within months. He recruited the Claretians specifically for their ability to minister in Spanish. But it turned out that Handly also wanted them to preach in English (and optimally German) to nearby farming communities. To clarify, priests everywhere celebrated the Mass in Latin, but delivered homilies and made announcements in the vernacular (or local language). Fr. Gete found the expectations in Kansas taxing: preparing a homily, or simply saying something to English-speaking Catholics, required time. He needed rest as he was coughing up blood within months of arriving in Dodge City. With Gete in bed, Vallvé anxiously requested the assignment of another Claretian who could speak some English to tend to the "Americans on the farms." Handly, meanwhile, focused on fundraising for a new Sacred Heart Church to serve the Anglo parishioners. He seemed more concerned with satisfying Euro-American Catholics in Dodge City and nearby communities, hoping to secure monies for the church in construction (designed by the lauded architect Ralph Adams Cram of Boston). Therefore, beyond some well-crafted fundraising pleas, Mexican people did not hold Handly's attention.

Fr. Serrano, whose English was strong, replaced Vallvé and so the Claretians completed their contracted year in Dodge City. In addition to ministering to the several hundred people in the Mexican Village, the small Claretian community oversaw the Mexican chapel in Hutchinson, 120 miles distant.[68] They regularly visited trackworker camps to the west including Ingalls, Copeland, and Elkhart (the latter 120 miles away); to the east, nearby Wright, Kansas. The Claretians were busy in Dodge City.

The Claretians' hope to establish a permanent *parish* in Dodge City, however, went unfulfilled. All they could call theirs was the Mexican Village, with its modest wooden church, heated by a stove that made one side too hot, the other too cold. Their promised year complete, the Claretians left Dodge City in 1916.[69] Still, seeds had been sown. Fr. Hilario Hernández, a Spaniard exiled from a diocese in Mexico, took over. He ministered for decades at the old wood frame church in the train yard. In 1949 he oversaw the erection of a new Our Lady of Guadalupe Church. The missionaries, Fr. Handly and the Claretians, had laid the groundwork for a lasting if long separate Mexican Catholic community. Dodge City, a diocese since 1951, today is home to the Cathedral of Our Lady of Guadalupe. Latino people comprise 65 percent of Dodge City's population. Given the prevalence of Mexican employment by the railroads, the

Claretians were familiar with trackworker settlements throughout the United States. In Chicago and New Jersey, missions among the traqueros gave way to permanent Latino parishes.

Fall 1918: Father Monasterio Goes to Tennessee

The influenza pandemic reached Nashville in September 1918 and sickened hundreds of Mexican workers at the Old Hickory Powder Plant. When Bishop Thomas Sebastian Byrne heard that these Spanish-speaking sojourners faced death without proper religious attention, he asked other prelates for help. The archbishop of New Orleans recommended that he contact the Claretians in San Antonio. Soon enough Fr. León Monasterio (1874–1944) boarded a Nashville-bound train.

Fr. Monasterio found his mission in the largest munitions plant in the world. Old Hickory was a sprawling industrial complex owned by the DuPont Engineering Company that produced powder for artillery and firearms. Multiple train lines snaked into the brand-new city; odd, acrid smells hung in the air. Monasterio marveled at row after row of neat, newly constructed workers' housing: thirty thousand people lived onsite. Most resident-workers, who were white, lived in the primary neighborhood, with its named streets, YMCA and YWCA, and school. 1,400 men, women, and children lived in a dedicated "Mexican Village" (which included some Puerto Ricans and Navajos). This Village consisted of thirty bunkhouse buildings, on a rise over the Cumberland River, close to the Plant's hospital. A larger "Negro Village" stood nearby. While Monasterio busied himself with prayerful visits to the sick and dying, he certainly noticed the inferior, segregated conditions in which nonwhites lived. Black and Mexican workers lived on nameless streets, in bunkhouses identified by numbers. The separate and unequal reality hardly surprised the Spanish priest, after fifteen years in this country.[70]

The Old Hickory News, the Powder Plant's paper, explained that "the Mexican has been a great help to the United States Government during the great war. While thousands of Uncle Sam's boys have been forced to go to war, many Mexicans have been available on different construction jobs throughout the country." The Powder Plant provided a mess hall and a club house for these workers, but apparently no church. The company paper highlighted Monasterio's mission in Tennessee. When the deadly influenza infected many in the Mexican Village, they sent for the Spanish-speaking priest. He spent a month there, "administering both to the physical and spiritual welfare of the afflicted persons."[71] On November 16, 1918, *The Old Hickory News* declared the flu over and thanked "Father O'Neil and Father Monasterio for their cheering visits and for their services at the death beds of our people. May they remember us as long as we will remember them."[72] After a month in Nashville, his mission complete, the Claretian returned, unharmed, to Texas. Monasterio carried out similar work during the 1924 bubonic plague outbreak in Los Angeles, as did fellow Claretian Fr. Medardo Brualla, who eventually contracted the plague and died.[73] When Monasterio passed away decades later, one superior opined, "Every individual is worth one," but to him, "Father León [Monasterio] is worth five." The Claretians recalled his spirit of sacrifice, always willing to visit the sick, at any hour.[74]

* * *

From the Claretians' global vantage point in 1902, "no one saw the importance for the Congregation of having Houses in the United States."[75] What began very tentatively with just two Spaniards preaching itinerant missions in rural Texas would gradually reorient the Claretians. The United States quickly became a large, vigorous province. As Spanish speakers, with more than a decade of experience in Mexico, the Claretians were well positioned to serve Mexican people. Places like Martindale, Texas, demonstrate how laypeople and Claretians could collaborate to foster strong foundations for Mexican Catholics. Fr. Inocencio Martín's steadfast involvement there embodied what many Catholics today call *accompaniment*, as his weekly stays demonstrated true caring and solidarity with the mexicanos whose lives were so circumscribed by the Texas cotton economy and its related racism. In Claretian memory, the year in Dodge City was a "failure" (*fracaso*).[76] In retrospect, though, we can see that the Claretians bolstered an emerging Mexican community that persisted and grew after their short stay.

Each of these rural and small-town missions came to life when the Claretians responded to a bishop's call—from San Antonio, Tucson, Wichita, or Nashville.[77] Bishops usually expressed their need as *linguistic*. The diocese lacked personnel capable of ministry to the Spanish-speaking population. This was true. But bringing the Claretians to staff churches also meant that existing parishes could avoid integration. If Mexicans could have their own capillas and catechism classes, Euro-Americans would not need to share the pews with them. Jerome, Prescott, and Dodge City vividly demonstrate the limits of Mexican-Euro-American integration in the early twentieth century.

The Spanish-born and -educated Claretians worked daily with the systemic racial stratification in a country—and often in a Catholic Church—that disdained Mexican people. Their ministries supported Mexicans' spiritual lives and built up respectability. But in that era they did not confront the racial status quo. Likewise, the Missionary Oblates of Mary Immaculate (commonly known as Oblates) carried out work in south Texas very similar to that of the Claretians; they also allowed racial divisions to persist within some parishes. As Gilberto Hinojosa describes it, the Church was both "timid and courageous" in its work with mexicanos in that era.[78] Some Claretian individuals lacked the empathy needed for missionary work. A subset of them looked down on Mexican people, carrying over the racial and classist views that originated in Spain, flourished in Porfirian Mexico, and prevailed in the early twentieth-century United States. As Fr. Torrente commented in his first year in Texas, mexicanos there "speak our beautiful language as poorly as they practice our faith."[79] His position of Spanish superiority was evident in sharing this observation with fellow Claretians.

The Claretians followed Mexican Americans and Mexican immigrants where work called them. Cotton fields and mines gave rise to some permanency; where towns existed, a church could stand. With time the Claretians grew better at navigating the hubbub of big cities, the doldrums of endless train trips, and some learned to drive automobiles. They grew accustomed to ministry in a land where the Catholic Church was marginalized, if not abhorred and mistrusted in many regions. They grew adept at filing insurance claims for torched churches, seeking the use of rooms in public schools, and at expressing their needs to American bishops—all of which required some fluency in English. Crucially in these first decades, the Claretians experimented with the notion of mission. The itinerancy of this period, which seemed in keeping with Anthony Claret's missionary drive, would wane, if not disappear, as the Claretians grew into an unexpected role as parish priests.

2

Building Urban Parishes

Refugios *and Spaces of Catholic Americanization*

It is not enough for the Priests in charge of the Mexican
people to speak well their language, Spanish, it is also necessary to like them and understand them, which is not so
frequently found.
—Fr. James Tort (1943)

Robert Alvarado sat amidst his second-grade classmates on the front
steps of the Navarro School in San Antonio for their class portrait in
1922. Born in San Luis Potosí in 1914, the boy's family had settled in the
lively if dilapidated Laredito neighborhood. Like many of the boys on
this picture day, Robert wore overalls, a sign of the limited income of
most San Antonio Mexicans. Yet even among the shanties and corrals
that housed Laredito's families, there was poor and there was poor. Robert wore shoes and he sat next to boys who did not.

A few blocks from Navarro School stood Immaculate Heart of Mary
Church, raised by the Claretians and the Mexican faithful in 1911. Robert
was present when the parish dedicated its three-story parochial school
in 1926. This time the twelve-year-old dressed immaculately in an altar
boy's black robe and white lace surplice, his black hair neatly combed
and gleaming. Squinting in the sun, he stood in the inner circle flanking
Archbishop Arthur Drossaerts and the Claretian clergy, with the school's
artful, double-arched doorway behind them. The public who gathered
for the ceremony included Mexican men in suits and ties, women draped
in dark rebozos, and girls in white dresses, their hair in tidy plaits. The
previous Sunday the priests reminded parishioners to dress carefully for
the dedication and specifically asked them to keep street urchins away
from the ceremonies ("niños y jovenes callejeros fuera!"). Still, barefoot
boys edged their way into the crowd and the day's formal photographs.

Immaculate Heart Church was part and parcel of its neighborhood. With this tight-knit and Claretian-administered parish supporting him, however, young Alvarado entered a life far beyond.[1]

Arriving 1,200 miles to the north, many thousands of newcomers from Mexico were starting new lives in Chicago, including Elidia Barroso. Born in Guanajuato in 1897, unmoored by the Mexican Revolution, orphaned, Elidia and her siblings sought refuge in Texas in 1917. For several years in San Antonio, she enjoyed attending Mass, fiestas, and rosaries at the Claretian-run San Fernando Church. Elidia followed family and her fiancé to Chicago in 1924. After marrying at the tiny, makeshift Our Lady of Guadalupe Church, near the South Side steel mills, the newlyweds set up housekeeping in Chicago's Near West Side. Through Claretian missionary efforts, Mexican Catholic worship soon emerged there. In 1925, Elidia happily went to Mass with her husband at a storefront church; Fr. James Tort presided. After many years of migration and uncertainty, Elidia felt settled enough in Chicago to fulfill a long-held desire: She requested a Mass for her parents' souls. She did so, in Spanish, to the Claretian priest. The Claretians began to minister at St. Francis of Assisi, an old German church nearby. Elidia was among their first parishioners. She joyfully recorded in her diary in December 1927, "I received the medal of Our Lady of Guadalupe in St. Francis of Assisi mission church. Fortunately, I am a member." The ceremony reminded her of when, at age sixteen, she was received as a Hija de María in Guanajuato. St. Francis of Assisi, Claretian-run through the 1990s, was the place the Barroso family paid homage to past generations and established new Mexican American lives.[2]

This chapter explores three cities where the Claretian missionaries arrived as strangers and grew deep roots in their parishes: San Antonio's Immaculate Heart of Mary (established 1911), Chicago's Our Lady of Guadalupe (1924), and Our Lady of Fatima (1949) in Perth Amboy, New Jersey. The Claretians evolved from itinerant missioners in the style of Anthony Mary Claret to builders of brick and mortar churches and related parish structures that answered to a larger diocese. The parishes reflect Latino Catholic life in three different regions of the country.[3] Mexican people and Spanish language were widespread in San Antonio. By contrast, the Mexicans were barely acknowledged in Chicago; in New Jersey, the Puerto Ricans were a similarly small (and maligned) population. In San Antonio, the Jesuits and Oblates carried out parallel work at Mexican parishes. In Chicago and Perth Amboy, the Claretians were the only clergy dedicated to Latino Catholic ministry. Overall I find more similarities than differences in these parish histories. Everywhere, the Claretians fostered embryonic parishes in working poor neighborhoods and, as a result, created stable, multifaceted institutions that anchored what outside observers called "slums" or blighted areas. Claretians put these Spanish-speaking parishes on the map as they hired architects, planted the seeds of parish societies, publicized beyond the parish boundaries, and created opportunities for lay leadership. I argue that the Claretians played a vital intermediary role between diocesan structures that embodied centralizing, Americanizing impulses and the desires of Mexican and Puerto Rican Catholics to nurture the culture of home.

Newcomers from Mexico and the Spanish Caribbean sought and found *refugio* in these US Catholic parishes and gained respectability as members. These parishes served as refuges for immigrant adults including Elidia Barroso—with homilies and novenas given in Spanish—and as spaces of Catholic Americanization for children like Robert Alvarado—with their scout troops, schools, sports teams, and Halloween parties. Claretian parishes served as a glue that connected immigrant parents and their US-reared children. These refuge parishes became home for multiple generations in this county.

A Church Meant for Mexican People: San Antonio's Immaculate Heart of Mary

At Bishop John Forest's invitation, the Claretians assumed the administration of San Fernando Cathedral and its parish in 1902.[4] But Immaculate Heart of Mary, their next parish in San Antonio, was truly special for the missionary congregation that envisioned and erected the church. The Claretians situated themselves in Laredito, a neighborhood known for poverty, the dirt and noises of multiple train yards, and the city's red-light district. In 1907, the Claretians built a handsome three-story brick residence with a spacious front porch that looked toward San Antonio's downtown and a quiet courtyard-garden behind it. While the new church would serve the city's poor, the Claretians opted for large, striking construction and incurred substantial debt. The Byzantine-Romanesque church, designed by respected San Antonio architect, Leo M. J. Dielmann—and built by Mexican workers, with a Spanish-language cornerstone—was blessed on August 11, 1912. The Claretians' gamble, to construct a big church for humble Laredito, paid off. In time, with regular fundraising among the new parishioners, the church was ornately outfitted with "the essential statues for a church meant for Mexican people."[5]

The disruptions of the Mexican Revolution led to tremendous growth of the city's Mexican population, including Robert Alvarado's family. Membership and sacramental attendance grew rapidly at Immaculate Heart of Mary in the 1910s. Catholic clergy also fled Mexico in 1914, with bishops and exiled Claretians overflowing their residence next to the new church. While nurturing the new parish, the Claretians also went outside the city to minister at dozens of rural sites. Priests regularly visited thirty-two "missions" beyond the city in 1914. From Helotes and Jourdanton, to distant Seguin and Cotulla, these temporary commitments stretched out into decades for the Claretians at Immaculate Heart[6] (see figure 1.3 and the appendix).

In 1926, the parish erected a free-standing school building, often described as "magnificent." Archbishop Drossaerts declared it the finest parochial school in his see. This was a striking pronouncement given the statewide practice of separate and decidedly subordinate schools for ethnic Mexican pupils. The school also housed a clinic for children and the poor in the parish.[7] The basement-level hall (*salón*) could seat 1,200 people and hosted concerts and plays that drew in parishioners and others. The parish showed movies, often of a Catholic bent, inspired by the screenings at nearby La Trinidad, a Spanish-speaking United Methodist congregation.[8] In 1926, people came to see newsreels ("hermosas peliculas") of the Jubilee Year and panoramas of the Holy Land. In 1929, the parish sponsored an afternoon and evening screening of *The White Sister*, a silent movie starring Lillian Gish. The parish complex became a beacon in Laredito.

The new church welcomed Tejanos and a multitude of refugees from the Mexican Revolution (1910–17) and the Cristero War (1926–29).[9] The Claretians delivered all the announcements in Spanish, from marriage banns and meeting times to details about the unending, varied fundraising activities. The Olivares family fled anti-clericalism and violence in their native Coahuila in 1917. Arriving in San Antonio, the elders told their sons: "Look for a Catholic church so we may thank God that we arrived safely." When the teens found Immaculate Heart of Mary, the family offered prayers of thanksgiving for their safe arrival from war-torn Mexico. Young immigrants made new friends and even met partners at the church. Damaso Olivares washed dishes at the Mexican Manhattan Restaurant and became president of the church's San Luis Gonzaga society ("los Luises") for unmarried men. The young señores of los Luises functioned both as a faith-based and social club. In 1923, for example, members debated the purchase of a radio, but chose instead to buy boxing gloves. Victoriana Aguiar worked in a pecan-shelling plant, but avidly participated in the Hijas de María, becoming its president. Victoriana and Damaso crossed paths in a group that "put on little plays in the church for the benefit of the church." Finding purpose and a new social world at the parish, the two devout Catholics and erstwhile actors married in 1928. Their seven children attended the new parish school. As one Olivares daughter recalled, "the Church was the center for us. Some other families would go to picnics. We would go to church."[10]

Many lay societies, mostly same-sex, emerged at Immaculate Heart. Take, for example, the devout mexicanas who came together as the Apostolate of Prayer (Apostolado de la Oración) on Sunday evenings at 7 pm beginning in 1915. The group selected officers—Presidenta, Secretaria, and Tesorera—with a vice-officer for each position. The women, married and single, greeted each other and their spiritual adviser, a Claretian priest, then began each meeting with a devotional reading. (In the 1930s, the members read aloud from the life of Anthony Claret in the years surrounding his beatification.) The group commented on the illness (or passing) of current members, urging prayers and visits. Members gave their dues, beginning at five cents minimum (raised to a dime in 1927). The treasurer totaled the weekly collection, dutifully reported and jotted down by the secretary. In the 1910s, they often collected at least seven dollars each week. Meetings ended formally as members recited the Our Father (*Padre nuestro*) and Ave Maria to the Sacred Heart of Jesus. The secretary recorded the basics of each meeting in a hefty, lined book, bound in dark red. She noted once that "the meeting was lively" ("la junta estuvo animada"). As the Apostolado's traditions began, the priest directed the officers to wear their sashes for the weekly meetings and at church. At Mass, these women occupied the first pews, directly facing the Sacred Heart.[11]

Apostolado members decided to order a specially made banner (*estandarte*) from Spain in their first year. The women excitedly awaited its arrival for months. Then customs officials in New York refused to release the banner until unexpected fees were covered, so requiring more donations. Nearly two years later, the members rejoiced to see the society blessed, banner and all, by Bishop John Shaw at their church. For decades to come, the women proudly displayed their banner at monthly Masses, the fiesta of the Sacred Heart, and carried it aloft in processions around the neighborhood, marching together. As a group they made plans for stands to be used for the fundraising fairs (*jamaicas*) that punctuated the year. They agreed to purchase flowers to adorn the altar, often prompted by a pastor's request. Apostolado members wore their medals to church events. The priest had membership cards (*cedulas*) printed and urged the women to carry one "to prove membership": at the cost of five cents. With pleasure, the members received holy cards (*estampitas*) of the Sacred Heart, tucking them into pockets and purses, adding the token to home altars, further connecting church and home.

The regular meetings and group communion nurtured connections and friendships between newly arrived women from Mexico and those for whom the parish was home.[12] In 1940, señora Manuela E. Villareal served as Presidenta, still the minutes affectionately describe her as *Manuelita*. Secretaries handled the dark red ledger with care and pride, passing their history from one officer to the next over forty years. For hundreds of women over decades, the Apostolado linked them more closely to new friends and to the Claretians, to their faith and to their parish. These early societies left a tangible legacy in their Texas church. The Luises and the Hijas de María together collected donations for a church window. Today, the sun shines through a quartet of stained-glass windows over the altar that bear their names, in Spanish, including the Apostolado and Archicofradía of the Immaculate Heart.

Damaso Olivares, onetime refugee and actor, served his parish as an usher during the Depression. The *ujieres* greeted people arriving for Mass; they walked down the aisles, pausing at each pew to extend the collection basket on a long pole, awaiting the hard-earned coins and dollar bills that parishioners placed into the basket. In the sanctuary's rear, these men emptied *la colecta* into a receptacle to be taken for safe-keeping and counting. The ushers, hair neatly combed, wore their Sunday suits (though not all with ties) and polished shoes. Few of these men wore a suit at their jobs. Damaso's son would recall that "even though we were poor . . . my grandmother and my dad and my uncles exercised a leadership role, not only in church, but also in the barrio. People looked up to them for advice on community and personal matters, on church activities, and so forth."[13] Mexican people fought hard to gain a foot-hold in the United States at a time when Anglo Texans would not call them "Mister."[14] Among the ushers and the broader parish community, men like Damaso Olivares gained the respect and trust of their neighbors, and they did so speaking Spanish. The twenty-four ushers posed for their photo, in orderly rows that surrounded the pastor and a statue of Immaculate Heart of Mary, notably with the two-toned brick walls of their church behind them. In a barrio of unpaved streets and adobe homes, Immaculate Heart of Mary Church provided a place to take a dignified photo.

Large processions from the parish circled the Laredito neighborhood. Devout laypeople, and the Claretians, made manifest their Catholic faith and respectability in well-orchestrated movements on fiestas for Corpus Christi, the Sacred Heart, and Our Lady of Guadalupe as well as connected to special novenas.[15] On a Monday in May 1937, the parish celebrated the graduation of eleven children from Immaculate Heart School. The priest announced at the early Mass, "today we are celebrating" ("Hoy estamos de enhorabuena"). The procession soon left the school, making a one-mile loop through Laredito's streets of San Luis, San Fernando, Concho, and San Saba. Joining the graduates, their teacher-sisters and the Claretians, were the uniformed members of the young women's group, the Hijas de María, holding aloft their banner. In case anyone missed it, the sounds of accompanying musicians drew people out from corner stores, sweeping the floors at the cantinas, or hanging the wash along the wooden fences.[16]

The annual December 12 procession to honor the Virgin of Guadalupe was a big affair. Take the 1948 "grandiosa procesión" that commenced at 3:30 pm. A police escort led the dozens of groups who overtook Laredito's streets. Damaso Olivares organized the altar boys and the car-

Figure 2.1 Ushers, Immaculate Heart of Mary Church, San Antonio, 1934. Source: Claretian Missionaries Archives USA-Canada.

rying of the Cross. The procession featured children: from a boy scout troop to a group of little *chinas poblanas* and "inditos" in their folkloric costumes. Fifty boys and girls formed a living rosary chain. Other girls dressed as angels. The adult societies took their places, including the religious groups, led by a banner bearer, including the female Apostolado and the male Cristo Rey. At the helm of the Holy Name (*Santo Nombre*) men was don Matilde Elizondo, a parishioner of some thirty years and owner of the iconic La Gloria bakery. Alonso Perales, prominent attorney, civil rights leader, and a founder of LULAC (League of United Latin American Citizens), led the Centro Social contingent.[17] An ornate float portrayed the apparition story and rolled through the streets. Then came the Claretians and the parish choir; behind them walked the faithful, united in their devotion and mexicanidad.[18]

What happened to Robert Alvarado (1914–2005), the immigrant and altar boy, whose story opened this chapter? With the strong support of his pastor Fr. Joseph Preciado, after graduation from Immaculate Heart grade school, he entered the Claretians' junior seminary in California.

Figure 2.2 Celebration following Fr. Robert Alvarado's first Mass at Immaculate Heart of Mary Church, San Antonio, 1939. Source: Claretian Missionaries Archives USA-Canada.

In 1939, he returned home to Immaculate Heart as a Claretian and an ordained priest, a first for the parish. Following his first Mass there as celebrant, hundreds of people made their way next door to the church hall in the school. Parishioners and friends of the Alvarado family filled five extra-long, white covered tables. Some five hundred people enjoyed a meal, lingering over bottles of soda pop and Pearl beer. Seated with family and friends, parishioners looked up at the photographer positioned high at a corner of the hall. The camera captured the array of people who found a home and community at Immaculate Heart. The women wore stylish, Sunday dresses, some with new hats for the occasion. Just a few older women appeared with heads covered with a dark rebozo. The men wore ties, some with a pin attached to the jacket signifying their membership in a parish society, including the ushers. Older folks, raised in a different era, tended not to smile, while the younger people, mostly raised in Texas, beamed for the camera. White-aproned women stood amidst the guests, removing dishes and tidying up. Imagine the chatter, mostly in Spanish, that filled the hall. Dressed in black, the Claretians, including Fr. Robert Alvarado, lined up near the stage. Altogether the photo captures a vibrant, San Antonio parish that had weathered migration, including exile from Mexico, the Depression, and now even had a bit of a middle-class sheen. That day marked a special milestone: joyfully coming together to celebrate Alvarado's entry into the priesthood, one of their own, in a time when there were few Mexican American clergy in the United States. Once an overalls-clad boy, Alvarado went on to a varied career with the Claretians. He served in Arizona, California, and Texas parishes, and also had a lengthy appointment at an urban parish in Panama, often representing the United States.

Devotion to This Church and Shrine: Chicago's Our Lady of Guadalupe Church

From their early perch in the Southwest, the Claretians had their eyes on the northern United States, especially Chicago. Fr. Domingo Zaldívar wrote to Archbishop George Mundelein in 1918 and pointed out that the city's budding Mexican settlement needed Spanish-speaking clergy. These initial inquiries went unanswered. In 1924, the archdiocese acquired a decommissioned wood-frame army barracks, moved it to the scrappy South Chicago neighborhood where the steel mills eagerly recruited Mexican men. The old barracks became Our Lady of Guadalupe Church, initially staffed by Fr. William Kane, SJ. Mundelein next attempted to staff the emergent parish with a priest from Mexico, Fr. Miguel García (who celebrated Elidia Barroso's 1924 wedding). García's reportedly "informal" interactions with women led to his dismissal within months.[19] Mundelein then decided to invite a religious order to minister to the Mexicans in his see; he debated between the Dominicans and the Claretians, choosing the latter. In October 1924, as the cold arrived, two Spanish Claretians settled into the meager residence. So began a century of ministry at Our Lady of Guadalupe and elsewhere in Chicago that dramatically impacted the growing Mexican colonia as well as the Claretian trajectory in the United States.[20]

South Chicago presented a new missionary challenge for the Claretians. In great contrast to San Antonio or East Los Angeles, Mexican people did not dominate South Chicago. Enormous steel mills hugged

the lake shore, trains pulling gondolas of coke cut through the neighborhood of aging homes, many of which served as boardinghouses. The
mills had drawn laborers from Europe until World War I. Employers
increasingly turned to Mexico when the war and then the immigration
quotas basically cut off entry after 1924 for people from eastern and
southern Europe. Mexicans comprised a minority in this polyglot area
as the Claretians settled in: just 7.6 percent of this neighborhood at their
pre–World War II height in 1930. Yet on some blocks near the church,
Mexicans made up 35 percent of the residents. South Chicago's Catholic
parishes were spiritual and community homes for Poles, Serbs, Croa-
tians, and other European immigrants and their offspring. Amidst the
more established European-origin steel workers and neighbors, Mexicans occupied a low rung and faced a degree of racialized disparage-
ment. Still, the steel mills came to prefer Mexican workers, and Mexican
families appreciated stable, year-round work in the city.[21]

The prospect of starting work in Chicago thrilled the Claretians. To
them Chicago was the "Rome of American Catholicism," with over two
thousand priests, ten thousand nuns, and an immense network of parochial schools.[22] Chicago had a history of supporting missionary work
overseas and in the less-churched parts of the United States. The Claretians knew this firsthand. Their Texas missions had received impactful
funds from the Chicago-based Catholic Extension Society.

The day-to-day realities of missionary work in Chicago proved so-
bering. Their base in South Chicago had its own difficulties. The little
wooden barracks-turned-church proved inadequate. The pipes froze.
The stove worked poorly, filling the air with coal smoke. Even the Polish handyman could not believe the meager, cramped circumstances
in which the missionaries lived. When African Americans purchased
nearby lots to build a church, the Claretians panicked at the prospect,
and argued that such proximity could not stand given "the antipathy that
the Mexican has toward the Black." The Claretians brought this concern
to the attention of local Catholic laypeople who bought back the lots
from the Black church. Archbishop Mundelein invited the Spaniards to
his New Year's Day reception for clergy at his *palacio*, as the Claretians
termed the north-side mansion. After the newcomers kissed his ring, he
asked, "are you going to the Mexicans all around Chicago?" His question
stunned the Spanish men given South Chicago's peripheral location. As

Fr. Sebastián Ripero recalled, "from this corner in the city's south, how could we attend to the Mexicans that lived spread out in the immense city?"[23] The Extension Society, it turned out, would not support the Claretians' initial steps. Extension's president explained, "Chicago even in one's wildest dreams, is not a Missionary Field." Fr. James Tort (1880–1955) countered, "I had never suffered so much in the deserts of Texas and Arizona as I have in the greatest and richest diocese, Chicago."[24] The thrill of Chicago wore off quickly.

No matter the Claretians' tenuous footing, they pursued their mission in Chicago. Beyond their ongoing work at Our Lady of Guadalupe, they established four catechetical centers throughout the city. They attempted to serve Mexican people in the distant cities of Waukegan and Milwaukee, one hundred miles north. Two of the railyard-based catechetical centers quickly evolved into chapels in rented storefronts, outfitted with old church furnishings (with financial help eventually won from the Extension Society). Elidia Barroso, introduced at the beginning of this chapter, began connecting regularly with Mexican Catholics at one makeshift capilla.

Fr. Tort, who we last saw in Prescott, Arizona, where he employed unorthodox methods to build a Mexican chapel, was sent to South Chicago in 1925, joining the two priests and a brother in their tight quarters. (They fashioned a room for him by dividing one bedroom into two tiny rooms, so small that Tort's bedstead had to be cut down in size.) Tort, heavily accented English notwithstanding, energetically made contacts wherever he could. With a Spanish-speaking Jesuit, he visited railroad camps and boardinghouses and created a census of resident Mexicans. Tort typed the list of names and addresses; the resulting seventeen-page document, more than nine hundred individuals, made his case regarding the numbers of Mexican people ripe for Catholic outreach. Tort worked with the Catholic Instructional League, mostly Irish and Anglo Catholic women, to arrange Christmas parties in the boxcar communities.[25] He maintained connections with sympathetic Chicago bishops. He kept the local politicians and business leaders informed of the plight of Mexican Catholics. Tort considered various existing properties and construction estimates to create permanent, brick and mortar churches for the growing Mexican colonias of South Chicago and the Near West Side. In 1926, the Claretians gradually eased their way into St. Francis of Assisi, an old German parish near the Loop, the city's multiple train stations and sprawling train yards.[26] Two years later, they inaugurated their own new church in South Chicago.

While the name *Nuestra Señora de Guadalupe* naturally beckoned mexicanos in Chicago, in its earliest years the parish struggled to retain committed members. Perhaps it was the colonia's financial instability and youth, the harsh winters, the uninviting wooden frame building, and maybe the initial Claretian staffing. For whatever reason, laypeople hesitated to make this church home. Attendance at Mass dipped during a heavy snowfall or during summer layoffs from the steel mills (when people left the city for work on sugar beet farms in nearby states). The Claretians revealed their own poverty in 1926 and from the pulpit asked the meager parish to donate coal, an extra room, and even a car to meet their own needs.[27]

The Claretians encouraged Mexican newcomers to align themselves with the South Chicago parish in ways that echoed lived religion in Mexico. Special Masses on the twelfth day of each month facilitated devotion to Guadalupe. The priests reminded people to bring a rosary to the Feast of El Carmen. While supporting Mexican devotions, the Claretians simultaneously nurtured American ways to become devoted parishioners. The parish initiated a Holy Name Society for the men.[28] The new society encouraged members to take part in colossal events for the International Eucharistic Congress in Chicago in 1926: one Mass at Soldier Field, another at Mundelein Seminary. In May 1927, twenty-five children made their first Holy Communion, after which a photographer captured a shot of the group—the future of Catholic Mexican Chicago. Then the children processed from the church to a nearby hall where they celebrated with ice cream and cake. The priests encouraged all to plan a fundraising jamaica featuring the raffle of an automobile (as advised by the Knights of Columbus). That first fair was poorly attended. Worse, people did not purchase enough raffle tickets. For eight Sundays after the jamaica, the priest announced that the raffle was extended, haranguing people to sell tickets.[29] American Catholic ways did not always work for Mexicans.

The outbreak of the Cristero War in Mexico, pitting the anti-clerical regime of Plutarco Elías Calles against clergy and most Catholic laypeople in Mexico, colored religious life in South Chicago, as it did in

San Antonio and Los Angeles. Historian Julia Young details how, "by the mid-1920s, Mexican Catholic religious devotion would incorporate a markedly political agenda."[30] With Catholic worship banned in 1926, hundreds of Mexican clergy—priests, bishops, female religious, and seminarians—went into exile in the United States, including Chicago. Our Lady of Guadalupe hosted an exiled priest with whom they mounted an annual novena to Nuestra Señora de la Esperanza, a rising devotion in Jacona, Michoacán. On occasion, the Claretians publicly decried the anti-Catholic events in Mexico. For example, as December 12 approached in 1926, the priests reminded Mass goers to prepare for the feast, "as there will not be Mass in the Guadalupe sanctuary in Mexico, accordingly we should celebrate as much as we can in this poor sanctuary." Several times the priests urged action, especially prayer and church attendance to counter Calles, whom they labeled a "Bolshevik" and an impious tyrant.[31] In 1927, the members of the Holy Name Society decided to take the "popular name of Vasallos de Cristo Rey," alluding to the Cristero struggle in Mexico. While the Claretians in Chicago, San Antonio, and Los Angeles hosted many exiled Mexican clergy, I have found few indications of exiled Claretians during the Cristero conflict. This stands in contrast to the many Mexican Claretians sheltered in 1914. The exiled Cordi-Marian Sisters did come to Chicago in 1927, partnering with the Claretian Missionaries. The "Mexican sisters" supported immigrant families for seven decades, providing childcare, kindergarten, summer programs, music classes, and catechism instruction.

Similar to San Antonio, people took part in countless processions at the South Chicago parish. At night, the laity carried candles. Many Decembers the faithful filed through the steel barrio's snow-covered streets to show their devotion to the Virgin of Guadalupe. Walking in formation they expressed their dedication to Cristo Rey and to the Sacred Heart of Jesus. They prayed for peace in Mexico. After 1929, parishioners walked together with the many Euro-Americans who demonstrated their devotion to the newly installed St. Jude.

Fr. Tort well understood that processions could be a powerful symbol of presence. In the year leading up to the opening of the new brick Our Lady of Guadalupe Church, he led parishioners to process from the old church on at least four occasions: the groundbreaking, the placement of the cornerstone, the dedication, and finally, the first Mass in the church

in September 1928. Tort meticulously planned for maximum attendance and publicity for these events in the city's English- and Spanish-
language press. Tort played up the terrible, anti-Catholic conditions in
Mexico.[32] Photographers captured the visiting cardinal and bishops
from Mexico and the Euro-American Knights of Columbus. Historian
Malachy McCarthy details how Tort orchestrated the participation of the
Mexican laity and the visible collaboration of English-speaking Catholics. Cardinal Mundelein spoke to the Claretians afterward. Impressed
with their efforts, he suggested that the Claretians "create a junior seminary to get vocations for our Congregation."[33] In an area that outsiders
judged dismal, "made for industry, not for men and women and little
children," Tort and the Claretians literally put the new Mexican church
on the map.[34]

Once installed in the new, spacious church at 91st Street and Brandon,
Our Lady of Guadalupe parish became a true center of activity. Lay societies formed, including the St. Vincent DePaul Society. The church hall,
in the basement, opened up the parish in a variety of ways. There the
parish hosted its first "bunco and card party" (noted in English, suggesting the attendees were Euro-Americans). On December 12, after many
Masses in honor of the church's patroness, the hall offered a spacious
place for an evening showcasing literary and musical talents (*Velada Lit-
erario Musical*). On Christmas Eve, parishioners put on a Nativity play
for children (*pastorela infantil*) in the salón until 2 am. Then people,
sleepy children in tow, ascended the stairs for a Christmas Mass at 3
am that filled the sanctuary (the Claretians recorded that "americanos"
comprised half of the attendees). On December 31, they observed with
satisfaction that "this year has been one of increased life and movement
for this house."[35]

The year 1929 brought tremendous changes to the new parish, especially with the introduction of the devotion to St. Jude Thaddeus.
With St. Jude, the "Mexican" church took on a decidedly dual cast.
On a day-to-day basis, the Claretians administered Our Lady of Guadalupe for Mexican parishioners, fostering a refuge in Chicago. At the
same time, under the same roof, the Claretians oversaw the shrine to
St. Jude. Many Anglo Catholics attended Mass for the chance to visit
the shrine. Euro-Americans dominated the multiple novenas to St. Jude
that the Claretians publicized throughout the year. The Claretians found

themselves catering to two avid groups: English-speaking and Spanish-speaking. While the church remained Our Lady of Guadalupe, many non-Mexicans simply called it "St. Jude's." The Mexican American boys' baseball team wore jerseys emblazoned with "St. Jude," with O.L.G. stitched above in much smaller letters.

Despite the economic devastation of the Depression and the threat of forced repatriation, most families in South Chicago persisted, making do with less.[36] When the steel mills reduced hours to two days a week, families built up extensive gardens (*milpas*) in empty land beyond the neighborhood, kids scavenged for pop bottles and coal, threadbare garments hung from clotheslines. City officials selected the St. Vincent DePaul Society to distribute aid to the needy, thus making the Mexican church a charitable hub.

The young Tejano priest, Fr. Leonard Cuellar (1909–78), provided a candid take on the Chicago parish in the 1930s. On December 31, 1937, he typed a long, chatty letter to his friends at Dominguez Seminary, his "Alma Mater" in California. "Dear Boys," he began and then how much he missed the familiar rituals and comradery at Dominguez, as well as the milder weather. A Chicago ice storm, with streets "just like glass," was a trial. He recounted the long hours hearing confessions and packed Masses on December 12 and Christmas. Of the musicians who came on December 12, Cuellar reflected, "of course, some of these fellows you never see them in church. They come on Our Lady of Guadalupe's Day, but after that maybe you never see them again." The young priest oversaw the parish Catholic Youth Organization and named the champions, Jesse, Joe, and Salvador, as exemplars of an emerging generation of Mexican American Chicagoans. While Cuellar wrote the three-page letter in English, filled with American slang and conjuring Irish accents, he regularly addressed the older pastor, Fr. Anthony Catalina, in Spanish.[37] Cuellar's bilingualism certainly helped in this busy parish that served Mexican immigrants, their Chicago-reared children, as well as a steady stream of English speakers from the neighborhood and beyond—drawn by the St. Jude devotion.

The South Chicago church became a second home as people from Mexico made lives anew. The Claretians at first had to coax Mexican laypeople into regular support. That changed over time as people took part in weddings, baptisms, funerals, and other rites of passage at

Our Lady of Guadalupe. On Sundays the priest declared the banns (*amonestaciones*) of couples soon to marry. Names and home towns in Mexico, deep in memory, were read aloud. Most of the engaged couples came from different towns and states in Mexico, meeting only in a boxcar camp, the sugar beet fields, or under the towering steel mills. Together they would birth an emerging Mexican Chicago, with history in different parts of Mexico, but raised in Chicago. They spoke Spanish at home and English was their public language of school, streets, and jobs. In 1940, a new gym was dedicated for Mexican American boys and girls. Parents enrolled their children at the Our Lady of Guadalupe School in a brand-new building in 1949. The parish, like the Claretians, embraced Mexican and American culture almost seamlessly in the mid-century.[38]

When the parish installed nine colorful, icon-driven stained-glass windows in 1956, it embodied the shared goals of Claretian clergy and the laity at Our Lady of Guadalupe. (Plain glass had served as windows since the church opened in 1928.) In the more settled and more prosperous postwar era, South Chicago Mexican Catholics could afford to support the sanctuary's beautification. With the leadership of Fr. Severino Lopez (1918–2012), himself a vocation from Our Lady of Guadalupe, the parish ordered unique windows from F.X. Zettler in Munich, at a cost of $1,800 per window.[39] On the sanctuary's east side, three windows brought to life the story of St. Jude, whose veneration was still expanding nationwide three decades after its founding by Fr. Tort. One panel, "the world is turning to Jude," portrayed an international group of devotees, including Africans and native Americans, and men and women with European features. The Immaculate Heart of Mary, the Claretians' special devotion, centered another panel.

To the west, four panels depicted the Virgin of Guadalupe's apparition to the indigenous Juan Diego. This miraculous story dates back to 1531. The windows made lifelike that iconic Mexican moment. At the rocky Tepeyac hill, with its radiant turquoise-green cactus (*nopalera*) tipped with amber flowers, the Virgin Mary appears, in a red gown and deep blue cloak appointed with golden stars draped modestly over her head. Juan Diego kneels below her, roses spilling from his dark mauve cloak (*tilma*). Another window showcased San Felipe de Jesús, missionary-martyr and Mexico's first saint, and St. Anthony May Claret.[40]

The mostly Anglo St. Jude League underwrote nearly half of the windows' cost, with other large donations provided by the mostly Mexican Holy Name Society and Archicofradía del Corazón de María. About 170 individuals and families contributed at least ten dollars to adorn their church, which evolved from a refugio in the 1920s to a place that was home in the 1950s. As Fr. Lopez predicted at the 1956 dedication, "these artistic windows will proclaim in their silent grandeur *your* love and devotion to this church and Shrine." Multiple generations have since visited Our Lady of Guadalupe: for prayer, for celebration, in thanksgiving, and in sorrow and in memory. Looking up from the pews, the windows' radiant colors and arresting iconography speak to the distinctive community that has called this parish home for a century.

How a Catholic Church Anchored Latino Perth Amboy

In the 1940s, the first Spanish speakers settled in Perth Amboy, New Jersey: an ethnically diverse, industrial city that celebrated its colonial roots. Fr. James Tort visited the area in 1943 and recognized the presence of Spanish speakers and Portuguese. The city had nine Catholic parishes. St. Stephen's served the Poles since 1893. The Slovaks dedicated Holy Trinity Roman Catholic Church in 1902; Our Lady of Hungary Church opened in 1903. In 1908, Ukrainians saw the dedication of their Catholic Church of Assumption. Not a single parish seemed aware of the newest arrivals from Latin America. The Bishop of Trenton, William Griffin, asked local clergy to support Tort in his mission to locate the scattered people.[41]

Tort returned in 1947 and, often traveling by bus, he located "over 30 Portoricans," families from Cuba, Ecuador, Peru, and Chile, and a sizeable, organized Portuguese community. He soon proposed a diocesan-sponsored Latin American Center.[42] The diocese purchased a two-family home at 441 Lawrence Street for this purpose and printed a trilingual handbill inviting people—in Spanish, Portuguese, and English—to come by for assistance of any kind; "if you cannot come, write us, and we will be more than glad to visit you at your home." On a chilly afternoon in November 1949, one hundred people gathered outside on Lawrence Street to dedicate the building as Immaculate Heart of Mary Mission. Neighborhood Catholics witnessed the event. With the Knights of Columbus as an honor guard, sheltered under a tent loaned by the Zylcka Funeral Home, Bishop Griffin, the Claretian provincial, Fr. Tort and five other priests blessed the new chapel and mission at 4 pm. As night fell, the clergy walked to a celebratory dinner at the nearby Portuguese Sporting Club.[43] The mission underway, Tort left within weeks for another assignment. The Claretian-founded mission grew into, I believe, the first Spanish-speaking parish in New Jersey.[44]

The mission initially struggled to find a clear path forward. Fr. Andrew Roy and Fr. Thomas Matin devoted themselves to Perth Amboy in the 1950s, but with different styles. Fr. Roy, born in Spain in 1911, but in the United States since 1932 (where he completed his studies with the Claretians), was new to parish work.[45] In 1948 he began the mission by poring through the local phone directory for "Latin named people"; starting with the As, he contacted the Arias household. He gradually assembled a census of the Spanish-speaking families and individuals.

Fr. Roy tended to describe Puerto Ricans as a challenge. In late 1948, he reported to the bishop, "the most serious problem here at Perth Amboy is presented by the Puerto Ricans." He complained of the many single men and women who led a "free life, that is, almost lawless." An attempted Puerto Rican club failed due to their "inconstancy and insincerity." Roy connected more easily with Euro-Americans. He lauded the Portuguese who "united to help us in their work." Roy persisted in framing the ongoing migration of Puerto Ricans as a "real and serious problem . . . alarming for Church and State."[46] As befit the mission, he served Puerto Rican people with interpreting, seeking better housing, obtaining food donations for needy families, and intervening with local authorities.[47] When Roy visited Puerto Rico in 1954, he seemed to gain a fuller sense of his Caribbean flock and a more positive framing. Newspapers in Puerto Rico showed him, smiling, as he received a Puerto Rican flag from Governor Luis Muñoz Marín, destined for his compatriots in Perth Amboy. When the priest delivered the flag, the photo from Perth Amboy appeared in *El Mundo* in San Juan. In these news stories the flag appears as an innocuous sign of a transnational community, but it also carried a more charged meaning as the United States repressed Puerto Rican nationalists.[48]

Fr. Roy's initial negative attitudes toward the Puerto Ricans mirrored common views about the perceived "problematic" strangers.

With an estimated two thousand Puerto Ricans in 1954, Perth Amboy had the highest ratio of Puerto Ricans of any New Jersey city. *The New York Times* highlighted local efforts to ease their entry. Puerto Ricans (described as "the problem"), pushed out of New York City, then moved to Perth Amboy, but supposedly they were ill-equipped to work and fit in. An experimental night school program stressed industrial English with the goal of preparing newcomers for work settings in New Jersey.[49] Throughout the northeastern United States, Spanish-speaking arrivals and their children struggled to establish themselves in a deindustrializing economy.

Fr. Thomas Matin (1900–1975) voiced no complaints about the newcomers who overflowed the Lawrence Street chapel and its Fatima Social Center. German-born Matin, with many years of experience in Mexican parishes in Chicago and Los Angeles, energetically expanded on the growing mission.[50] He quickly attended to the devotional traditions of the Puerto Ricans. He shunted aside the Fatima League with its mostly Euro-American membership. The Holy Name Society replaced it and soon attracted many dozens of Latin American men. Matin moved decisively to find more adequate space for the ever-larger community. He convinced the diocese to support his emerging parish's takeover of the old Church of the Assumption (vacant after the founding Ukrainians moved to a new location). To make the church more attractive to his parishioners, Matin obtained a statue of St. John the Baptist, patron saint of Puerto Rico. In June 1956, he blessed the statue, following with a "traditional *verbena*": a fundraising fair on the parish grounds. He reported that Mass attendance at the newly renamed La Asunción church multiplied from sixty people to eight hundred. To increase attendance at the popular Día de San Juan, Matin sought the bishop's permission to hold a Sunday afternoon Mass so allowing farmworkers to join the celebration.[51]

Fr. Matin stood pleased, in his white straw hat, among increasingly large groups of children who took part in summer programs at Asunción. Girls wore white anklets under their sandals, the boys in gym shoes or scuffed lace-ups—some climbing on the yard's stone wall. When these children made their first Holy Communion, Matin preached a traditional sermon (he called it a *fervorin*) at the Mass. To support the surging population, he located Spanish-speaking nuns, found a convent for

Figure 2.3 Children in summer program, Fr. Thomas Matin (top right), Perth Amboy, New Jersey, n.d. Source: Claretian Missionaries Archives USA-Canada.

them, and obtained their funding from the diocese.[52] Notified of new arrivals in Perth Amboy, the Claretians sent each a letter and a leaflet, enclosing a picture of La Providencia (Our Lady of Providence). A home visit followed the mail. In his copious letters, reports, and press releases, Matin never disparaged Puerto Ricans. He simply worked to bring them into the Catholic fold, to meet their needs as adults and young people, be it at Immaculate Heart of Mary, Our Lady of Fatima, or Asunción—all names of worship spaces in Perth Amboy administered by the Claretians into the 1960s.

The Claretians reached out to Puerto Ricans who lived in the surrounding countryside, whether through missions held at chicken farms or in vacant shops. From 1955 on, Fr. Matin doggedly built up a makeshift mission center in Cassville, first in a converted restaurant on Route 528; by 1960, the bishop dedicated a free-standing church named for St. Anthony Claret. The Claretians created missions in nearby counties that became parishes: Cassville (St. Monica's), Lakewood (St. Anthony Claret), and Lakehurst (San Juan Bautista). Matin produced a Spanish-language brochure that asked, "Que hago? Adonde Voy?" ("What should I do? Where do I go?"). The simple leaflet urged people to call the rectory at 441 Lawrence, but included addresses and schedules for Mass, confession, and catechism instruction at the four Claretian-staffed centers. A hand-drawn map demonstrated how to arrive from New Brunswick, Freehold, and Lakehurst. The leaflet encouraged people to avail themselves of the sacraments, to get involved in parish societies, and reminded them not to attend non-Catholic churches. To those who followed this guidance, the leaflet promised, "This way you will go along the path of true happiness, goodness and justice. And all other things will be given to you in addition."[53]

Latin Americans, mostly from Puerto Rico, kept arriving in Perth Amboy throughout the 1950s and 1960s. Consider some individuals from Guayanilla, a rural district on Puerto Rico's southern coast. Anabel M. spent fifteen years as an assembly worker at Metex Corp. in Edison. She was a communicant at Our Lady of Fatima Church in Perth Amboy, where she led as president of the Asociación de Apostolados. Anabel was also president of the city's Puerto Rican Women's Civic Organization. Luis I. came to Perth Amboy as a twelve-year-old. For decades he was a machine operator at Goldberg Scrap Metal in Perth Amboy; he was also a cabinet maker and mechanic. Virgilio F. left Guayanilla at age eleven. After serving in the Army during the Vietnam War, he worked as a forklift operator for thirty years. He was a member of the International Brotherhood of Teamsters, Union Local 210. Albertina T. arrived at age thirty-two. She was a homemaker and a parishioner of La Asunción Church. Margarita S. came to Perth Amboy in 1953, at age fifteen. She was a seamstress at the Individualized Shirt Company and a member of the International Ladies Garment Union. At Our Lady of Fatima Church, she became a Eucharistic Minister and helped found the Grupo de Oración Carismático. Rubén, Anabel, Luis, Virgilio, Albertina, Margarita: They all worked, dreamed, waited, and they found a new home in Perth Amboy. Many found a refuge and a second home at church.[54]

The Claretians became go-to people for information on the Latino population. When Puerto Rican youth and Perth Amboy police clashed during a series of hot August nights in 1966 over enforcement of an anti-loitering law, the city was on high alert. Recent years had seen urban uprisings in Harlem, Philadelphia, and Watts in Los Angeles. The Hall

Avenue riots, as the skirmishes were known, laid bare the simmering sense of injustice between brown youth and the white police force. The local paper editorialized that "Calm and Reason Must Prevail," quoting Fr. Raymond Bianchi (1926–2015), pastor at Our Lady of Fatima, on the Puerto Ricans' grievances. A reporter for *The Evening News* even phoned Fr. Walter Mischke, Fatima's pastor from 1960 to 1966, in Chicago for his perspective on the riots.[55] One reporter mentioned that a "small group of parishioners from Our Lady of Fatima said the groups were no larger than usual on a warm summer evening."[56] Bianchi took part in a public forum that week, he visited the mayor's office, and generally urged non-Latino Perth Amboy to understand the perspective of young, Spanish-speaking immigrants. "In Puerto Rico they're accustomed to standing around on the streets," Bianchi explained. He even drew connections back to Greek and Roman history and traditions of people talking in the marketplace. "It's in their blood," asserted the priest.[57]

While the press widely quoted the Claretians, Puerto Ricans in Perth Amboy were hardly voiceless. They spoke up at public forums and wrote letters to the local paper that asserted their citizenship. The Puerto Ricans, despite reaching 20 percent of the local population, clearly found their place contested. Just days after the unrest, Nicholas Orengo, a parishioner at Our Lady of Fatima, wrote to the Bishop of Trenton to expose multiple ways that other parishes did not welcome Latinos ("go to the Spanish Church"). At least one parochial school would not enroll Puerto Rican children. "None of the local priests showed any kind of interest towards our pastor, Rev. Bianchi, during the 4 day riots." Orengo added, "if the local priests are like this you will not have to guess how the parishioners are."[58] At this tense moment, the Claretians would continue their unique role as intermediaries, trusted both by Spanish-speaking parishioners and by the Euro-American establishment.

The Claretians and their parishioners had made the best of inadequate, improvised spaces in Perth Amboy for two decades. The diocese always supported the mission with cars, the purchase of buildings, and renovations. Nonetheless this fast-rising parish still lacked a fitting space in the late 1960s. Its original chapel and rectory, the converted two-family house on Lawrence Street, was always insufficient for its membership; it was demolished circa 1967 to widen the ramps for the Outerbridge Crossing to Staten Island. In March 1968, the Claretians opened a new parish center downtown in a renovated two-story commercial building (338 Smith Street). The 1914 building encompassed living quarters for Claretians and for nuns, classrooms for catechism and sodality meetings, as well as a chapel. Two hundred adults attended English classes at the center, in collaboration with the local Board of Education. But Masses remained at Asunción, the old Ukrainian church. As the Latino population showed no signs of slowing, the parish dreamed of a church of their own that would allow their Catholic community to thrive.

On a picture-perfect day in September 1968, people lined downtown Perth Amboy's Smith Street to watch the Desfile Hispano Americano, a parade organized by Our Lady of Fatima parish. Puerto Ricans made a strong showing. The Guayanilla Social Club's float cruised down the street; white-gloved young women waved at spectators from atop a vivid green hill, with faux palm trees, a *casita*, and a red hammock that swung in the breeze. The Puerto Rican Community Council festooned a convertible with red streamers and the American flag. Dominicanos had a significant presence in the parade. On foot, a woman in a flowered mini dress and a white-suited man proudly carried a large Dominican flag. Behind them marched Dominicans of all ages. Latino-owned businesses joined the parade. Migdalia's Bridal Shop showed off a tuxedo-clad groom linking arms with a bride in a white gown, veil and all; the pair topped the wedding cake-like float. The Quiñones Travel Agency's float conjured a jet plane in flight. The festival's *reina*, Miss Hispano America was perched on a red throne. In a butterscotch yellow gown and white stole, she waved to all along the route.[59]

The Hispanic parade included staples of old Perth Amboy. Five high school marching bands, led by baton twirlers, wound their way through the downtown. A contingent of police officers marched in formation. A pair of baseball players solemnly bore a large photo of the late President John F. Kennedy. In Perth Amboy, long home to the Irish, Slovaks, Hungarians, Jews, and Poles, the Spanish-speaking community had clearly come to stay, "flooding our city with music and flags."[60]

Catholic elements of the new and thriving community could not be missed. The float for Nuestra Señora de Fatima parish featured women in an array of folkloric costumes, a nod to the city's diverse Latin American origins. The parade's largest group was the Holy Name Society. In jackets and narrow ties, eighty men processed in three dignified rows—with a traditional banner at the front. This highly organized society brought together Spanish-speaking men, keeping them connected to their faith and their new-found parish.

Perth Amboy mounted a parade with an even larger Latino population in 1970. Fr. Bianchi, the Grand Marshal, in a charro suit with a matching sombrero, was all smiles on Smith Street. The Claretians, Our Lady of Fatima parish, and the "Spanish community" sponsored a Latin American Heritage Banquet at the ZPA, a Polish hall.[61] Bianchi gave the invocation. Guests dined on prime rib and stuffed cabbage rolls. The sounds of Puerto Rican–born Chuito Velez and his orchestra filled the hall: mambos, boleros, and "Dancing Bugaloo" from his recent album. Mayor James J. Flynn, then in his fifth term, spoke. Attendees applauded the new reina, Miss Linda Marrero. The evening's proceeds added to funds for a long-anticipated new church.

The dream became reality at the site of a closed bottling plant on Smith Street. On September 19, 1971, the new Our Lady of Fatima Church was dedicated. The church's groundbreaking and opening garnered much attention in the Perth Amboy and regional press, often based on Claretian-penned press releases. The diocese had chosen to support brand-new church construction at a time when Perth Amboy's overall population was stagnant and declining. The city's old Euro-American parishes clearly were in decline. Did the diocese consider transferring one of those to the Claretians? This was a low point for church construction in the United States generally, more so in inner city neighborhoods.[62] The Claretians recognized the great need and the potential of Perth Amboy's Latino population and they successfully made the case for new church construction to the diocese.

After another procession, people poured into the new Fatima sanctuary, which seated 720 people, for a bilingual liturgy. Frs. Matin, Roy, and Mischke returned for the dedication and first Mass. Santo Nombre men, Apostolado women, and families with roots in many parts of Latin America filled the pews that fanned out in a semi-circle. They marveled at the sanctuary's clean lines and uncluttered views. The sanctuary embodied the Vatican II ideal that "the church building is the house of people"; like a modern house, "roomy, bright, pleasant, restful, open," allowing people to "see each other, hear each other rejoice in each other's presence." The up-to-date church, built to enable the laity's active participation in the changing Catholic Church, probably took some getting used to.[63] Still, after twenty years in temporary worship spaces, católicos now had a modern, spacious home in Perth Amboy.

A year later, the parish had four Claretian priests and six Mexican sisters "totally committed to the catechetical and social work." The sisters, with thirteen lay teachers, ran the CCD program that served eight hundred children each week. Fr. Luis Turon asserted that Spanish-speaking Perth Amboy was 95 percent Catholic, if not all practicing. (Five Spanish Protestant churches had three hundred members total.) At Fatima, the largest parish societies included the Holy Name, the Dominican Hijos de Altagracia, the Apostolado de Oración, and the Hijas de María. Other active societies included Young Christian Students, Niños de la Cruzada Eucarístico, and the Christian Family Movement. Hundreds of people had taken part in cursillos.[64] The freestanding parish social center had a large gym that hosted plays, concerts, retreats, and banquets. The social center was—and remains—a busy place. The Claretian stamp on downtown continues. The old, makeshift parish center from the 1960s was attractively rehabbed as the Claret Center in 2019.

Since Fr. Tort's arrival in the late 1940s, the Claretians had always advocated on behalf of the once small population of Puerto Ricans, often problematized by the local press, city, and police. The Claretians created spaces in which the community could grow, where mutual aid was offered, and dignity maintained, on Sundays or in weekly meetings. The large, modern buildings downtown were a highly visible sign of católicos' arrival and respectability in Perth Amboy.

* * *

This chapter explored how Spanish-speaking parishes emerged in the cities of San Antonio, Chicago, and Perth Amboy. These parishes shared many characteristics. In each one the founding laity were emigrants and exiles in a strange land, far from the rancho or barrio that they had called home. Moving to the United States meant confronting a new language, often facing ethno-racial subordination, and getting accustomed to a city that seldom felt like home. For some, finding a new home could be as basic as attending Mass or murmuring prayers before a familiar icon such as La Providencia or the Virgin of Guadalupe. As these new members became immersed in the parish, by joining a theater group or building a parade float, serving as an usher or donning the sash of the Apostolate of Prayer, the church often served as a substitute pueblo or rancho that provided new affective and social ties. The lay societies became channels to dignity and empowerment.

The Claretians rose to the challenge of establishing parishes in dioceses throughout the country. Many of the Claretians were themselves immigrants: Frs. Tort and Roy from Spain, Fr. Matin from Germany, Fr. Bianchi from Italy. They did the groundwork of visiting families in boxcars and scattered apartments, learning of their needs, and then initiating regular worship often in provisional spaces, such as a repurposed barracks or a two-story house. In 1920s Chicago and 1950s New Jersey, the Catholic hierarchy barely glimpsed the nascent Spanish-speaking population. The Claretians penned reports and letters in English that forced the local chancery and other Catholics to see the emerging need. In each case, the Claretians convinced diocesan authorities that barely coalesced communities deserved proper, dignified churches in unlikely spaces such as a barrio of unpaved streets, under the shadow of the steelyards, or on a site vacated by a bottling plant. When the churches opened their doors, the Claretians met the spiritual needs of arrivals from Mexico and the Spanish Caribbean, while attending to the generation coming of age in the United States. Immaculate Heart of Mary in San Antonio, Our Lady of Guadalupe in Chicago, and Our Lady of Fatima in Perth Amboy stand today as vital Catholic sites of refuge.

The Claretians demonstrated a special knack for connecting with their new parishioners. As Fr. Tort reflected to American bishops in the 1940s, "It is not enough for the Priests in charge of the Mexican people to speak well their language, Spanish, it is also necessary to like them and understand them, which is not so frequently found."[65] Tort was spot-on. Most Claretians radiated warmth and understanding and that drew parishioners. Running busy city parishes meant unending tasks: from writing homilies and preparing people to receive sacraments, to choosing (and paying for) replacement windows, ordering cases of beer for a parish festival, and keeping an eye on the building loan from the diocese. All the while they lived in community with fellow Missionary Sons of the Immaculate Heart of Mary, Claretians, with daily prayer and monthly spiritual exercises. For many, community life could be a buffer to the stressors of parish administration and the loneliness that many priests face. For some men, "a little bit of community life went a long way," and they chafed at the daily expectations.[66] After 1940, the rising number of American Claretians—who could maneuver and minister in English and Spanish—proved essential to the province's accomplishments for decades to come.

3

Communicating in Two Languages

Race and the Emergence of the US Province

El ideal que debe de tener es cuidar a todos los mexicanos, y no descuidar a ningun Americano.

The ideal is to care for all the Mexicans, and not to neglect any American.
—Fr. James Tort (1929)

As a youngster in South Chicago at the start of the Depression, Severino Lopez was a newsboy for the *Chicago Herald Examiner*. For three cents he enjoyed the Westerns at the neighborhood movie theater, after which he and his brother played cowboys, "slapping the sides of our corduroy pants to imitate the sound of horses' hooves." Some summer days, Sevy walked north for over two miles, skirting the steel mills, to Rainbow Beach where he collected *verdolagas*, a plant that was greatly prized by Mexican cooks. He gently packed handfuls of the greens into brown paper bags. Back in his neighborhood surrounding Our Lady of Guadalupe Church, he went door to door and sold them to pleased families for five cents a bag. The proceeds went to his mother. The Lopez children spoke English at school, but their immigrant parents insisted on Spanish in the home. He served as an altar boy with three buddies at the Claretian-run church and often helped Fr. James Tort with mailings of pamphlets and letters to promote the new devotion to St. Jude, patron of impossible causes. When Sevy expressed an interest in the priesthood, his religious family supported him and Tort arranged to enroll him in the sole Claretian seminary in the United States at the time. On July 25, 1932, the feast of St. James (and Fr. Tort's birthday), Sevy, his altar boy friends, and their families gathered at their church for a prayerful send-off, seeking Nuestra Señora de Guadalupe's protection. At the Santa

Fe Station downtown, the thirteen-year-old boarded the train with his friends. They waved farewell to the Mexican crowd on the platform. The trip took more than three days, as the boys were bound for Dominguez Seminary, near Los Angeles. Twelve years would pass before Sevy Lopez would next see South Chicago and his family.[1]

For a boy used to the soot and rotten egg smell from Chicago steel mills, the California seminary was a lush and spacious Eden, with orchards and playing fields. Sevy told himself, "I'm staying here!" ("Aqui me quedo!"). These young teens had to acclimate themselves to the rigors of study, obedience, and many hours of silence, like any junior seminary of the era.[2] Sevy pushed through these challenges, but other Mexican American boys, one by one, either left or were dismissed by the seminary prefects. The faculty and administrators—like the American province at that time—were comprised entirely of Spaniards. Many decades later, Lopez reflected on how the faculty's inflexible rigor drew upon their own training in Spanish seminaries.[3] The Spanish Claretians saw themselves as white and, generally, saw the Mexicans as non-white. The Spaniards' "*de facto* racism toward a good number of Mexican students" may have driven out many seminarians, including Sevy's friends from Chicago. Many Spanish priests, "specifically those in charge of formation, were of the opinion that greater efforts should be made to establish a *purely American province*, toward Anglo-Saxon candidates, *los hueros* [sic], 'the light ones.'"[4] Lopez speculated that his own light complexion partly explained his advance to the novitiate. As the province trained its first cohort of US-raised Claretians in the 1930s, being a Mexican American seminarian sometimes meant experiencing the discomfort of "the feeling that I do and do not belong." Lopez termed this feeling of social and cultural insecurity as "el poche syndrome"; *pocho* is the common phrase and spelling used among ethnic Mexican people.[5]

Lopez did become a Claretian and was ordained in 1944. Taking the train home to Chicago twelve years after his departure, he stopped in Phoenix to celebrate Mass at a Claretian parish. The church filled to see him, as a "newly ordained priest of Mexican descent was a rarity in those days." Back at last in his childhood parish, Our Lady of Guadalupe, he celebrated two Masses. First, he presided over the monthly Communion of the St. Jude Police League with an English-language homily. Then the parish mexicanos came for a noon Mass with a Spanish-language homily. At both, the sanctuary was filled with joyful people eager to see their parish son in his white vestments.[6]

Fr. Severino Lopez (1918–2012) had a productive career, mostly in parish ministry in Chicago, California, Texas, Georgia, and elsewhere. He joined a select group of Claretians approved to attend the 1950 canonization of St. Anthony Mary Claret. Spanish-born Claretians, middle-aged and older, comprised most of the US delegation. Lopez was the youngest of the American Claretians to attend the canonization and the only Mexican American. In Roman piazzas, he stood out with his gleaming dark hair and stylish sunglasses.

This chapter explores the rocky road to becoming an American religious community, from 1902 into the 1950s. Following the Mexicans from cotton fields and copper mines to steel mills and factories required that the Claretians exhibit self-sacrifice, humility, and persistence. In the pioneering era, they were *all* Spaniards, mostly involuntary migrants, far from home and unlikely to return there. Their families in Catalan and Basque lands faded to hazy memories. In addition to their primary work to missionize to Spanish-speaking people, each claretiano in the United States struggled to learn fluent (or passable) English. They whittled their traditional two surnames to a single one, ideally one that americanos could pronounce. (Note that some Euro-American Claretians also anglicized their surnames. Richard Toczydlowski became Fr. Todd. Eugene Galecki became Fr. Grainer.) The Spaniards had to acculturate to American ways, including the mores of lived race in the United States.

Initially I planned to focus on language in this chapter, highlighting the Claretians' ability to maneuver in English and Spanish. But research about language uncovered a more complicated, often contradictory story about race and mission. When Anglo Catholics did not want to share pews with Mexican co-religionists, as described earlier, the Claretians often conceded to those wishes and to forms of segregation in the pre–WWII era. Yet ideas and practices regarding race were never uniform. Civil rights crusader and Claretian parishioner Alonso Perales spoke more boldly than the congregation itself. He asserted in 1952, "for the Claretian Fathers, segregation is something repugnant that they consider to be arbitrary, completely contrary to the doctrine and teachings of Our Lord Jesus Christ."[7] As the new province became less Spanish and more American, ideas and practices regarding race evolved.

In the 1930s, a steady stream of home-grown Claretians enrolled at the American seminaries: think Severino Lopez and Robert Alvarado, but also men with Polish, Irish, and German surnames. By 1950, this province was no longer markedly Spanish, but a largely American group of religious—including Mexican Americans—who served Spanish-speaking people. The province, at the same time, harbored a prolonged ambivalence about its mission: whether to concentrate on Hispanic ministry or to reach whiter, wealthier Catholics. Some Claretians wanted the sense of arrival and status that came with aligning themselves with white American Catholics, so taking on judgmental attitudes about the católicos they served. The seminaries recruited boys by enticing them with a future as *missionary* priests in far-off lands, while shrouding the ties to Spanish-speaking ministry in the United States in the recruitment process. I argue that, this ambivalence notwithstanding, the majority of Claretians demonstrated a fundamental sense of empathy, connection, and accompaniment with their Latino flock.

Learning English and Building Networks

The Claretian Missionaries arrived in the United States in 1902 precisely because they were a Spanish-speaking missionary order. As Henry Granjon, Bishop of Tucson, put it to the Claretians, "You speak the language of these poor people."[8] When the Spaniards took over predominantly Mexican parishes, they soon realized that English-language proficiency would also prove essential. This fact seemed extraneous to the sending province of Mexico and the receiving US dioceses. When Frs. Camilo Torrente and Mariano Luisilla arrived to preach in Texas, as we saw earlier, they fumbled their way through encounters with English speakers. Torrente, among the province's great chroniclers, later made sport of their blunders and lack of preparation. When he was selected for the missions in Texas, he suspected that the random English words picked up at university in Spain would prove inadequate. He hired a tutor (*el buen Mister*) who gave lessons at the Hotel Washington in Mexico City. In ten days, he learned little and convinced himself that his feeble English amounted to "worse than nothing" for the Texas trip. His tutor correctly warned him, "when you arrive in the United States, you won't understand a thing. You will need two years to forget the accent and rhythm of the Spanish tongue." When promised an oyster dinner on the Texas Gulf, Torrente heard *hostias* and wondered why communion wafers would be served; a big plate of oysters appeared before him and he understood his error. For decades Torrente enjoyed sharing stories of these linguistic missteps with confreres and seminarians.[9] His anecdotes highlighted the Claretian pioneers' agility and persistence when they faced challenges in their new missions.

The congregation was determined to learn and utilize English in this foundational era while, simultaneously, the Spanish-language ministry remained their bread and butter in the parishes. From their initial post in San Antonio in 1904, the missionaries reported to their confreres "right now we limit our sphere of action to *la raza latina*, but in time we want to open way to *la raza anglo-sajona*." This goal would require improving their English skills, "whose pronunciation is so difficult to obtain."[10] Even early on, the Claretians' missionary aims were not circumscribed by language. The Scalibrinians provide a useful contrast with their aim of preserving faith via preserving the Italian language of the immigrant-laity.[11]

The Claretians studied English, sought US citizenship, and established connections with larger Catholic networks in their new country in order to best advocate for the Mexican laity.[12] A superior at San Marcos instituted group English lessons for the priests and brothers in 1916. He directed the community to carry out their monthly spiritual exercises, a day devoted to prayer and reflection, in English as well as Spanish.[13]

Three Spanish Claretians stand out in the quest to create a functionally bilingual province. Frs. Domingo Zaldívar (1877–1939), Eugenio Sugrañes (1878–1942), and Jaime Tort (1880–1955) all trained at the same Claretian seminary in Catalonia. All arrived in the United States between 1906 and 1914, where they remained for the rest of their lives. Like most Claretians of their era, each one anglicized his name, signaling their willingness to adapt to their new home.

Fr. Eugenio Sugrañes became Eugene Sugranyes. After a year of serving in Mexico, the twenty-seven-year-old was sent to San Marcos, Texas, in 1906 to establish a Claretian community. That parish (today St. John the Evangelist) always served English- and Spanish-speaking parishioners; the pastor needed to speak English to deliver the homily, read the

Figure 3.1 Meeting of Provincial Chapter, 1935. Frs. Zaldívar (sitting, fifth from left); Tort (middle row, seventh from left); Sugrañes (top row, fourth from left). All present were Spaniards. Source: Claretian Missionaries Archives USA-Canada.

announcements, hear confessions, and direct the club for Catholic students in the college town.

Handling business such as banking or the insurance agency required English proficiency, as did corresponding with the bishop, filing annual reports, and seeking funding from the Chicago-based Extension Society. Sugrañes, a bespectacled man, often lost in his thoughts, had an intense personality that offended some. Fellow Claretians praised his determined language study that resulted in "knowing English so perfectly that he could communicate with anyone." Accordingly, superiors sent him to start Claretian ministry at San Gabriel and La Placita in Los Angeles, and to far-flung Yuma, Arizona, and Newman, California. Sugrañes wrote regularly for English-language Catholic papers and magazines as well as books on the history of San Gabriel Mission and a biography of Anthony Mary Claret. One American bishop reportedly said that Sugrañes "knows English better than I do." Upon meeting him, American readers and history buffs were surprised to encounter a "humble Spanish priest."[14]

Fr. Domingo Zaldívar (soon, Dominic) arrived in the United States in 1909, at age thirty-two, after nine years of ministry in Portugal. The Claretians hoped that he would minister to California's Portuguese immigrant population. Working in Los Angeles in the 1910s, he came to speak English fluently. Attractive and well-groomed, a capable and tact-ful administrator, Zaldívar easily gained the trust of others, including American bishops and the wealthy *californio* Dominguez family (who became crucial benefactors to the American Claretians). Appointed su-perior of the Claretians in the United States in 1918, he pushed them in new directions that better rooted the Spaniards in American soil and created educational structures for their successors.

English figured prominently in Zaldívar's daily actions as well as his larger plans. Confreres usually wrote to him in Spanish from California and Arizona. As superior, he responded in English. Under his watch, they issued their first publication, *The Claretian*, in English; the Clare-tians would inaugurate several national magazines for English-speaking Catholic readers. When priests did not advance in their language acqui-sition, Zaldívar sent certain individuals to a private Catholic school to "learn English among Americans, not in the Mexican parishes that we administer and offer little help to that end."[15] Some Spaniards struggled greatly with English and superiors placed them in parishes dedicated solely to Mexican ministry.

The forward-thinking Zaldívar realized that the congregation needed to re-brand themselves for the United States. The formal title, the Con-gregation of the Missionary Sons of the Immaculate Heart of Mary, was simply too much for Americans unfamiliar with the group. He proposed a brief, simpler title that remains to the present: "Claretian Missionaries."

English would dominate at the new schools begun under Zaldívar. Creating a Claretian House of Studies in Washington, DC, adjacent to and affiliated with Catholic University, was a significant action for in-clusion and respect in Catholic America. It opened in a modest frame house in 1922. A larger, more modern structure replaced it in 1958. This brick building, designed for the Claretians, featured classrooms, a dor-mitory, chapel, and other common rooms. Study in Washington became an enriching perk for professed Claretians readying themselves for or-dination and for mid-career priests to obtain a doctorate. The House of Studies also provided a useful stop for newly arrived Spanish priests.[16] In 1924, the iconic californio property at Dominguez, just south of Los Angeles, began a fifty-year run as a seminary. At that Edenic school, seminarian Sevy Lopez found English to be the language of classes and dorms, sporting events and work details.

Zaldívar wanted to position the Claretians more deeply in the American landscape. Envisioning a nationwide ministry, he repeatedly sought to place his men into missions in the Archdiocese of New York (but was ignored). The Claretians angled for St. Louis and Detroit, also without success. The desire to follow Mexican immigrants into the Archdiocese of Chicago required a long game of contact, correspondence, and visits with Archbishop George Mundelein. Zaldívar's persistent efforts to establish a Claretian presence in Chicago finally succeeded in 1924.[17] Chicago broadened the Claretians' prospects in so many ways. They ministered to all of Chicago's Spanish-speaking Catholics through 1960. Chicago also became the fertile ground of the St. Jude devotion which connected to English-speaking Catholics across the country. The devotion led to the establishment of St. Jude Seminary, which attracted hundreds of students in the Midwest and eastern United States.

Fr. Jaime Tort had the most visible influence on the evolving Claretian project here. He spent four years in Mexico before anti-clerical threats and violence forced him to disguise himself in secular clothing and a beard. Fleeing in 1914, Fr. Jaime became Fr. James in the United States.[18] At age thirty-four, learning English could not have been easy. He spent his first decade ministering in rural Texas and northern Arizona. The province sent Tort to Chicago in 1924 to lay the groundwork for Mexican ministry. He epitomized the determined missionary ("who can never be at a stand-still"). Lopez remembered that "Tort did not speak English well, but he was a great communicator." He further mused, "He had a lot of well-to-do friends. There was something in him that appealed to people. Maybe it was his straightforwardness, and his zeal to help the unfortunate."[19] Tort persuaded Chicago power-holders—the archbishop, the mayor, industrialists, Irish Catholic women, and the police—to support Catholic ministry and, in time, three churches for the growing Mexican colonias under the Claretians' stewardship. Tort's remarkable talent for networking in Chicago proved fruitful in subsequent years.

Promoting St. Jude

In the early twentieth century, the Claretians ministered almost exclusively to Mexican people and gained a reputation among them as go-to priests. The Claretians fostered devotions to their own patroness, the

Immaculate Heart of Mary, holding novenas and founding the archcon-fraternity from little Martindale to Los Angeles. These devotions had a certain appeal, but never beyond their parishes. Mexican laypeople always exhibited much greater attention to the Virgin of Guadalupe.[20]

Fr. Tort tried a new devotional focus and put the Claretians on the US Catholic map with his highly effective promotion of the St. Jude devotion starting in 1929. After the move into the new Our Lady of Guadalupe Church, the Claretian priests cajoled mexicanos, Sunday after Sunday, to support their parish. The looming church mortgage weighed heavily on any plans. In an oft-told story by the Claretians, hoping to attract more visitors, in early 1929 Tort acquired additional statues for the church: St. Therese de Lisieux ("the Little Flower") and the then-obscure St. Jude Thaddeus. St. Jude, holding Christ's image at his breast and a flame above his head, symbolizing the Holy Spirit, began to draw visitors to the church, especially from beyond the Mexican parish. By fall, Tort scheduled a novena to the "forgotten apostle" that culminated on his feast day, October 28. The next day, the stock market crashed, marking the beginning of the Great Depression. With steel mills laying off parishioners and parish income plummeting, Tort worked double-time to promote the St. Jude devotion for Catholics all over Chicago and beyond. Women of European descent, not mexicanas, crowded the new shrine. In scholar Robert Orsi's words, St. Jude had "no particular significance to the Claretians, unlike their founder [Claret], whose cult the order was never able to promote successfully in the United States."[21]

Tort drew partly from Anthony Mary Claret's playbook—use the printing press—coupled with modern American methods of market-ing and direct mail. Initially he printed pamphlets and other notices at the parish; altar boys, including Sevy Lopez, stuffed envelopes and distributed handbills for upcoming novenas outside of parishes around the city. Tort organized a St. Jude's League; he requested and received Cardinal Mundelein's approval for the Claretian-run organization in November 1929. In 1932, he organized the Police Branch of the St. Jude League for the Chicago Police Department, and it came to encompass members of the State Police and other members of law enforcement. Chicago police were men who took on gangsters with submachine guns, endured three-hour gun battles, and, they boasted, finally killed the criminals. Grisly tales of this sort, the Police League and Tort believed, would prove to policemen "that they had a real though invisible defense from their newly chosen heavenly Protector, St. Jude Thaddeus."[22] Police League members participated in huge processions on Chicago streets before taking communion en masse; the city's Catholic mayors, Martin Kenneally and Richard J. Daley, often joined this show of law, order, and piety. The Claretians began publication in 1935 of *The Voice of St. Jude*. The monthly magazine bore the masthead, "A Catholic Monthly—Official Organ of the National Shrine of St. Jude. Rev. James Tort CMF Editor."

Amidst the Depression's hardships, the many novenas (nine days of special devotion) brought thousands of laypeople to "St. Jude's," as outsiders tended to call Our Lady of Guadalupe Church.[23] The Claretians conducted the shrine events in English, inside the Mexican church, as Spanish speakers at that time were not drawn to Jude. The clients of St. Jude, men and women, became walking advertisements for the saint's help, often far from Chicago, amplifying the Claretians' new devotion and soon drawing substantial donations.[24]

Danny Thomas, the affable entertainer and early television personality, became the best known of St. Jude's clients. Raised in a Lebanese Catholic family in Toledo, Thomas had witnessed dramatic personal vows to saints. His own mother, when faced with a sick baby, got on her knees, begging "Please, God, spare him and I will vow to you [that] I will beg pennies from door to door for a whole year to give to the poor. Spare my baby." And as a young man trying to break into radio with a baby on the way in 1937, Thomas recalled, "I was so down-and-out in Detroit ... I accidentally learned about the almost unknown St. Jude Thaddeus." A drunk stranger shared the story of his wife's miraculous cure from cancer after the man prayed to St. Jude. The stranger told Thomas of his bargain with St. Jude. "If he answered my prayers, I would tell everyone I could about this forgotten saint." So inspired, Thomas made his own bargain with Jude: "I asked him to show me my way in life, and I vowed to build him a shrine." Thomas moved to Chicago, changed his name (from Amos Muzyad Yaqoob Kairouz), and soon his career took off.

Tellingly, St. Jude's reputation reached Danny Thomas through word of mouth; he still had not visited the national shrine in South Chicago. At a church near his northside Chicago apartment in 1942, he found a pamphlet announcing a novena at the shrine. "I'm suddenly finding out that he [St. Jude] already *had* a shrine in the very city to which Fate had taken me." As Thomas's fame grew—and with it, a good network of Hollywood stars—he acted on Samuel Cardinal Stritch's suggestion to raise funds for a children's hospital to fulfill his promise to St. Jude.[25] In his memoir Thomas dedicated seven passages to his evolving devotion to St. Jude, but never mentioned visiting the shrine itself. The Claretians did develop a relationship with the successful star, who headlined fundraisers and appeared in publicity photos at the shrine. Thomas even starred in a 1959 promotional film for the Claretian Missionaries titled *For Heaven's Sake*, filmed on the set of his popular show *Make Way for Danny*.[26]

While people of Mexican descent knew Claretians as their parish priests, most Anglo Catholics learned about the Claretians via the veneration of St. Jude and related publications. Like most believers in St. Jude, Danny Thomas was English-speaking and had no affiliation with the Mexican church where the saint's reputation arose. The Claretians, beginning with Fr. Tort, aimed their publicity at Anglo Catholics, and only incidentally at Spanish speakers. Their magazine *The Voice of St. Jude* was an English-language publication. The monthly featured a range of articles, as well as selected testimonials by lay Catholics who attested to the saint's positive impact on their lives. Most subscribers lived well beyond the parishes where the Claretians worked. Reading the magazine allowed them to learn all about the Claretian missionaries and their young American seminarians.[27]

Fr. Tort understood how the budding devotion could support the Claretians' mission to Spanish speakers. Two years into the Depression, he typed a letter (in Spanish) to his provincial in California. Tort recognized the mounting dedication to St. Jude in South Chicago and "to all Americans. But we want to grow it more." He sought to expand the distribution of flyers from a "publicity center." Tort argued, correctly, that promoting the Shrine "could be an immeasurable help to the Province, given that *the Americans* continue to give us enough to cover all costs." He toggled back to the Mexican parish that housed the shrine, noting that the recently decorated church was a "beautiful thing." Tort acknowledged that these enhancements had been done by the Mexicans, easy enough "now that they were unemployed."[28] Tort went back and forth in his ministry to two lay groups, who spoke different languages. "The ideal is to care for all the Mexicans, and not to neglect any American," he reported to the Claretian leadership.[29] Tort's optimism and vision of the Claretians in the United States led to another grand project. Despite the inauspicious hard times crippling Chicago—and the two Mexican parishes there struggling to keep the lights on—Tort and the Claretians envisioned a seminary to form missionaries in the heartland.

Nurturing American Vocations

In 1937 the Claretians dedicated the new, three-story St. Jude Seminary in Momence, Illinois. After driving fifty miles south of Chicago's Loop, the last stretch on the rural Dixie Highway, parents and invited donors marveled at the red brick seminary, trimmed in grey-white sandstone, with a large cross at the top. Two circular stone escutcheons bore the congregation's coat of arms and their founder, Anthony Claret, recently designated "Blessed" by the church, a step toward sainthood. Atop a tall pole, the American flag waved in the breeze that also carried the smells of neighboring Illinois farms. On fifty-eight acres, this seminary impressed parents as a healthy place for boys to study and grow, especially compared to the city streets they left behind. After the dedication, the visitors departed, and Fr. Martin Sanz sat down to report to the provincial in California, "Everyone greatly praised the building." He added with satisfaction, "the time has come that the Claretians will be something in these lands."[30] With "these lands," Sanz likely meant Chicago and the Midwest. Rooted in Texas and California for thirty years at that point, the Claretians had worked in Chicago for only a decade. His phrasing also suggested that by launching a seminary that would train American Claretians, the congregation would gain notoriety and respect in the United States.

It took six years to accomplish completion of this postcard-worthy seminary. Fr. Tort began scouting locations for a seminary in 1931; he first looked north of Chicago, where Euro-American friends had land to donate. Cardinal Mundelein, with his grand archdiocesan seminary in the far northern suburbs, blocked any plan that might compete geographically.[31] The Claretians settled on a foreclosed farm south of Chicago in Momence in the Diocese of Joliet. Approved by the provincial office in California, they purchased a modest farmhouse on twelve acres

Figure 3.2 Postcard, St. Jude Seminary, n.d. Source: Claretian Missionaries Archives USA-Canada.

in May 1933. A small Claretian contingent rushed to open the doors in three months, with the modification of a quickly built addition.[32] The St. Jude Police League, with its steadily employed membership from across Chicago, largely underwrote Tort's latest project. Four boys enrolled in September and so began nearly forty years of high school–level education at St. Jude Seminary. Of that first class of four boys, two became Claretians: Frs. Patrick McPolin and Walter Mischke.[33]

In their zeal to open the seminary, the Claretians blundered at this original location. The first four academic years became a comedy of errors. The makeshift chapel at first had neither monstrance nor pews. The Catholic church in Momence donated those; a nearby convent offered an old laundry machine. After Christmas vacation, only three pupils returned. So began a saga of retention challenges at the rustic seminary.[34] The remodeled farmhouse remained inadequate, even after installing electricity. The Spanish priests, who had previously served in Texas or California, grumbled in early 1935, "we are covered in snow, although with heat, the place is very small. Boys have no way to entertain themselves inside." Scabies afflicted the boys that spring and they returned to their Chicago homes to heal, shuttering the seminary for a month. To improve hygiene, the Claretian brother bought a new washer and the farmhouse sink was connected to a sewer. Amidst these crises Fr. Joseph Puigvi sought recruits for the next year. He drove north each week to visit Chicago parochial schools and talked to seventh and eighth grade classes. When the seminary re-opened, two families withdrew their boys, fearful of more contagion and commenting on the lack of high school type study. Families visited, but the deficient physical plant left many shaking their heads. The Claretians admitted many shortcomings amongst themselves.[35]

The early teaching staff, all educated in Spanish seminaries, struggled to deliver the well-rounded curriculum expected in American high schools. To do so required more faculty prepared in modern methods and who could teach in English. The priests came to realize that high school enrollment was much more prevalent in this country than in Spain. Attaining state accreditation for the Illinois seminary was essential, as the families demanded it.[36] The superior worried, "Everybody aware [of our 5-year course of study] looks down on us as backward Spanish."[37] Yet during the third academic year the new superior of St. Jude Seminary, Fr. Aloysius Ellacuria (1905–81), blithely reported that the postulants (candidates for a religious order) now wore cassock and sash, both black, on Sundays and feast days. Seeing the boys so dressed, Ellacuria boasted, "surely gives them a fine likeness of tiny Claretians."[38] Tiny Claretians aside, the seminary staff stressed the urgent need to build a proper school, with actual classrooms. The breaking point came in January 1936, with three weeks of intense cold ("Everything is frozen"). The priests noted that "the postulants had ice skating very often." Then, the heating broke down, forcing the suspension of classes. The Police League, seminary champions, took an interest. The search for a new location for St. Jude Seminary began in earnest.

On a sunny November day in 1936, the Claretians broke ground for the new seminary on a farm, just north of Momence. Bishop Joseph Preciado, a Claretian visiting from his see in Panama, blessed and broke the ground. A photographer captured the group at the ground breaking. Just behind the bishop stood the bespectacled John Stege, captain of the Chicago Police Department and a major seminary supporter, cupping his shovel. Fr. Ellacuria, in cassock topped with a lacey, white surplice, and Fr. Anthony Catalina in a suit and collar, held their shovels. Seventeen St. Jude boys in their smart dark suits filled out the group. And so the Spanish Claretians put down roots in the Illinois prairie, the dried corn stalks of fall's harvest behind them.[39]

This same season the Spaniards received grim news from their homeland. The Spanish Civil War led to the murder of 271 Claretians, including the fifty-one martyrs from the seminary at Barbastro in August 1936.[40] For months, letters that recounted the bloodshed to their Spanish congregation made their way to communities in California, Texas, Arizona, and Illinois. In November, Fr. Aloysius Dot, serving at Momence, received word of the death of his brother, also a priest, at the Claretian foundation at Selva del Campo. Killed by "Communists," the late priest was another of the Claretian martyrs and thus a brother to all in Momence. Fr. Tort was among the many Claretians who had studied at the Barbastro seminary. He wrote Spanish and English books on the tragedy, bemoaning the loss of life and young missionaries. While grieving the martyrdom of dozens of Claretians in Spain, the leaders here simultaneously understood the necessity of training their own in the United States.[41]

In Illinois the Claretians moved ahead, leading the boys to plant hundreds of trees around the seminary-in-construction that would become shady groves in the decades ahead. In December the postulants sang carols before the Christmas tree at the first seminary. The next fall a three-story seminary welcomed a new, expanded group of boys, of whom some would become American Claretian priests. By 1958, St. Jude Seminary could boast of forty-five ordinations among its graduates.

The early seminary administrators—Spaniards all—fretted over how best to combine the "seriousness of our Claretian religious spirit with American customs."[42] Once in the new seminary, from 1937 on, life at St. Jude Seminary certainly assumed a more American feel. The Black Knights played basketball and baseball. Bookish boys avidly published their monthly paper *The Stepping Stone* and *The Judean* yearbook. Others took up ornithology and stamp collecting. Everyone watched movies. The students enjoyed field trips to a local bakery, the Statesville prison, or a big day out at Chicago's Riverview amusement park or the Indiana Dunes. Yes, the boys wore black cassocks when they took part in liturgical events at Our Lady of Guadalupe or St. Francis of Assisi, such as singing at a funeral or joining a procession for the St. Jude Po-

Figure 3.3 St. Jude Seminary basketball team, 1950s. Source: Claretian Missionaries Archives USA-Canada.

lice League. Back in Momence, however, there was no uniform; some boys wore their letter sweaters. Enrollments increased, with most boys coming from Euro-American parishes in Chicago, but also nearby Joliet, Wisconsin, and Indiana. Fathers drove down for father-son communion Sundays, followed by a breakfast. Mothers, especially from nearby Irish parishes on Chicago's South Side, organized a St. Jude's Mothers' Club that took on special projects at their sons' school and became a fundraising arm. American Claretians filled more and more of the teaching and administrative positions in Momence after 1940.

The seminary, in time, had few apparent connections to the congregation's origins in Spain. In October 1955, St. Jude's celebrated the Feast of the Immaculate Heart of Mary with Mass: a tradition since the congregation's founding in 1859. After the Mass, though, a treasure hunt awaited the boys. Divided into groups, they competed to find boxes of candy bars. This involved "searching in trees, under railroad tracks, in the swimming pool." (Boys named Torres and Cervantes led the winning teams.) Later the students enjoyed a wiener roast and watched a spy movie starring James Cagney. American customs and culture had decidedly penetrated "the seriousness of our Claretian religious spirit" at Momence.

The Claretians' relationship with Chicago police officers also shaped the midwestern seminary. The Police Branch of the St. Jude League, Fr. Tort's creation, supported the seminary from the prairie ground breaking through decades of expansion. With thousands of members and open pockets, the Police Branch supported each addition: the gymnasium building, a convent for sisters, a freestanding chapel, and a faculty residence.[43] The league members recommended boys for the school. When St. Jude boys went on to the priesthood, league officers ceremoniously presented newly ordained Claretians with wristwatches.

The Police Branch picnic was the seminary's big fundraiser. Chicago policemen and their families drove a good hour or more and comprised most of the crowd numbering in the thousands. On a July Sunday in 1935, 1,400 corned beef and cabbage meals were sold, washed down by beer. Arriving that evening: "a lady client of St. Jude's came to the picnic all the way from Chicago walking."[44] Once the seminary moved to its new grounds, so did the picnics. Police Branch members had a chance to wander about the fruits of their Catholic brotherhood and the Claretians' work. The trees grew taller and fuller each summer; under their shade, hundreds of tables beckoned in grassy groves. The seminary's enrollment increased to near one hundred students. In 1958, the Police Branch of the St. Jude League claimed eight thousand members. That year, visitors toured the new gym with its indoor pool. Outdoors they spent freely at refreshment stands; the kids enjoyed carnival rides. The Claretians celebrated an open-air Mass. Police precinct baseball teams took over the diamonds and vied for the trophy presented by Chief Lyons, the Police Branch president. As evening came, some visitors danced in the gym. At 8 pm crowds drew near the main stage, awaiting the crowning of the event's boy king and girl queen. Clutching raffle tickets in perspiring hands, thousands anticipated the picnic's climax: the announcement of the fortunate winners of trips to Las Vegas and to Europe. The day's proceeds would seed the fund for a new seminary chapel.[45]

Ground breaking for the new chapel was a much-photographed event. Older Police League men, clad in suits on a sunny day, posed with shovels, together with Fr. Patrick McPolin (1916–2012), one of the first St. Jude students and longtime chaplain to the Chicago police force.[46] League members returned to Momence for the chapel's dedication in late 1958. In the strikingly modern, almost spare chapel, the police donors filled the pews, many with their wives in stylish hats reminiscent of Jacqueline Kennedy, a few in fur coats. Everything that day seemed a great remove from the Claretians' origins in Spain. Distant too was the Depression-era origin of the St. Jude devotion. Nary a soul could recall the original seminary's chapel: simply a hallway in the frame farmhouse, with some potted geraniums, not even a monstrance.

When Frs. Sugrañes, Zaldívar, and Tort advocated for English-language skills, they paved the way for the American seminaries and for US-born and -educated Claretians. Using English allowed the Spaniards to build and sustain relationships with English-speaking Catholic supporters which, in turn, supported the Claretians' ministry. The Claretian Missionaries, as their name indicated, offered boys a future as missionary priests overseas, in exotic lands. The ties to Spanish-speaking ministry in the United States remained shrouded in the recruitment process. The promotional film, *For Heaven's Sake* (1959), went so far as to create a faux-mission field in Central America, with Euro-American boys dressed as natives, an Illinois waterfall as their backdrop. One-time St. Jude seminarian and writer Patrick Reardon considers that the US Claretians in essence had two orders, "the Spanish-language ministry and a more American ministry including *U.S. Catholic*, the police chaplain, and the parish in Fairfax, Virginia."[47]

"To Enroll Boys of All Races?"

The deep investment in the Illinois seminary, in addition to the decade-old seminary in California, reflected the Spanish Claretians' sense that the eastern United States would yield more vocations and of "better quality."[48] From 1933 to 1936, for example, every single postulant at Momence had a Euro-American surname. The Spaniards who ran the seminaries in the prewar years preferred the white students—possibly implied in the phrase "better quality." No matter the preference, the California seminaries did enroll good numbers of Mexican American pupils.

The junior seminaries in Illinois and California shared strict guidelines for proper conduct, prayerfulness, and study.[49] Young Sevy Lopez mastered the expected obedience, even when it chafed. Other teens rebelled in ways small and large; some graduated and continued on toward the priesthood, most did not. First-year classes were large, but much reduced by the fourth year. Lopez, for example, entered Dominguez in 1932 in a cohort of twenty-one, three of whom advanced to the novitiate. At St. Jude Seminary in 1960, similarly, the freshmen numbered forty-three, with just four boys in the senior class.[50] Retention was a perennial challenge at the Claretian schools, as at minor seminaries run by many religious orders.[51]

When Lopez looked back on attrition during his seminary days in the 1930s, he came to believe that some Spanish priests effectively blocked boys with darker complexions from continuing, with the goal of establishing "a purely American province" in which Anglo-Saxons would predominate.[52] Let's consider Lopez's barbed assertion of colorism.

Claretian leaders engaged the issue of racial inclusion at their Provincial Chapter meeting in 1935 (see figure 3.1). They posed the question, in Spanish: "Is it convenient to enroll boys of all races?" For applicants of good physical, intellectual, and moral standing, the Spaniards decided not to "reject anyone of the Spanish or *mejicana* race, and generally those of the European race." In essence, the Claretians made a clear statement of Mexican inclusion. By contrast, they avoided the question of *all* races.[53] The Claretians remained silent at that point on potential African American or Asian Claretians; those students entered after 1960.

The policy of Mexican admission to seminary was clear. Daily practices at the seminaries, especially around language, offers clues about the Claretians' inclusive if assimilationist expectations.[54] Conversation in Spanish among postulants was prohibited for decades at Dominguez and Del Amo—schools long run by Spaniards. From the vantage point of our times, a no-Spanish policy for students seems mean-spirited and, furthermore, shortsighted. Afterall, most American Claretians would serve in the dozens of Spanish-speaking parishes administered by the congregation at midcentury.

The English-only policy, as recalled by Mexican American seminarians, was an expectation: "it wasn't prohibited so much as we just didn't do it." Still, Mexican American postulants resisted the dominant culture. Amongst themselves, they joked in Spanish, beyond earshot of priests and Anglo students. Talking about home and family, anything personal, remembered Henry Olivares, "we would always use Spanish." Notably, the pre–Vatican II seminary discouraged private friendships and contact with family. Instead staff encouraged silence and sublimation of strong personalities in these teens.[55] A fair number of Mexican Americans enrolled at Del Amo and Dominguez. They experienced a double standard: a no Spanish-language expectation for them as students, while the Spanish brothers and priests who lived at Dominguez spoke in Spanish among themselves into the 1950s.

Louis Olivares, a native of San Antonio and Immaculate Heart of Mary parish, faced the English-only policy upon enrolling in 1948 at Del Amo Minor Seminary (part of the Dominguez complex). Like Severino Lopez in the 1930s, the thirteen-year-old set out on a long train ride to California, in the company of two Mexican American recruits from San Antonio. They likely chatted in a mix of Spanish and English as they made their way west. As they accustomed themselves to the seminary's rigors and life without their families, Olivares did so alongside boys from similar backgrounds. Students adapted to anglicized names. Luis had become "Louis" by his teacher-nuns in grade school.[56] Rafael Chen, a Panamanian student of Chinese descent, learned to answer to "Ralph" at Dominguez.

Scholar Mario García believes that the seminary and "the Claretian order were not by any stretch a racist institution or organization." But in the lived experience at the seminary, ethnic differences appeared, for example, in the self-selecting sports teams of Irish-, Polish-, and Mexican-origin students. Some Anglo students received certain privileges from the Spanish priest-prefects. Some of the Spanish Claretians looked down on their Mexican American students as less developed than people from Spain, and they demonstrated as much. Some boys felt the sting of microaggressions, others did not.[57]

Facing the condescension of their Spanish teachers, prefects, and novice directors, a good dozen Mexican American boys persisted in the prewar seminary. Severino Lopez, Henry Herrera, Leonard Cuellar, Robert Alvarado, Michael Montoya, Richard Treviño—all born to immigrant families in the 1910s, all educated at Dominguez. All became Claretians and ordained priests. Each served several turns at Hispanic parishes. Claretian provincials also tapped them for service that earned a higher profile. Cuellar (1909–78) served as a military chaplain for the 814th Aviation Engineers Battalion as they fought through Tunisia, Sicily, Naples, and on to Rome.[58] Alvarado, once an overalls-clad schoolboy in San Antonio, went off to a high-profile placement in Panama with Bishop Joseph Preciado.

Fr. Henry (Enrique) Herrera (1918–1996) had a rich career with the Claretians. Born in El Paso to parents from Guadalajara and raised in Los Angeles, Herrera filled out the Dominguez application in pencil ("I want to be a priest") and entered the minor seminary at the age of ten. By his teen years, he drew avidly and constantly. In doing so, Herrera defiantly ignored the guidance for study hall that warned against "wasting time in useless things, drawing pictures, etc."[59] Pages and pages of his doodles and cartoons chronicle his experience at the seminary and novitiate. He drew likenesses of professors who bored him. He created scenes that expressed feeling overwhelmed by study and afraid of failing exams. Herrera's drawings suggest a free spirit, not a young man who would choose the priesthood in the 1930s. Despite year after year of Spanish Claretian sublimation, Herrera maintained his sense of self, including his Mexican heritage. At one point in his formation, he listed his languages as "English, slang English, Spanish, slang Spanish, Latin, and Hebrew."[60]

Following his ordination in 1942 and study at Catholic University, the provincial assigned Fr. Herrera to Guardian Angel parish in El Paso, Texas, where he worked with Mexican American youth. He coached the girls' volleyball team to a championship in 1948–51. Subsequent assignments suggest anything but a second-class status for this Mexican American priest. He twice earned plum appointments as a missionary in the Philippines. Herrera became the principal of San Gabriel Mission High School in 1963, when few schools had Hispanic principals. Furthermore, this high school had an Anglo-majority student body (including Kenny Loggins, the popular singer-songwriter ca. 1970–90, whom Fr. Henry directed in the choir). In the 1980s he avidly served in migrant ministry in central Oregon; in Phoenix he celebrated the Spanish Mass broadcast by Univisión. Herrera's decades of varied service demonstrate that the provincial leadership recognized talent regardless of ethnicity.[61]

In contrast to the California seminary, my research on Momence did not reveal a no-Spanish policy. The Illinois seminary enrolled a much lower proportion of boys from Spanish-speaking households than the parallel school in California. In many years, no Latino boys attended there. In 1960, five boys with Spanish surnames were enrolled at St. Jude's, of seventy-two total. Given the seminary's proximity to the Claretians' Spanish-speaking parishes in Chicago, why did so few Latino boys enroll? The Claretians generally recruited at Anglo parishes across Chicago. Some boys came recommended by Chicago policemen, thereby replicating the large number of Irish American students. Some boys appeared because their mothers were great "clients" of Jude and learned about the seminary in monthly issues of *The Voice of St. Jude*. Boys enrolled there from families named McPolin, Peplansky, Brummel, Cirone, and Kirk. Only occasionally did a Rodríguez or Valadez arrive at St. Jude's. St. Jude alumnus Reardon recalls, "because there was so little time for talking, we tended to talk to those guys in our class or guys we were on sports teams with or worked with in some jobs, such as publishing *The Stepping Stone* or, say, building the hockey rink." He remembers Mexican peers with whom he played baseball. School yearbooks and newspapers give every indication of Mexican American boys joining the mix—commended for their friendships, athletic ability, or studiousness. St. Jude Seminary began to enroll African American students in 1965. Of those years, Reardon considers "the Mexican and African-American guys were pretty quiet and retiring. I suspect they felt foreign, and I suspect they were treated, maybe unconsciously, as foreign."[62]

Advertisements for St. Jude Seminary punctuated the Claretians' English-language publications. Tellingly, no similar vocation ads appeared in *La Esperanza*, the Claretian Spanish-language weekly that ran for decades. Latino boys who enrolled at the Illinois and California seminaries, with few exceptions, came from Claretian parishes. Bishop Placido Rodríguez (1940–) immigrated from Mexico to Chicago at age twelve and realized then "I wanted to be a priest." At his new parish, St. Francis of Assisi, he talked with the parish priest, Fr. Thomas Matin and the vocation director, Fr. Richard Bartlett. He left home to enroll at St. Jude's in 1955. "Seeking the Claretians was providential," Rodríguez reflects, "not every seminary took Hispanics at the time. But with the Claretians, no problem."[63]

The Claretians did not emphasize Spanish-language study at their seminaries. The language curriculum instead stressed Latin, with forays into French, ancient Greek, and Spanish. A year of Spanish was the most a postulant could study during the high school years. At points, even this was optional. Michael Cody graduated from St. Jude Seminary in 1945 and then Dominguez with no Spanish coursework, yet he later taught Spanish Basics as a faculty member at St. Jude's. Others muddled their way through a year of basic Spanish with Fr. Tort, recalled by a few as a less-than-compelling teacher. Until 1965 at least, such was linguistic formation in a province with an ambivalent ministry to Spanish-speaking people. On this shortcoming, Bishop Rodríguez comments, "to speak Spanish was a given as a Claretian, but not crammed down your throat."[64] In comparison, the Redemptorists required Spanish in their US seminaries after 1902 with an eye to mission work in the Caribbean.[65]

The Adventures of Albert Daube

When eighth-grade boys chose to enter Dominguez, Del Amo, or St. Jude's, few Anglo Catholics understood that the Claretians' mission was primarily to Mexican people in the United States. Albert Daube, a son of Chicago's North Side, enrolled at St. Jude's in 1936. Archbishop Juan José Maíztegui of Panama—the first Claretian named an archbishop since Claret himself—and his much younger secretary Rev. Louis Lawler CM visited the seminary the next year. One evening the visitors talked informally with the boys about their work in Panama. "We enjoyed every word of both the Archbishop and Father Lawler," wrote fifteen-year-old Albert, adding, "We retired that night thinking of all the trials and sufferings one must experience in the life of a Missionary Priest."[66] The Claretians' label as *missionaries* attracted a good many boys, if little understanding that a future mission might well be carried out in Yuma, Arizona, East Los Angeles, or Chicago's Back of the Yards neighborhood.

Albert Daube was likely an exception to this obliviousness. He better understood the relevance of Spanish for Claretian work than many of his peers. He chose to complete his studies for the priesthood in Chile (supposedly for health reasons) where he was ordained in 1947.[67] Assigned to work with the young people at San Antonio's San Fernando Cathedral parish in 1948, the youthful Daube gained a reputation for "untiring effort, burning charity, boundless kindness." He likely spoke fluent Spanish. With a "sunshiney disposition," on top of his assigned duties with the parish youth, Daube quickly connected with the Archdiocesan Office for the Spanish Speaking, organized an athletic club for San Antonio's shoeshine boys, and started a Newman Club for students at Tech High School. At the students' Easter Sunday picnic on Lake McQueeney, boats overturned. The young priest saved two students from drowning. Attempting to save eighteen-year-old Pauline Govea, Daube himself drowned. This tragic story of sacrifice spread through the San Antonio press in both languages.[68] His pall bearers included several of the city's notable Mexican American leaders (civil rights attorney Alonso Perales, future congressman Henry B. Gonzales) and Damaso Olivares, father of Louis and Henry, both training for the priesthood with the Claretians. The shoeshine boys formed an honor guard at the cemetery. The province lost a promising priest who should have had decades ahead and the ability to work capably in English and Spanish. Albert Daube (1922–49) would be remembered, in Chicago, California, and Texas, as the first American Claretian priest to pass away.[69]

* * *

Early leaders issued directives to use the English language in many affairs and they planted the Claretian mission in US soil with their seminaries, publications, and the St. Jude devotion. In 1941, they noted with satisfaction when the word "Claretian" gained a place in an English-language dictionary.[70] Communicating in two languages undoubtedly enabled the Claretians to create a wide network of support and to foment devotions among Latino and Anglo Catholics. After the 1950 canonization of Anthony Mary Claret, the pioneering Spanish priests—now aging and passing the baton to their American successors—could rightfully claim that the Claretians had become something in these lands. Claretians in the United States were no longer a markedly Spanish community, but largely an American group of religious that included an unusual number of Latino men. In the second half of the twentieth century, they developed a distinct English-speaking ministry that at times received greater emphasis than the Spanish-language ministry.

When the Claretians met in their Provincial Chapter in 1953, they agreed unanimously that "the history of the Province should be written at all costs" and further, their history should be translated to English. (Those present presumed the history would be written in Spanish.) The Chapter also adopted this measure: "Our pastors should be able to speak well both English and Spanish. The students should cultivate assiduously the language or languages they will have to use with the faithful."[71] Their own seminaries nevertheless did not stress Spanish language and even undermined its use among native speakers. For a handful of Claretians, catering to pious Anglo Americans and cavorting with Hollywood stars at fundraisers seemed to eclipse their core mission in the United States: ministry to Spanish-speaking people. The eventual absence of Spanish leadership, Vatican II, changes in the Claretian formation program, and the Chicano movement all coalesced to allow more probing discussions of mission.

4

Working in the Shadows of Empire

Missions in Panama and Guatemala

America is an extensive and very fertile field and in time more souls bound for heaven will emerge from America than from Europe. This part of the world [Europe] is like an old vine, producing little fruit, and America is a young vine.
—Anthony Mary Claret (1869)

It is hard to understand how people like President Nixon, Cabot Lodge and Pope Paul would put their finger on Izabal, Santo Tomas, our bishop and our program—but it has happened.
—Fr. Richard Todd (1971)

Anthony Mary Claret's missionary fervor to steer "more souls bound for heaven" inspired the Claretians to travel, sacrifice, and innovate.[1] The US province, itself a mission territory at the dawn of the twentieth century, would send its own men to distant lands. Foreign missionary work excited many teens enrolled at Claretian seminaries. For some the mystique began earlier, at home, where their parents read about Catholic missionaries' overseas work, be it Maryknolls, Jesuits, Redemptorists, or others that fanned out to Asia, the Caribbean, or Latin America in the early twentieth century.[2] Claretian bishops in Panama visited the American seminaries to narrate slide shows and talk with the boys about the active missions, reachable only by plane, motor boat, or slowly paddling up rivers. These meetings inspired missionary impulses as boys thought about "all the trials and sufferings one must experience in the life of a Missionary Priest."[3] As a missionary congregation, the Claretians highly touted their work beyond American shores.

At midcentury, the US province administered missions in the Philippines, China, Japan, and Panama. Bent on "A World to Win" for Catholicism, the Dominguez seminarians planned a Missions Fair in 1949. A young priest, Richard Todd (1927–2021), penned an impassioned essay "Claretians are Missionaries" in 1954. He profiled the Claretians' intrepid work in violent areas of the Philippines, conjuring comparisons to the historic sacrifices of Fr. Isaac Jogues, a Jesuit martyr in New France, and Franciscan Fr. Junípero Serra's untiring efforts in Mexico and California. St. Anthony Claret's own missionary calling and "his thirst for souls" fit right in. Todd mentioned Panama's four hundred islands of San Blas, home to a "colorful Cuna population that is one-fifth Catholic." He reminded readers that Christ's call, "'to teach all nations,' inspired the Claretians to advance the Church's frontiers."[4] In these early Cold War years, the Claretians' foreign missions also reflected American Catholics' sense of international responsibility and concerns regarding the spread of Communism.[5]

This chapter explores the Claretian missions in Panama (1927–52) and Guatemala (1965–98). Both projects intersected with US imperial ventures, whether intentional or not. Their efforts fit into a larger history of foreign missionary clergy in twentieth-century Latin America.[6] The Claretians wrote letters from both countries that detailed arduous travel by *cayuco* (canoe) to far-flung communities to celebrate baptisms in churches with thatch roofs, to lead processions, and to bless new schools. Malaria, tropical heat, and fearsome animals tested their physical and mental health. The Panama missions, staffed largely by men from Spain, embodied traditional, hierarchical Catholic projects in lands believed to be exotic. By the time the Claretians launched their mission in Guatemala in the late 1960s, great change had arrived for the Catholic Church: in the United States, globally, and especially in Latin America with its seismic shift to experimenting and acting in a spirit of liberation. I argue that comparing histories of the Panama and Guatemala missions reveals the Claretians' resolve to work in challenging circumstances and their capacity to accompany marginalized people. Fr. Todd would have his chance "to teach all nations" when he joined the team in Guatemala. The Claretians would remain in Guatemala in the 1980s, during a horrifying era of mass killings by the military, backed by the US government. An estimated two hundred thousand Guatemalan civilians were killed. Employing liberationist approaches, the Guatemalan missions would in time influence the Claretians' stateside ministry.

Marketing the Panama Missions

The US Claretian province had a multilayered presence in Panama for twenty-five years, if very few American Claretians on the ground. Fr. Juan José Maíztegui, a Spaniard, was named the Vicar Apostolic of Darién in 1926, after fifteen years of work in the United States. Maíztegui became archbishop of Panama in 1933 until his passing in 1943. In 1927, the US province took over administration of the few Claretian personnel in Panama. Soon after, Claretian priests and brothers—almost entirely Spaniards—took on a challenging mission among Guna people at Narganá in the San Blas islands, known as Guna Yala today.[7]

When readers of *The Voice of St. Jude*, a Claretian monthly magazine, paged through the August 1935 issue, many paused to examine the large black and white photo of a bishop flanked by four children, in front of thatched huts. The bishop, a bit corpulent, strains at his black cassock, but smiles benignly notwithstanding the enervating heat. The scene, more familiar in *National Geographic*, drew readers to "An Appeal

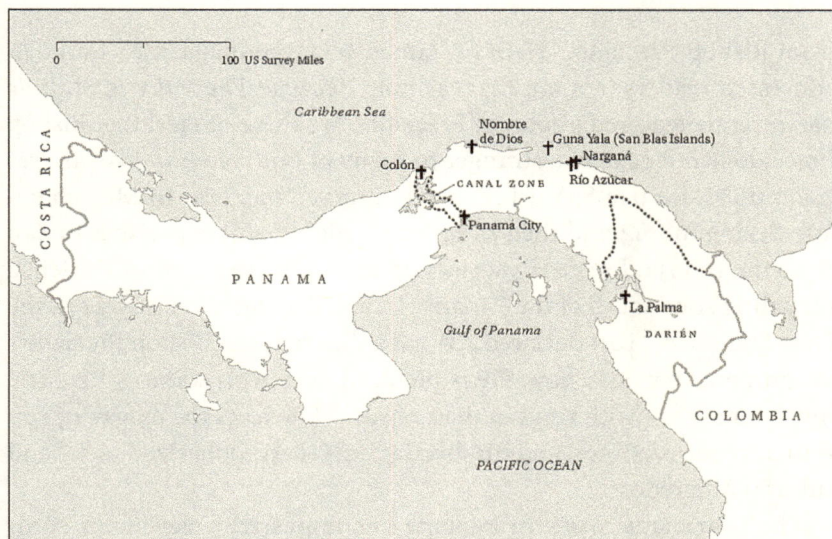

Figure 4.1 Panama: Claretian residences ca. 1940. Each residence served dozens of dispersed missions. Much activity described here occurred in the Guna Yala archipelago, centered on Narganá. Historic documents refer to the region as the San Blas Islands. Map by Molly O'Halloran.

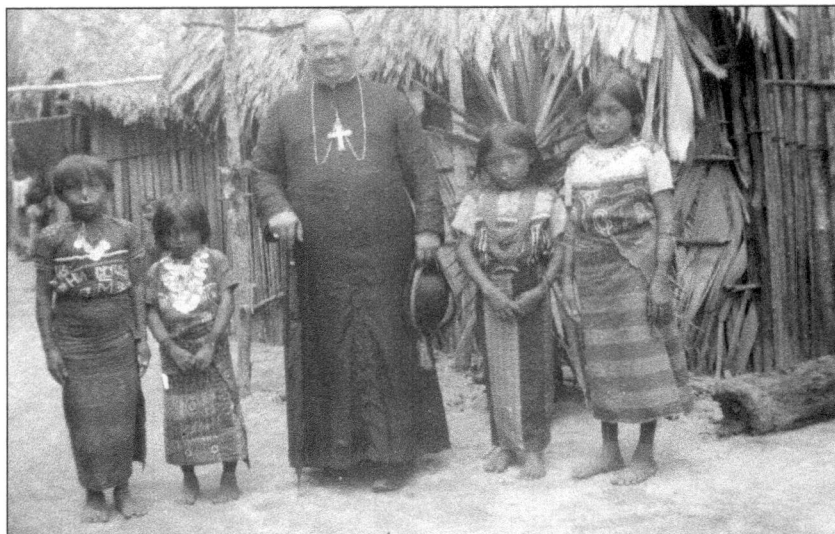

Figure 4.2 Bishop Joseph Preciado with children, Panama, 1935. Source: Claretian Missionaries Archives USA-Canada.

from Bishop Preciado." Here Fr. James Tort, the magazine's founder, addressed readers in a familiar fashion. Because *The Voice of St. Jude* had recently featured photos of Preciado, "we therefore feel that Bishop Preciado is not exactly a stranger to many of our readers." Joseph Preciado (1886–1963), a Spanish Claretian, served one year in Mexico before fleeing in 1914 and then assigned to highly visible parishes in San Antonio. In 1934, Preciado was named the Vicar Apostolic of Darién, a sprawling zone south of the Panama Canal. During his "last year in the Lone Star state," Tort declared, "What a difference in Bishop Preciado's assignment then and now. He is pictured here with some of his little Indian charges—with rings in their noses."[8] For years the magazine ran similar reports, photos, and funding appeals that emphasized racial and cultural differences.

The Claretians' work in Panama encompassed seven main communities. The urban parishes in Colón and Panama City looked much like their American counterparts with large, well-appointed churches and comfortable rectories. Photos of urban confraternities and processions included many Afro-Panamanians and a visible Chinese Catholic presence. The five Claretian houses in rural Darién and Guna Yala each served dozens of dispersed missions. Bishop Preciado visited these places annually by small plane, motor boat, and even in a cayuco. In the simple mission residences, he enjoyed conversing with his fellow Claretians, some of whom he knew from seminary days in Spain. Photos of Preciado with native people regularly appeared in Claretian publications and fundraising material. In 1937, *The Voice of St. Jude* presented native adults building new chapels that needed altars, images, and bells. Preciado directly appealed to American readers to open their pocketbooks: "it should also be an investment for you . . . [offering] dividends for all eternity." Donations for the "poor Vicariate" could be addressed to Preciado simply as Bishop of Colón, Republic of Panama, or to Fr. Tort at the Shrine of St. Jude in Chicago.[9]

Preciado's persona and career continually refreshed connections between the Panama missions, the American Claretians, and their parishioners. He generally spent half the year in the United States, visiting Claretian communities and fundraising. His ongoing visits, for example, spurred La Placita, a Claretian parish in Los Angeles, to donate the funds to erect a church in Buena Vista, Panama.[10] As a Spanish-speaking bishop, he confirmed thousands of Mexican American youth in Chicago, San Antonio, Phoenix, and other cities. Preciado spent more time in Texas, California, and Illinois, year after year, then he did in the far-flung missions among indigenous people of Panama.

Reports of these stateside trips often mentioned his berth on the Great White Fleet, the ships of the United Fruit Company. United Fruit had a reputation for upholding dictatorial regimes, with US military backing if needed, and harming people and land throughout Central America and the Caribbean. Pablo Neruda's 1950 poem distilled long-simmering grievances against the American company. "With the bloodthirsty flies came the Fruit Company, amassed coffee and fruit in ships which put to sea like overloaded trays with the treasures from our sunken lands."[11] Bishop Preciado happily boarded these ships, often as the company's guest.

The Claretians sent hundreds of photos north for fundraising purposes: images that suggested success and progress in the Panama missions. The photos often contrasted savage bodies with civilized bodies, to demonstrate the mission's success in reducing the indigenous people to civilization. This colonialist framing was common in many mission settings, including the Claretians in South America.[12] Examining the photos and appeals against internal documents, however, a sad charade emerges. Most of the priests, by and large men from Spain, mistrusted and disdained indigenous people, referring to them as "little Indians" (*los indiocitos*). The midcentury missions in Panama, administered from California, relied on Spaniards whose ethnocentrism often overwhelmed their Christian spirit.

Enemigos del misionero: Working in Guna Yala

The young Fr. José Berengueras (1902–51) arrived from Barcelona in 1928, after a year spent teaching in a junior seminary, to establish the original Claretian mission on the island of Narganá in Guna Yala. Five Franciscan sisters came at the same time to staff the school. For the next eleven years, Berengueras dedicated himself to building churches, chapels, and schools. He learned the Guna language and methodically recorded his linguistic work (completing a Guna grammar in 1933). He became the first of several Claretian priest-scholars in Panama.[13] Berengueras shared his experience in the region in *El auxiliar del misionero de Darién* (1936; republished in 1946), a sort of "Mission Work for Dummies," in which he detailed the many, many "enemies of the missionary." A future arrival might expect the climate's unrelenting heat and sun. But the manual further warned of the dangers of the air and especially the water as a challenge for drinking, bathing, and travel that led inevitably to unwanted baths, seasickness, and wet clothing. Berengueras cautioned readers who might swim in the sea or river to take a companion, as he mentioned the drowning of Fr. Fortunato Muñoz on Easter Sunday in 1926.[14] He detailed the missionary's most numerous and feared enemies, *los animales*: many types of loathsome insects, bats, and snakes. Tropical diseases plagued the missionaries. Even local foods could be an enemy; Berengueras listed the "good fruits" versus "harmful fruits." Everything about coastal Panama spelled discomfort and danger.

The missionary traveled constantly, usually by water. At journey's end he faced awkward entrances and stays in native villages. Staying with a family brought challenges, including the near impossibility of taking a siesta. The nights were worse, especially during a fiesta. Berengueras detailed his great suffering as "dances, shouting, songs, the most monotonous music, fights, profanity" resounded in the dark, blocking sleep: "it is a horror." Even leaving a village had its trials as native youth might follow the traveling priest. Should one suffer this in the field, Berengueras counseled, "just remember Christ in his passion."[15] The experiences of earlier Catholic missionary writers, from the Jesuits in New France to Anthony Mary Claret, echo throughout *El auxiliar*'s pages.[16]

Fr. Berengueras showed a penchant for endless labor in the missions, often in tandem with a Claretian brother. The priest erected a wooden chapel in Río Azúcar and he built tables and benches for missions lacking furniture. To better feed the children at the Narganá boarding school, he acquired two parcels of land (which the government forced native owners to cede). He then cleared the spiny palms and other forestation from the sites, burned the land, and planted ñame, yucca, and plantains. For Berengueras, church building was a positive strategy to fend off a wave of Protestant activity in the region. He not only directed these building projects, but acted as bricklayer and carpenter in fifteen such projects in his eleven years. To encourage others to join him, he often worked at the front of the projects. On his "free days," Berengueras traveled by cayuco to neighboring islands of Río Azúcar, Río Tigre, and Tigantikí to teach catechism in the schools, spread religious songs, and "to encourage all to become Christians." He worked to stop the spread of unmarried couples (*amancebados*) and Protestants, pursuing them day and night. Throughout all, the priest wrote copiously and in diverse formats: his Guna grammar, songs in Guna language, Claretian devotional readings, and essays for *La Esperanza*, a Spanish-language weekly in the United States. All this fervor and labor took its toll. After eleven years in the islands, tuberculosis sent Berengueras to the United States for rest and medical treatment.[17]

Brother José Benet (1891–1946) worked alongside Berengueras in Narganá for many years, predating him with several years of service in Claretian communities in the cities of Panamá and Colón. When his confreres returned from a long day of mission work, the brother welcomed them, asking "What would you like to eat?" and dutifully went to the kitchen. After the meal, Benet offered extra servings. He installed the first electric plant in Guna Yala and learned to operate the mission's first motorboat. His memorialist painted Benet as a "model Brother" who used his skills as electrician, mechanic, bricklayer, and sacristan as well as cook. He credited Benet with the preparation and gardening for the Narganá boarding school. (Fr. Berengueras hardly did this hard project solo as his memorial depicted.) Benet's unceasing work had costs, breaking his health over time. He was a pious spirit and devoted to the Immaculate Heart of Mary, which he nurtured by reading little volumes that dated back decades, lovingly packed in the luggage of Panama-bound Claretians. The Guna people affectionately recalled Benet with the nickname *aisapi*, meaning "the young friend."[18]

Most Claretians in midcentury Panama felt a deep discomfort with the targets of their efforts: native people. Missionaries from Spain (and just a few from the United States) struggled to learn basic Guna. In the villages, they faced people shoeless, with rings in their noses. The outsiders could barely keep these people apart, struggling to recall (and pronounce) names. Most Claretians saw a people given to drunkenness, thievery, and laziness. "They are prideful," wrote Berengueras, "believing themselves superior to outsiders, especially to the blacks," so alluding to another layer in Panama's diverse population. Two decades after establishing the missions, the Claretians claimed to have baptized only three thousand Guna (who numbered around twenty-four thousand). The disappointing data notwithstanding, Berengueras called the Guna mission "a glory for the Congregation and the Vicariate." He encouraged missionaries to work with faith and unlimited patience: "Don't go to destroy customs, but to Christianize." The Guna, whatever their perceived deficiencies, held a much higher place for the missionaries than the Chocos who lived dispersed and largely unclothed in the Darién mainland.[19]

Two decades after Claretians' arrival, Fr. Antonio Román weighed in on the Guna missions in a frank letter to the provincial in Los Angeles. He bemoaned "the shortage of triumphs, the lack of statistics and accomplishments to describe," compared to what Claretians elsewhere reported. Despite the missionaries' efforts, "these people of the tropics" felt that baptism alone sufficed. Baptisms, teaching catechism, and some building projects were all the Claretians could claim. Román confessed that the missionaries were "sliding from normality." The priest's sad confessional typified the rural missions in the mid-1940s. Fr. Jesús Serrano (1902–97), a level-headed administrator (who would become a bishop), detailed a constant shortage of staff as men fell to long bouts of malaria and pulmonary trouble, a few left the congregation, and some mission residences were barely habitable. Generally, Serrano reported, the missionaries' spirit was "very depressed."[20] For whatever reason, the US province sent few of its own men, just Frs. Robert Alvarado, a Mexican American vocation from San Antonio, and Edward Kolb (who did not speak Spanish).

When the Guna Went to California

Fr. Jesús Erice (1911–90) stands out in the midcentury as truly believing in the Gunas' humanity and potential. He arrived in 1940 from Spain and spent his whole career in Panama. Amidst his confreres' gloom and sense of impotence, Erice exhibited energy and a true desire to communicate with the Guna, taking novel steps to cultivate indigenous Catholic leaders. Upon arrival in Panama he dug into Berengueras's Guna-language grammar. By 1942, Erice ended a typed report on native schools with a handwritten aside, "I am preaching in Indian every Sunday."[21]

Since their arrival in the 1920s, the Claretians had accepted the Panamanian government's request to administer the public schools for Guna youth. The government plan followed the 1925 Tule Rebellion in an attempt to pacify native people, integrate them into the nation, and move them, gradually, to modern ways. Early twentieth-century Panamanian leaders, wary of Protestants and English speakers, chose the Spanish-speaking Catholic Claretians for this task.[22] Mission superiors frequently admitted that the schools faced "imminent danger," as families hesitated to enroll or send their children. The Claretians, acting as government employees as well as missionaries, made at least a pretense of educating the children. Photos showed the schools as active places. By 1942, Erice proactively initiated educational projects. He oversaw the day schools and a boarding school with the Franciscan Missionary Sisters at the helm.

Yet Erice wanted more. He envisioned a new trade school (*artes y oficios*) in Narganá dedicated to teaching skills that would be useful to indigenous people. He proposed training native catechists. "The boy who has grown with us for four or five years should continue growing at the Fathers' side as well as in a US parish, if we want him, one day, to serve with us in the Mission." Erice floated plans to send Guna youth to California for study, drawing upon the examples of Protestant Gunas educated in the United States.[23] This last vision became reality in a few years.

On September 20, 1946, four indigenous men boarded a Pan American Airways clipper bound for the United States, to embark on studies at the Claretians' Dominguez Seminary near Los Angeles. Laurencio Montero, "an exceptional indigenous boy" and graduate of the Narganá boarding school, may have been the youngest, at eighteen. Francisco Ávila was twenty-six, taught school, learned to tailor, and expressed interest in the priesthood. (The relatively open-minded Erice did not entertain the young man's dream.) David Rodríguez, also a teacher, was in his thirties. Francisco Salazar completed the group, despite the fact that Erice did not see a future in him. The Guna men would not follow the regular course of study at Dominguez, rather, the priest wanted them to study Spanish, music, typing, geography, and science. Simply by being in a Claretian community, the young men would pick up "our piety" and English. Their studies abroad would prepare them to return to the missions as better-trained teachers and catechists. The men left contentedly, Erice reported, because in California they would be with "el Padre José [Berengueras] or *Padir Ose* as they called him. (Note this affectionate reference came seven years after Berengueras departed Panama to recover his health in the United States.) Before leaving Panama, the four dressed in suits and ties, posed for a photo surrounding Bishop Preciado and Fr. Erice.[24]

Throughout the fall, Erice repeatedly wrote to his confreres in California, seeking updates about the Guna men. Finally, after five months Berengueras responded. Their education was not advancing as hoped: "Not even the Indians know what to do." The Claretians did not provide what the four men needed. Erice felt that a better plan, centering study in Spanish, would be to send promising Guna men to Colombia. But he confessed to Berengueras, "there is a lack of the right sort of Indians" (*faltan indios correctos*). Erice, normally the optimist, worried that native people's widespread drunkenness and incorrigible nature would prove a stumbling block.[25] Laurencio ("Larry") Montero did graduate from Del Amo junior seminary.[26] But otherwise, I have found few clues about the Guna group's experience in California. The experiment was not repeated. A handful of non-indigenous Panamanians did study at Dominguez and became priests.[27]

A plan to educate a different sort of Panamanian boys emerged in 1947. Some Claretians enthusiastically proposed a new seminary in the center-west of the country. Fr. José Correa (1909–2003), a *panameño* educated by US Claretians, had his eye on a property in Chupampa, with a healthy climate and enough land to build a spacious seminary like Dominguez. The proposed seminary could help meet the scarcity of priests in the region. He clarified that the future school would enroll "white boys (Spaniards); they aren't wealthy, but their families can cover the costs of clothing and board." The proposal came with a hand-drawn map of the possible seminary layout. Correa added a postscript: "Fr. Erice offers three or four Indians to work in the house and grounds."[28] It seems that nothing came of this plan. The proposal alone indicates that many Claretians in Panama believed that natives could function as servants, but not as future priests.

Fr. Erice launched a new project in 1947: publishing a typed, bilingual (Guna and Spanish) magazine, *Juventud Sanblaseña*. The periodical continued through 1951 at least and embodied this Claretian's belief in Guna youth as capable of progress, if slowly.[29] Still, the Panama missions reduced Erice's buoyancy; after eight years there, he too sent demoralized letters to his provincial.

The American administration of the Panama missions lasted twenty-five years. Panama became an independent Claretian province in 1952. Bishop Preciado stayed on until his retirement in 1955 and Robert Alvarado remained through 1958. Overall the Spanish priests seemed beaten down by the "enemigos del misionero." The Claretians did little to prepare their men with language and cultural study, seemingly ignoring the diligent efforts of early scholar-priests Berengueras and Manuel Puig.[30] Since that time, the Vatican has named Claretians in a string of Panamanian bishops, including Fr. Jesús Serrano. Current publications by the Panamanian Claretians celebrate Fr. Erice's work and demonstrate that, in time, the province supported native Catholic people in meaningful ways. Social media posts allow a glimpse at the intercultural ministry rooted in the Guna Yala.

Consider this unexpected legacy of working in the shadow of empire. The Special Operations Research Office, at the service of the US Army, prepared an overview of the San Blas people in 1964. "At Nargana, as a result of missionary influence, nose rings have been done away with, and most of the women wear western dresses instead of native costumes . . . Many of them speak Spanish and a goodly proportion of them think of themselves as Panamanians rather than Indians." Further, many Guna were Catholic. The Special Ops report aimed to serve US military planning; it cited published work by Frs. Puig and Erice.[31]

"We Must Move": Reinventing Mission in Guatemala

Fr. Richard Todd, an accordion-playing young priest from Chicago, was taken with the Claretians' missionary spirit. He wrote with admiration of their intrepid work in distant, often dangerous lands. He play-acted the role at a mission fair in 1949. Dressed in a spotless black cassock, he kneeled before a fierce "native" boy in the doorway of a thatched cottage, surrounded by supposedly pagan items.[32] For the next two decades his dreams of foreign missions remained only dreams. Photos show Todd, properly attired in white surplice over black cassock, at the dedication of the new Claretian novitiate in Indiana or blessing the roses before the Guadalupe Mass at a Chicago parish. His missionary inclination finally found an outlet in Guatemala, where he joined the recently established mission in 1967. At age forty, Todd put his calling to work, as well as Vatican II exhortations to update the Church. In impoverished, isolated eastern Guatemala, he collaborated with an array of Claretian clergy, Catholic sisters, and lay volunteers who opened themselves to new ways of working as a parish team. Dressed now in khaki pants and a short-sleeved, button-down shirt, Todd sat in a circle of working poor native and mestizo men, discussing Catholic teaching and learning about their lives.[33] The thatched roof homes and chapels that he visited were not a play setting at a mission fair, but the challenging reality of building a Christian community in a long-neglected part of Central America. The team was dedicated to creating a new, local church in Guatemala that was much more than physical buildings, but would also nurture the talents of local women and men. During Todd's seven years in Guatemala, the smell of roses and candles in Chicago churches seemed a lifetime away.

In 1964, conversations in the Claretians' eastern province[34] based in Chicago circled around Vatican II, urban renewal projects, and the chances of a winning season for the White Sox. At birthday gatherings in the St. Francis and Our Lady of Guadalupe rectories, at St. Jude Seminary celebrations, and around the water cooler at the US Catholic office, talk kept coming back to a possible new mission in Latin America.

The popes exhorted US and European Catholics to turn their attention to Latin America with its exploding population, poverty, and possible move to Communism. With the Cuban Revolution' triumph in 1959 and Fidel Castro's turn to the Soviet Union, the change became a close reality. The Vatican urged the wealthier, well-staffed centers to commit to share 10 percent of their resources to bolster Latin America.[35] The Claretians knew of San Miguelito, an experimental parish taking shape near Panama City, backed by the Archdiocese of Chicago.[36] The Chicago Claretians yearned for a new project to pull them out of a sense of stagnation and restlessness.

In August 1964, Provincial Eugene Grainer sent a seven-page, single-spaced letter to the Claretian General Government in Rome requesting a new mission territory in Latin America. "A foreign mission would be an effective and speedy remedy to these feelings of frustration." Further, a mission would help attract vocations. (Richard Todd, notably, served as the Vocations Director at the time.) The memo turned to Latin America as the proposed mission's location, citing the papal call to serve the region. But the letter stressed an American view of things. "American Foreign Policy, with its 'Alianza por [sic] el Progreso,' which has sharpened attention on the needs of Latin America in the social and economic spheres. The climate, therefore, is geared to Latin America." Finally, the petitioners stressed "our own Spanish background" and familiarity with Spanish language, as evidenced every day in their busy parishes in Chicago and Perth Amboy, New Jersey.[37] The first meeting of Catholic Inter-American Cooperation Program (CICOP), which gathered two thousand people for a convention in Chicago that year, surely stirred up these plans.[38] The General Government was not convinced, suggesting work in English-speaking places, such as India or Nigeria. Chicago countered that they would aim for Venezuela (rejected again), but soon proposed a mission in Guatemala. This time, the Congregation approved the desires of the hard-to-ignore eastern province, with the substantial proceeds from its publications and the St. Jude devotion. Despite scant knowledge of the Central American nation, it took just a year to start operations in Guatemala. So began a three-decade presence that would remake Guatemala as well as the US Claretians.

Learning about Guatemala and selecting a diocese for the mission presented a puzzle to the Chicago-based Claretian leaders. Without an internet search engine or Wikipedia, this meant sending off many letters to gather information. Fr. Grainer sought help from Fr. John Considine MM, director of the Latin American Bureau, in Washington, DC.[39] He wrote to the Jesuits and Maryknollers on-site in Guatemala. In early 1965, he and Fr. Robert Leuver flew to Guatemala to get the lay of the land. They seemed blissfully unaware of the United Fruit Company–instigated, CIA-sponsored overthrow of the democratically elected Guatemalan government in 1954, and the simmering military repression since. In a rented Volkswagen Beetle, they covered 1,800 miles in eight days.[40] With mixed feelings, they decided to set up missions on the isolated Atlantic coast, several hours east of the capital, in the diocese of Izabal. The tropical climate and disease-prone area worried the Americans. But the fact that people there lacked regular contact with Catholic ministry drove them toward their new mission. No foreign missioners had yet arrived in Izabal in contrast to many other regions of Guatemala.[41] As they weighed pros and cons of each possible site, the decisive factor was Bishop Constantino Luna OFM, an Italian, who welcomed the Claretians. Grainer and Leuver found Luna "honest, sincere, zealous and saintly . . . easy to communicate with."[42] Initially the Claretians wrote the bishop in Spanish; upon noticing that he was reading *Time* magazine, they gladly switched to English. Twice that summer Luna visited the Provincial House in Oak Park, Illinois, as the bishop-host and Claretian helpers built a mutually beneficial relationship. Three hand-picked Claretians prepared for the field by studying Spanish language and Latin American culture with other Catholic clergy in Puerto Rico; in their white cassocks, they posed for an amiable portrait. Knowledge of Spanish, they innocently assumed, would serve for Izabal.

The pioneering trio all had roots in Chicago and St. Jude Seminary in Illinois. Anthony Briskey (1921–78), age forty-five, had long served in East Asian missions. Roger Bartlett (1925–2018), age thirty-seven, had taught at St. Jude Seminary. Greg Zimmerman set out at age twenty-nine. The provincial gave them a formal send-off and blessing at the seminary on a cold Sunday in January 1966, with current students in attendance. Grainer declared, "What we are witnessing today is not so much an act of sacrifice . . . it is an act of charity, an act of love." He called upon St. Paul, asking, "How shall they believe Him of whom they have not heard? And how shall they hear without a preacher? And how shall

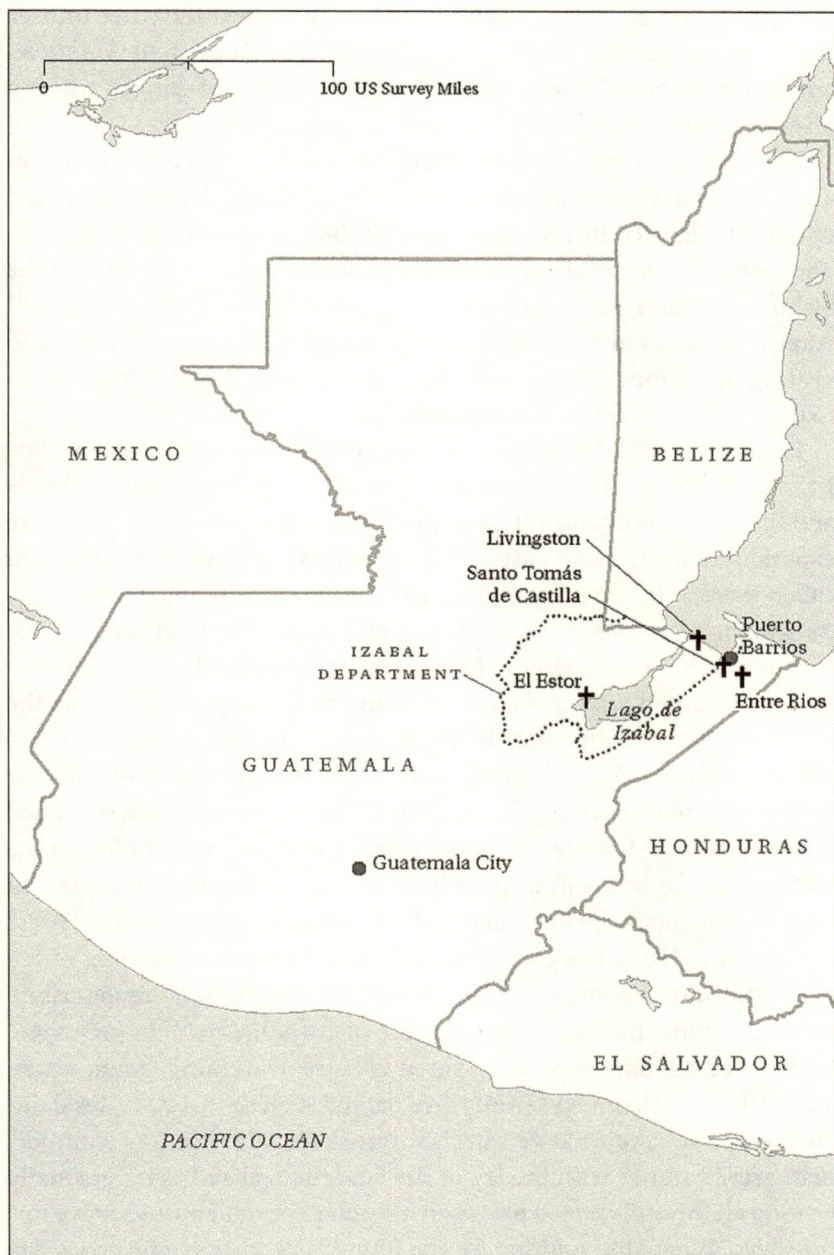

Figure 4.3 Guatemala: Diocese of Izabal and Claretian missions, ca. 1970. Map by Molly O'Halloran.

they preach unless sent?"[43] Grainer privately warned the three priests, "don't go native." His perhaps joking caution embodied an American ambivalence about Latin America: an inferior place of danger, where a priest could lose a sense of his training and discipline.

With suitcases packed with vestments, medicines, books, and fire-arms, the Claretians boarded the first of three planes. When they landed in Guatemala City, Bishop Luna awaited the Americans on the tarmac. The new arrivals' Spanish proved serviceable, a pleasant surprise to the bishop. Zimmerman enthusiastically reported, "this bishop is tops."[44] After a few days in the capital, stopping at the Maryknoll Center and visiting the homes of well-to-do American expats, the trio drove down to their mission field on the Atlantic coast.

From their initial residence in the isolated town of Livingston, Frs. Bartlett, Briskey, and Zimmerman fanned out to nearby Santo Tomás and the *aldeas* (outlying villages). Briskey, the senior member and more experienced missionary, pastored to the Afro-Guatemalan people (often called *moreno* in the documents, or Garífuna) who populated Livingston's unpaved streets.[45] He wrote to Chicago seeking financial support for a generator, boats with outboard motors, and a pickup truck. Eventually he wanted a motorbike, explaining to Chicago, "believe me the hills are getting higher and the road longer." Bartlett based his activities in Santo Tomás, including the creation of a fishing co-op and the John F. Kennedy Farming Co-op, projects aimed to provide a sustained income for local families.[46] Zimmerman, the youngest, set off into the hills, hiking for hours in tropical bush to reach indigenous villages and offer sacraments, hopefully on a "definite schedule of Masses, baptisms" in the many aldeas. His goal in those first months was in keeping with a pre–Vatican II missionary push, as Susan Fitzpatrick-Behrens describes, of "establishing the Romanized practice of Catholicism."[47] In June 1966, he devoted six days to visiting three villages, traversing "mud, water, and rock"; he celebrated seventy-five baptisms, with three Masses daily. He learned to take a native catechist translator with him. As Zimmerman grew familiar with the lay of the land, he realized that personally visiting all these dispersed places on a regular schedule would prove impossible. "What's the solution for the future? Catechists (who can speak Quiché)."[48] Spanish, it turned out, was not sufficient in Izabal.

Figure 4.4 Frs. Greg Zimmerman, Anthony Briskey, and Roger Bartlett, Guatemala, 1966. Photo by Edward Lettau. Source: Claretian Missionaries Archives USA-Canada.

Chicago sent professional photographer Ed Lettau to document the Guatemalan mission within months of its establishment. Striking black and white photos of this new kind of mission that brought "religious, social, and economic help" filled Claretian publications and fundraising materials for years. Lettau showed Bartlett, clad in khakis and boots, conversing with fishermen on the beach or farmers, in barely patched clothing, squatting in a banana grove. Photos presented Briskey tending to the parish health clinic, operating the short-wave radio, and chatting with the townspeople standing in their doorways or leaning out their windows. Zimmerman paddled a boat up a jungle river and leaned over the desks of catechism students in an aldea, sunlight pouring through the slats. In these photos, the white cassocks appear only on liturgical occasions. Beyond that, these priests always wore casual, street clothing, appropriate for men working in a tropical setting. Lettau captured them in a rare moment of rest and community, jammed into a cramped porch, enjoying a beer and apparently each other's company.

In reality, the three priests seldom acted as a cohesive community. Within months, the priests fell into persistent in-fighting. Egos were at play, but at the heart of disagreements were fundamentally different strategies in their Catholic mission. Overall, the Claretians in their first year in Izabal acted on a range of priorities, from attempting to establish Romanized Catholic practices to the proto-liberation theology of the co-ops to alleviate poverty.[49] Briskey observed Zimmerman, away weeks at time in the aldeas, and felt the young man needed to slow down his work. The older priest harshly commented that there was "no hurry to convert the whole Indian tribe who did not see a priest for centuries." Zimmerman, for his part, wanted to find ways to "unlock[ing] doors to our sleeping Christian community." He took the Vatican II teachings to heart, passionately declaring "we must move."[50] While the mission stood on shaky ground, somehow the Claretians had managed to set it up, from the vague original plan for an unnamed Latin American setting to staffing two main sites, in just eighteen months.

Building an *Equipo Pastoral*

The mission personnel grew from three priests and a handful of lay employees to an expanding cast of characters. Fr. Richard Todd, finally a foreign missionary, Fr. Thomas ("Don") Moran, and Brs. Richard Wilga and Richard White arrived from Chicago; several Claretian priests from the English province would join them. Lay volunteers, some for a summer and others for a year or longer, joined the emerging team. Brian Doran, an architect and Catholic lay volunteer from London, devoted two years (1968–70) to planning and construction of mission-related buildings. Marie Egan, a volunteer from Chicago, opened and oversaw a health clinic in lakeside El Estor and trained midwives.[51] Crucial to the expanding group, female religious from three different American congregations joined the emerging Claretian teams (*equipos*), working day in and day out, to promote education and health among the area's poor and indigenous. Female religious worked in some ways with greater freedoms as missionaries then did the priests.[52] In team meetings, Sisters Ida Herricks OSB and María Elena González RSM had equal say in shaping pastoral plans.[53] Priests, sisters, and lay volunteers together celebrated birthdays with a rum and coke and a sing-along or went to the movies at Puerto Barrios. The assemblage further widened circa 1970 as Guatemalan women and men took on increasingly active roles as leaders. The sisters and the Claretians smiled as Spanish-speaking town dwellers (*ladinos*) and Q'eqchi' speakers studied, prayed, and graduated from cursillos, a spiritual training for lay leaders. Hundreds of them trained further to become catechists, health promotors, and midwives. A different, more empowered Izabal was emerging in the Claretians' first decade. Similar transformations were unfolding in Catholic mission fields elsewhere in Guatemala, often with much larger numbers of American clergy at work.[54]

The Claretians in Guatemala generally demonstrated a willingness to experiment with the possibilities of Catholic life and to foreground social justice. The Claretians donned vestments to celebrate Masses, whether in cinderblock churches in town or open-air, palm-thatched *champas* in the aldeas. Most days they wore street clothing as they organized building projects, taught catechism, set up model gardens, and wrote grants to fund their experiments. (Brian Doran, the architect-volunteer, noticed that, in contrast to the Claretians, the resident priest in Panzós always wore his cassock.) Clothing-wise and speaking fluent Spanish, these American priests could have been the older brothers of the Peace Corps workers sprinkled throughout Central America. The changing wardrobe signaled more profound changes at work.

Initiatives in Latin America, perhaps more than the changes from the Vatican, influenced the Claretians in Guatemala. While training in Ponce, Puerto Rico, or Cuernavaca, Mexico, the missionaries got to know men and women from different religious orders and diverse regions.[55] The Claretians avidly read reports from San Miguelito, the Archdiocese of Chicago's experimental mission in Panama. Three Chicago priests, most notably Fr. Leo Mahon (influenced by his work with Puerto Ricans in Chicago), envisioned a community of "laity sharing in the priesthood of Christ." The San Miguelito team proposed a year-long moratorium on the Mass in 1963, proposing instead "a truly relevant form of Christianity."[56] Catholic circles in Guatemala discussed the out-of-the-box thinking at work in San Miguelito; Fr. Bartlett visited the Panama parish circa 1967. After two years in Guatemala, Fr. Todd similarly asserted "the laity should be put in the first place after the priests who have the ministry of the Word." With the emergence of lay catechists and other female leaders, Todd envisioned "a future church for Guatemala." The bishops in Guatemala and elsewhere in Latin America supported this approach and encouraged the Church to act on a "preferential option for the poor."[57]

Many of the Claretians avidly took part in local and Latin American programs to carry out a liberationist church. Frs. Zimmerman and Briskey participated in a cursillo on the Second Vatican Council at the Maryknoll Center in the capital in 1966. In 1970, Todd waxed enthusiastically about the small Christian base communities (known as *comunidades eclesiales de base* or *CEB*) and pastoral teams after a week of renovation, led by Colombian priest Edgard Beltrán of CELAM (Bogotá-based *Consejo Episcopal Latinoamericano*). In 1971, Frs. Gerald Leatham and James (Ned) Kennedy (of the Anglo-Irish Claretian province) took part in month-long seminars in Colombia.[58] Sr. Ida Herricks took a social approach of *conscienización* as she trained leaders in literacy, health, cursillos, and sewing.[59] Brazilian educator Paulo Freire popularized this pedagogical process in which critical social consciousness develops, liberating the oppressor and the oppressed.

This spirit of intentional collaboration and experimentation emerged first at Santo Tomás. Todd found it frustrating that some Claretians stuck to familiar forms of ministry at the other Claretian outposts. "If people do not want community, you can do nothing to force it." He confessed to his provincial in Chicago, "This whole thing about forming community is the real test and proof of religious life. I never realized this more than I do now."[60]

Building upon lengthy, monthly meetings of female religious and Claretians, the pastoral team at Santo Tomás created a ministry plan in 1971, to assist "people in the tradition of the *liberating* gospel of Jesus." They would not take part in "'hand-out' programs which produce a dependency. This spirit does not reflect liberation of people." The team encouraged "natural leadership" from the laity and community development.[61] This new approach to ministry took many forms including schools for Mayan children and for adults, practical training in carpentry, sewing, and midwifery, literacy and cursillos. In time, these activities bore fruit.

A Claretian-directed training center, the *Centro de Capitación*, also known as Campo de Dios (Field of God), had tremendous reach and impact on Santo Tomás and small communities dispersed in Izabal.[62] More than five hundred men and women participated in monthly trainings of several days each, over a period of years. The Claretians had multiple goals as they developed this center near their Santo Tomás church. To fund the new buildings, Todd sought and secured grants from the United States Agency for International Development (USAID) and from the Catholic-based Adveniat and Catholic Relief. Todd played to each agency's bent, for example, explaining "instead of accenting catechetics, capitation was the keynote for USAID."[63] Capacity building or development work, in a secular sense, brought in foreign aid.

Upon enrollment, the would-be catechists and health workers offered biodata that vividly showed the limited infrastructure and poverty of eastern Guatemala. These trainees were modest people, of whom about 35 percent were illiterate. Those who could read and write claimed between one and four years of school. About 40 percent spoke Q'eqchi'. Most men stated their work in agriculture simply as farmer (*agricultor*) or day laborer (*jornalero*); about one in fifty worked in a trade such as carpenter or bricklayer. The women worked in the home. Many trainees lost multiple children to endemic illness, an outcome of poor sanitation and lack of medical care. A surprising number of people who enrolled at the Centro were migrants. As a result, many places in Izabal lacked the traditional structures of indigenous Guatemala.[64] Despite all these obstacles, these people made their way to Campo de Dios.

To reach the training center, people traveled by cayuco from Punto Palma, an aldea on the coast, and Cuatro Cayos, an island in the Río Dulce; from the Santo Tomás wharves, they walked several blocks to the parish and the Centro. *Catequistas* named José and Juan, Manuel and Mateo walked several hours from Peñitas, Tamagás Creek, and other isolated aldeas before flagging down a bus to Santo Tomás. The men slept in bunk beds, atop a handwoven mat, in a roofed but modest dormitory made of concrete blocks (designed by volunteer Brian Doran). The male catechists-in-training (in groups of fifty) arrived on Thursdays and stayed through Saturday, before heading home. Champas served as classrooms. There students sat at simple tables and benches, poring over workbooks with their Claretian and female religious teachers. Alongside catechetics, lessons included agriculture, first aid, and social studies. In 1970, the first class graduated, yielding eighteen male catechists.[65] A visiting Claretian praised the Centro's work "in preparing native catechists, future deacons, and even future native priests."[66] The women came in much smaller numbers and bunked in a "model house" built on the parish grounds.

The missioners laid out different goals for male and female trainees. They saw men as future leaders in catechetics, conscientization, and literacy work. The women also trained in conscientization and literacy work, in addition to moral formation, health, and sewing. But the Centro trained women to *assist* their community's male catechist. The women were split into urban and rural programs. Both groups visited the Centro for a week at a time to study. By 1971, some of the lay women led the sewing programs and assisted in well-baby clinics.[67] For their enrollment at the Centro, many women agreed to have their portrait taken. In postage-stamp sized photos, the Angelicas and Isabels, wearing a floral-patterned dress or lace-trimmed blusa, often smiled for the camera as they embarked on a challenge that changed their lives and often their communities.

Andrea Santiago De Xitumul wore her hair in two neat plaits and smiled broadly for the camera as she started her studies at the Centro in 1971. She was a Q'eqchi'-speaking migrant who settled in in El Estor in her childbearing years. The lack of medical attention for indigenous women there led to the loss of six of her children. She became active in church activities in the Claretian era. "Seeking an opportunity for a *proyecto de capacitación,*" to better El Estor, Mamá Leya (as she became known) studied midwifery. As she shared with a journalist at age seventy-nine, amidst humble laughter, in 1978 "six of us graduated. Some *compañeras* (comrades) were not that pleased because, even today, I can't read or write." At the suggestion of Marie Egan, the long-term lay member of the Claretian team, Mamá Leya opened a modest clinic in her own home where she attended over one hundred births a year. Illiteracy notwithstanding, this midwife has taught women to take control of their pregnancies.[68] The Claretians, partnering with female religious and lay volunteers, dedicated themselves to training in new skills and, moreover, building a sense of agency.

Mission During *la Violencia*

Historians tend to date the state-sponsored violence in Guatemala to 1978, with the Panzós massacre in which Guatemalan soldiers killed between thirty and 106 peasants. As early as 1970, however, the culture of repression made its way into letters and diaries associated with the Claretians. Team members noted aggressive military blockades and rumored actions by the right-wing *Mano Blanco* squads. Presidential elections unleashed great uncertainty. The Claretians had some sense that their Centro de Capitación would draw negative scrutiny by the Guatemalan government. In March 1971, a government informant infiltrated an information meeting in the capital; from there he was chauffeured off to inform the president. Three days later, someone ripped the tabernacle out of the wall in the Puerto Barrios church, leaving it exposed on a nearby playing field. Fr. Todd described all this surveillance and intimidation in a letter to the provincial in Chicago. He realized that outsiders had been nosing around the mission for five months. "It is hard to understand how people like President Nixon, Cabot Lodge and Pope Paul would put their finger on Izabal, Santo Tomas, our bishop and our program—but it has happened." Mistrusting the Guatemalan mail, Todd asked a visiting American doctor to take his alarming report out of the country.[69] The development of the foreign-controlled Exmibal mining operation near El Estor in 1973 also stirred up tension in the Claretians' backyard.[70]

Yet mostly the 1970s hummed along with a functional equipo pastoral: church buildings erected, schools opening, and more and more Guatemalan catequistas trained and working in the aldeas. Claretians in formation came from Illinois and California to work for the summer or a year. Telephone service reached Livingston. The Claretians could envision a time when their efforts to build a native Church in Izabal would "put us out of a job."[71] Word of violence against Catholic clergy in Central America—especially the assassination of Archbishop Óscar Romero and the murders of missionaries Maura Clarke, MM, Ita Ford, MM, Dorothy Kazel, OSU, and lay volunteer Jean Donavan in El Salvador in December 1980—sent a chill through the Izabal team.[72]

In 1981, *la violencia* descended upon Izabal, especially El Estor and nearby aldeas. Pablo Bac, age thirty-six, was a farmer and catechist in

Chicipate. He also led community efforts to protect land there. On February 6, a squad shot him and left him dead on a roadside.[73] The area team discussed Bac's murder and the random shootings of "leftists" just one block from the church in El Estor.[74] Landowners and the military targeted catechists for their work in conscientization. Fr. Chris Newman, an English Claretian who worked closely with the catechists in the mobile team visiting the aldeas, faced persistent threats; urged by the team, he quietly exited the country in March 1981. In nearby Quiriguá, Fr. Tulio Maruzzo, an Italian Franciscan, was murdered on July 1, along with catechist, Luis Obdulio Arroyo Navarro.[75] That same month fourteen people were massacred in La Llorona, an aldea of El Estor, including three catechists. Fr. Carl Quebedeaux, then a recently ordained priest, reported that the massacre targeted supposed guerrillas, "but they were not, just good people who also were defending their land rights, seeking a way to secure titles to their lands."[76]

In tense meetings, the team debated safety plans, rumors of military squads, and how they would carry on their mission. They rescheduled evening Mass to daylight hours, urged members to avoid solo travel, and considered how to best serve the survivors from La Llorona. In the case that all missionaries were asked to leave the country, what would they do? ("No decision was reached," repeated the minutes month after month.) The military carried out a regular plan to intimidate the clergy and churchgoers. Parish employees reported that fifteen soldiers had entered Campo de Dios one night, firing guns outside. Several soldiers stood inside the Livingston church, leaving after the sermon; within days they returned, asking about the type of meetings held there.[77] To avoid possible confiscation by the government, the team agreed that the information cards (*fichas*) pertaining to five hundred catechists and trainees should be secreted out of the county. Fr. Milton Alvarez (1944–2024), a Livingston native, took the documents with him when he traveled to Chicago in August 1981. The team as well as the region were justifiably rattled, but no Claretian fled the country after Newman. "We should not abandon the people in the villages" agreed team members, but they also understood that preaching liberation theology would "bring grave problems." They puzzled over how to take their work underground.[78]

The military violence continued. In January 1982 Felipe Caal Mucú, a fifty-one-year-old catechist trained at Campo de Dios, knew he was being watched. He told his daughter, "I don't know why, I haven't stolen anything, yet they want me for my work as a catechist and for the land committee. I don't know which of these jobs makes them hate me, but they hate me." Military men found Felipe and shot him in the head on January 23, 1982. They also murdered five family members, including his nine-year-old daughter, Mercedes.[79] Three months later, four more catechists, who began their religious commitment as cursillistas in Santo Tomás, were killed. In October 1982, soldiers abducted seventeen men in the aldea of Caxlanpom. The disappeared persons (*los desaparecidos*) included two catechists.[80] The violence continued in 1983 with the assassination of catechist Felipe Ich Caal. Part of the mobile team, Felipe worked closely with Fr. Newman, Sr. Ida Herrick, Marie Egan, and fellow native catechist Ricardo Yat. On February 26, 1983, as he offered the Word in his village church, armed men interrupted the service, forcing him out. After beating him, the soldier shot Felipe in the head. Witnesses described that Felipe's blood flowed and took the form of a cross. His brother Emilio Ich Caal, a catechist, was killed later that spring.[81] The Guatemalan military's campaign of violence, often referred to as genocide, killed an estimated two hundred thousand civilians.[82]

Government repression and violence, largely sanctioned by the US government, greatly diminished the Catholic Church in Guatemala.[83] Throughout the country, reportedly 1,169 religious were killed or disappeared, of whom 921 were lay catechists. Between 1979 and 1981, the number of priests in Guatemala declined from six hundred to three hundred.[84] Livingston and Santo Tomás were spared government killing, while El Estor and vicinity experienced the brunt of the violence likely due to the land disputes and its indigenous majority population. As I write, the Vatican is reviewing a case that advocates for the beatification of "los mártires del Vicariato de Izabal": fourteen individuals, most of whom were catechists. Other area catechists beyond those memorialized in the proposal were tortured, disappeared, or killed in these years.

Fr. Edmundo Andrés (1931–2020) arrived in Izabal in the midst of la violencia. Andrés, a Spanish Claretian who joined the US province of the East in 1959, had devoted most of his career to teaching and campus ministry. Then, entering his fifties, he became a parish priest in a most insecure place and time; he served a total of fifteen years in Guatemala. Andrés fearlessly wrote petitions on behalf of detained parishioners. He addressed El Estor's military coordinator, calling him out on the rampant abuses of authority and the ongoing acts of violence against civilians.[85] Everything the Claretians had built in Guatemala was in danger, but, undaunted, Andrés protested. In time, the violence waned. The last of the catechist-martyrs, Luis Che, was murdered in October 1985.

A Future Church for Guatemala

In 1990, Fr. Andrés returned to Izabal after a three-year period in Perth Amboy, New Jersey. San Pedro, the parish in El Estor, prepared to celebrate its centennial. Andrés composed a prayer, in poem form, for the occasion that recalled one hundred years of beauty, building, and sacrifice as generations past built lakeside El Estor. "The work has been and always will be to create a united people." Andrés urged the people of El Estor "to overcome ignorance, cure ills, to draw and open new roads, to liberate the enslaved, to give all a just dominion." The priest struck a conciliatory tone, while insisting on justice and unity as the community looked to the future.[86]

In 1991, the Claretians celebrated twenty-five years of mission in Guatemala. A festive Mass was concelebrated in a large champa in an El Estor park, bringing together nuns, catechists, native people, ladinos, and a dozen Claretians from the United States and England. Returnees Frs. Todd and Moran formed a semicircle with current mission priests Frs. Dan Vogt and Edmundo Andrés: all in white vestments, topped with stoles, handwoven in bright colors. Along with the chalice and other communion vessels, a basket of fresh corn, another of oranges, and a pair of wooden cayuco paddles sat atop the altar. Two laypeople gave *testimonio* at the Mass about the Claretians' impact on their local communities and paid tribute to team members Marie Egan, Srs. Miriam Simon, Mary Braun and others. María Alcaria Santiago recalled when the clergy invited her to assist in the parish clinic. Over the course of five years she trained at Santo Tomás, at first illiterate, but learning to read and write in the school for adults. Now with two decades at the parish clinic, María knew first-hand the difference this clinic made for the many impoverished people. Eduardo Chavarría shared his appreciation of the Claretians and the team who trained catechists in Q'eqchi' and Spanish, and also built schools and churches in the aldeas. He praised

Figure 4.5 Fr. Edmundo Andrés celebrating liturgy at an aldea, Santo Tomás de Castilla, Guatemala, n.d. Source: Claretian Missionaries Archives USA-Canada.

the Claretians' leadership and ability to earn the affection and so the collaboration of people in town and aldeas. The result was "an active and enthusiastic church" in which "together we have lived days of happiness and days of sadness" ("Juntos hemos vivido días alegres y días de dolor"). The celebration continued as darkness fell, with fireworks and hot air *globos* lofting into the night sky. One balloon exploded, landing on the champa used earlier for Mass, further lighting up the El Estor sky.[87]

With that site scorched, the faithful returned the next day to San Pedro church, to witness another mission achievement: the ordination for the first indigenous Claretian, Fr. Manuel de Jesús Sam Cabnal. Bishop Gerardo Flores presided over the Q'eqchi'-language ceremony, with a secondary Spanish translation. Indigenous people filled the church an hour before the service. The new priest was the son of a local indigenous catechist, Juan Sam. Fr. Sam was assigned by his Central American provincial to work in the Darién Mission of Panama, where the Claretians worked a century ago. Today Darién is staffed mostly by Central American men, trained in Claretian seminaries, in Central America. "Padrecito Edmundo" Andrés remained in Izabal until the

Claretians left in 1998, after thirty-two years. I found no clear discussions of the eastern province's decision to leave Izabal. Declining US Claretian personnel numbers likely played a part, as did the growth of the Central American province.

* * *

The Claretians took their missions abroad in a prolonged series of stark encounters, well beyond their comfort zones. Linguistically and culturally challenged, the missionaries endeavored to bring Christianity and an imbedded church to people at a far remove from their worlds as Spaniards and as Americans. While planning this chapter, I had expected the missions in Panama and Guatemala would share a history. In both places, the Claretians carried out their missions under the shadow of the United States. The superficialities of thatched roofs and cayucos notwithstanding, my research uncovered two vastly different histories. The Guatemala enterprise began with no connection or advice from the Panama missions only a decade earlier. Panama was the Spanish Claretians' project. Guatemala was truly a product of the Americans, or more precisely, men educated at St. Jude Seminary in Illinois. In Panama, the missionaries were generally apprehensive of indigenous people; up to the 1950s, they negatively assessed Guna people's potential. In midcentury Panama the Claretians seemed at ease with US influences. On top of American control of the Canal Zone, the United States maintained approximately twenty military bases there. Bishop Preciado and Fr. Alvarado attended Fourth of July gatherings at the embassy. The two welcomed a smiling Vice President Richard Nixon on his 1955 visit to Panama.

When the Claretians arrived in Guatemala in the late 1960s, Catholic missionaries were growing critical of American imperialism. Ivan Illich (who directed the Mexican school where Fr. Todd trained) caustically wrote in 1967 that "through the U.S. missioner, the United States shadows and colors the public image of the Church. The influx of U.S. missioners coincides with the Alliance for Progress, Camelot, and CIA projects and looks like a baptism of these!"[88] The Claretians in Izabal sought and received aid from US government sources, but they were hardly agents of American neocolonialism. And they were hardly radicals. Yet by the early 1970s, the Claretian team was beginning to glimpse the shadowy connections between Washington, American economic power, and the Guatemalan state.

The Claretians recognized the human potential and capacity in Guatemalan people of different ethnicities. In doing so, they helped individuals find a voice and communities to build infrastructure—together, they created Church. The Claretian mission accomplished a great deal in Izabal given their relatively low personnel numbers.[89] The three decades in Guatemala, with clergy circling back and forth, would inspire and impact the Claretians in the United States, moving the province to an apostolate explicitly dedicated to social justice.

5

Re-Imagining Mission

Challenges and Opportunities in the Wake of Vatican II

Claretians, modern followers of a modern Saint, prepare to
minister to a changing world.
—Robert Bishop (1969)

Somos Iglesia unida en pluralismo. Voz de los que no tienen voz.
We are Church united in pluralism, voice of the voiceless.
—Ordination invitation (1978)

This ordination and first Mass felt like a new, livelier era. Even the invitation on copper color paper felt joyful. The cover declared, "Somos
Iglesia Unida en Pluralismo, Voz de los que No Tienen Voz" with no
translation. A drawing showed the united parish community forming a
semicircle, arms linked, of family, bishop, and a nun. Opening the invitation, one found a Mesoamerican motif along the top border. Below
a photo of a smiling, mustachioed Rosendo Urrabazo (1952–). "The
Urrabazo family and the Claretian Missionaries gladly invite you to celebrate with them the ordination and first Mass." The events would take
place in April 1978, at St. John the Evangelist Church in San Marcos,
Texas. Ordination invitations were usually staid, professionally printed
on ivory cardstock, and minimally adorned with a cross or lilies. This
photocopied invitation was simple, heartfelt, and profoundly Chicano.

Urrabazo's ordination itself was a joyous affair presided over by
Bishop Patricio Flores—the first Mexican American bishop, a Tejano.
The bilingual ceremony included a mariachi choir. Family members
from San Antonio, St. John's parishioners, and fellow Claretians filled
the gleaming, new sanctuary. Cordi-Marian Sisters drove ten hours from
Topeka, Kansas. To all, Fr. Urrabazo offered a warm "MUCHISIMAS
GRACIAS!"[1] Held in San Marcos, the Claretians' second parish in the

SOMOS IGLESIA
UNIDA EN PLURALISMO
VOZ DE LOS QUE
NO TIENEN VOZ

Figure 5.1 Ordination invitation, 1978. Source: Rosendo Urrabazo personal papers, Claretian Missionaries Archives USA-Canada.

United States, the 1978 celebration embodied the currents afloat as both the Chicano movement and Vatican II colored the Claretians' work.

This chapter explores the US Claretians from the early 1960s through the mid-1980s, or the wake of Vatican II with Rome's provocation to renew and to connect with a changing world. This *aggiornamento* (updating) unleashed new styles of thought, language, and action that modified long-standing hierarchies in the church. John O'Malley SJ, an influential scholar of the Council, emphasizes the new *discourse* that emerged, with equality words ("people of God"), reciprocity words (partnership), and words that signaled interior reflection (charism, conscience). The Church moved from "commands to invitations, from laws to ideals . . . from coercion to conscience, from monologue to dialogue, from ruling to serving, from withdrawn to integrated, from vertical to horizontal . . . from static to ongoing, from passive acceptances to active engagement." Historian Colleen McDannell considers "the spirt of Vatican II" in terms of its *reception* in the United States, via laypeople, their parishes, and clergy. The new ways of being Catholic varied depending upon region or parish. When predictable practices were "replaced by the spontaneous and fragmentary," it did not sit well with all Catholics. For many other Catholics, "aggiornamiento dovetailed nicely with the sixties' questioning of authority."[2] Like American Catholics generally, the Claretians initially varied in their acceptance and meaningful integration of Vatican II ideals. The Chicano movement added another challenge.

With their long-standing dedication to the poor and the immigrant, certain Claretian ministries presaged the changes that reformed the Catholic Church. For example, the Claretians promoted cursillo, a spiritual training for lay leaders that became popular in the 1960s.[3] They worked in inner-city, Latino parishes since their arrival in 1902, essentially acting on what became known as the "preferential option for the poor." The Claretians reached the height of their membership in the mid-1960s, with American men heading both the eastern and western provinces.[4] But the Claretians suddenly faced a soul-searching drop in prospective members (as did most Catholic orders). The Claretians overhauled their seminary training, bringing future priests into regular contact with the wider world. They experimented with team ministry, community development programs, and missions serving migrant workers. Priests encouraged actions in support of social justice, including the cause of the farmworkers and undocumented people.

The Latino population, the Claretians' special mission field, grew exponentially in the 1960s and beyond. The number of parishes that needed Spanish-speaking clergy overwhelmed many dioceses. The Claretians, for their part, spread out to new territories, taking on campus ministry in Louisiana and Long Island and English-speaking parishes in Colorado and Virginia. They sent men to Guatemala, the Philippines, and West Africa. They also remained in most of their historic Latino parishes, but these communities faced challenges of urban renewal, highway construction, and deindustrialization. Young people glimpsed new identities—as Chicanos, as La Raza, and as Brown Berets and Young Lords—and new ways to seek more, with church occupations, marches for *la Causa*, and blowouts from school.[5] The era brought on so much more than Vatican II–inspired theological debates. I argue that, with time, the Claretians opened to new ways of thinking and experimentation, new ways of being Church, while continuing their accompaniment with Latino Catholics.

Embracing the Times: Renewal!

Some Claretians were hyper-involved with the Second Vatican Council in its era. Seminarians, today in their eighties, look back on its texts, voices, and debates as formative. For others, despite the great media coverage from Rome, the Council was far away. A single Claretian from the United States, Fr. Basil Frison (1912–2002), took part directly as a *periti* (expert). The most visible Claretian at the Council, Cardinal Arcadio Larraona, a Spaniard, was part of the conservative minority; he was not a figure with whom most American Claretians identified.[6]

In 1961, Fr. Eugene Grainer became the first American to serve as provincial superior of the Claretians' eastern province (predating the first session of the Second Vatican Council by a year). Compared to his Spanish predecessors, Grainer had a more modern, more open approach. He contracted social scientists and advertising firms to produce strategies to move the Claretians productively into midcentury America. He cast a broader and more democratic net than previous superiors and sent out questionnaires to elicit ideas and opinions from province members. Good management and keeping up with the times perhaps motivated Grainer more than the theological debates coming from Rome. At the start of his term, he appeared in his clerical suit and collar, hair neatly clipped, as he presided at St. Jude Police League parades or at fundraising galas with Danny Thomas. By the late 1960s, he let his hair grow a bit longer and often wore cardigans and other secular clothing. Many American Claretians addressed letters to "Gene," replacing the traditional "Provincial Superior."

Claretian Publications, Chicago-based and essential to the identity of the province of the East, underwent a great transformation in the 1960s. Editors updated titles, format, and content of internal newsletters and magazines alike. The popular monthly *The Voice of St. Jude* (begun by Fr. Tort in 1935 as the "Official Organ of the National Shrine of St. Jude"), changed its name twice. Briefly published as *St. Jude*, a 1963 subscription ad featured a photo of young, well-dressed couples conversing around a modern coffee table, captioned, "If it's worth talking about . . . you will find it in St. Jude, A Magazine of Men, Events, and Ideas." The Claretians then settled on *U.S. Catholic* in September 1963. As the magazine's editor, Fr. Robert Leuver, explained to fellow Claretians, *U.S. Catholic* sounded important. The new title "makes use of the preemptive psychology so highly valued in advertising and promotion, in that it automatically sounds like a major publication."[7] Longtime subscribers noticed as the publication minimized its devotional content. The pages of letters that extolled Jude's miracles were gone.

U.S. Catholic, with its large format, glossy paper, and startling covers, aimed to be a prestige Catholic magazine featuring mostly secular authors. In 1963, readers found articles on the Peace Corps in Guatemala and the model integration of Marynook, a Chicago South Side neighborhood. In both content and style, *U.S. Catholic* grew increasingly punchy and provocative, publishing writers well-known beyond Catholic spheres, such as Bob Greene and Mike Royko, artist Franklin McMahon, and photographer Edward Lettau. An article titled "Understanding Homosexuality" appeared in a 1966 issue. In 1970, it tackled nuns' liberation, Catholic Pentecostals, draft counseling, Vietnam War dead, and young people and the Mass. And readers responded, sending letters of support and criticism that often filled several pages. Readers and editors embodied the Vatican II emphasis on dialogue. The magazine promoted itself in 1970 as "For Catholics who welcome a changing Church and who believe that asking intelligent questions is more necessary today than seeking the comfort of easy answers." *U.S. Catholic* looked and read like *Look* for American Catholics, but asked its readers to question the world.[8] American Catholics faced much more than theological debates. Families, schools, and clergy waded through intense feelings on youth culture, the Vietnam War, and movements to open up civil rights for Black and Brown people and for women.[9]

Claretian Publications initiated a new venture to address these overwhelmed lay Catholics. They published hundreds of pamphlets between 1965 and the late 1980s that embodied the eastern province's embrace of renewal. These colorful pamphlets were accessible in cost and content, and emblematic of a changing Catholic America. Titles ranged from changes brought about by Vatican II such as *Am I Still a Catholic: A Look at Catholic Beliefs Today*, to practical parenting advice such as *How to Prepare Your Child for First Communion* (and its translation, *Cómo preparar a los niños para la Primera Comunión*). Other pamphlets echo the anxieties of the rapidly changing cultural landscape, such as *Let's Talk Sense about Black Americans*. Each year the Claretians published as many as twenty pamphlets for distribution to laypeople across the country. Brightly colored covers and simple titles in modern eye-catching fonts beckoned readers. These post-conciliar tracts demonstrate a clear shift from the earlier devotional literature that, for example, propagated devotion to the Immaculate Heart of Mary or promoted the Rosary. Despite the changing form and content, these pamphlets form part of the Claretian Missionaries' ongoing communications apostolate, dating back to Anthony Mary Claret's own publications and dissemination a century earlier.[10]

The Claretians' embrace of the times was also apparent in its internal publication. The *Bulletin of the Province of the East* assumed a new format. Beginning in 1964, a striking, minimalist drawing graced each bimonthly issue. In 1966, the bulletin became the *CMF Eastern Province Newsletter* and looked more like a typewritten, interoffice memo. "The OLD bulletin is dead! How do you like our new format?" Fr. Edward Ryan, provincial secretary, cited the Vatican II Communication decree on the "rapidity" of news and the utility of "fairly continuous communication" as inspiring the nimbler diffusion of news in the province.[11] Within a few years, the western province communiques followed a similar update.

Claretians in Chicago gathered for Fr. Grainer's installation as provincial superior for a six-year term in November 1962. He addressed his confreres, reflecting upon "my own stream of consciousness" and pledged to apply "general principles of management." He addressed the need for renewal in the congregation, "at a time when lay Catholics are finally awakening to an awareness of a sense of community they enjoy with one another in the Church." He mentioned reading Fr. John Fichter SJ's new study, *Religion as an Occupation* (1961); the book pushed him to ask what emphasis, or charism, set the Claretians apart. Going back to Claret, he underlined their Founder's "super-natural zeal."[12] Vatican II's first session was barely in the rear view, yet its language seeped into Grainer's reframing of this nineteenth-century congregation.

The Claretians, especially in the east, avidly followed the news from Rome. At the St. Jude Seminary library, the faculty pored through Xavier Rynne's "Letters from Rome" in *The New Yorker*. Fr. Mark Brummel (1933–) recalls these stirring times, with "the talk about birth control, celibacy. Exciting time in the Church—a lot of moving in different directions."[13] At Catholic University (where Claretians completed advanced studies), mimeographs of just-translated decrees and major papers such as *Lumen Gentium* and *Gaudiam et Spes* replaced some time-honored texts, opening up the syllabi.[14] The provincial leadership hosted aggiornamento lectures at their Provincial House in leafy Oak Park. James

O'Gara, *Commonweal* editor, visited in 1965 to speak on "layman expectations from the Church in the post-conciliar epoch."[15] The same year, Grainer and two other Claretians attended the second meeting of the Catholic Inter-American Cooperation Program where they heard liberationist clergy from Latin America. Beginning in 1966, a steady stream of news traveled north from Guatemala, where the Claretians immersed themselves in experimental liturgy and teamwork, as explored earlier.

The spirit of Vatican II was present as two dozen Claretian priests gathered in Washington, DC, for the eastern province's first chapter meeting in 1968. The timeless hierarchy began to crumble as the priests decided unanimously to allow observation by the brothers and students residing at the House of Studies. The clergy smiled about their public relations success, gloating over the reported great growth in recognition "of the name 'Claretian' in all sections of the People of God in this country" due in part to *U.S. Catholic* and the campus Newman Centers. The leadership admitted that "nevertheless, we do not have a clearly defined and specific image for Catholics at large to identify us."[16] The very admission of an image problem broke with many decades of certitude. The problem was not easy to resolve given the Claretians' diverse ministries. But the 1968 chapter also asserted confidently that the eastern province was "undoubtedly at the vanguard in adaptation and experimentation in the forms of religious life in the Congregation." For the first time all province members directly elected their government.[17]

Virtually the entire membership took part in their assembly at St. Jude Seminary in April 1969. They dug deep into the Spanish-speaking apostolate in Chicago. They considered experimenting with worker-priest arrangements, which provoked much discussion. For example, would worker-priests eventually marry? Fr. Michael Cody (1927–year of death unknown), who had proposed the worker-priest experiment, told his fellow Claretians "This is not everybody's bag right now, but hopefully it will be in the future." Open discussion about testing the Spirit via experimental ministries—along with cigarette smoke—filled the assembly days and long talks into the night at St. Jude Seminary.[18]

The province's biggest concern was personnel. In the late 1960s, suddenly priests were leaving the congregation, many men left the novitiate, and enrollment at St. Jude Seminary plummeted. The seminary closed in June 1969. In 1970, the province sold the Illinois property, beloved

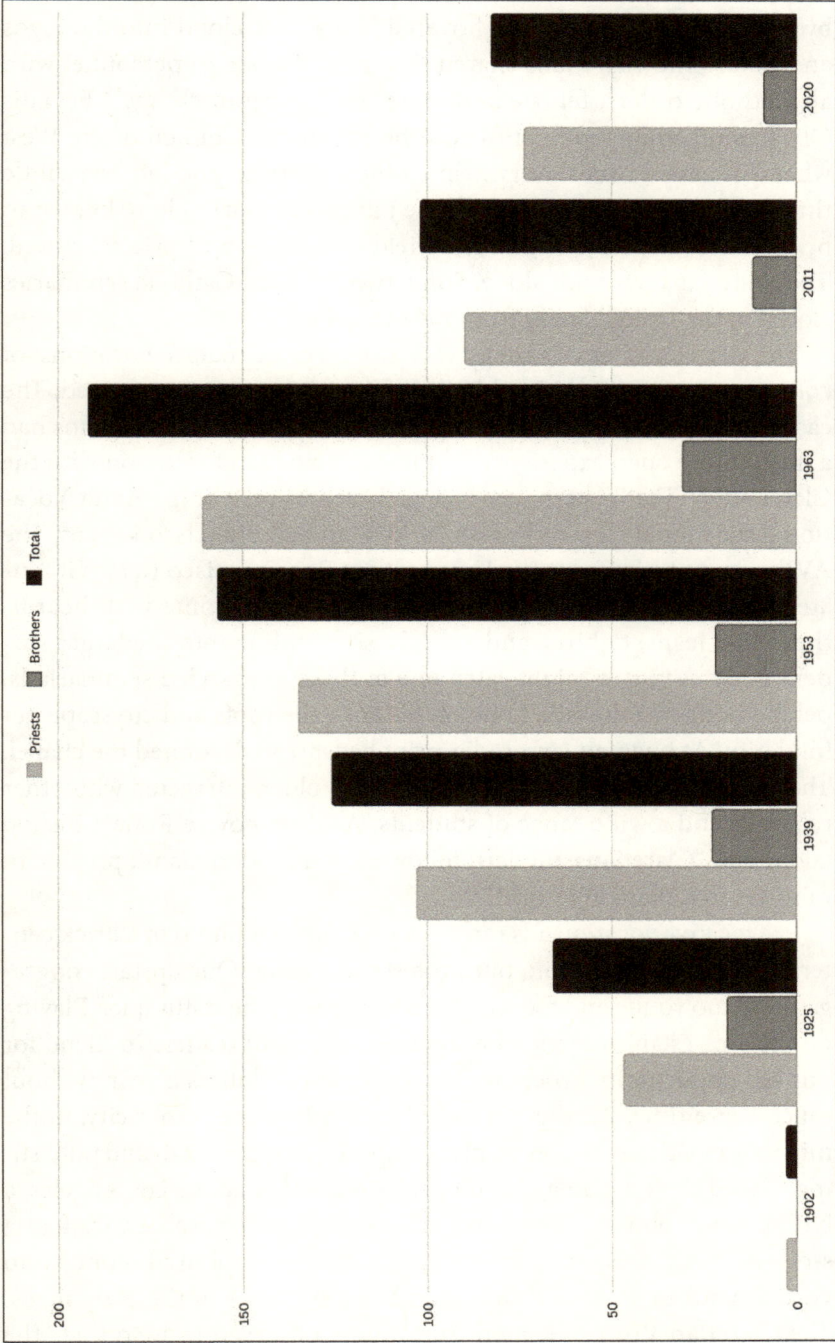

Figure 5.2 Claretian Religious in the United States, 1902–2020. These numbers include only fully professed members, not students and novices. During the era of the dual provinces (1953–2011), the Province of the West was larger. For example, in 1963, the West had 112 members and the East had ninety. The 2020 data include religious in Canada as well. Source: Claretian Missionaries Archives USA-Canada.

by many. The vocation crisis hovered like a dark cloud into the 1970s and 1980s. The Claretians shared this great decline in personnel with all Catholic orders, female and male, and diocesan clergy.[19] Fr. Luis Olivares remembered his time on the Provincial Council of the West when personnel issues overwhelmed the leadership and left "very little time to do any vision-setting."[20] The junior seminaries, long known to be resource-intensive with a low yield of novices and priests, closed. The Claretians were not alone. Some two hundred Catholic seminaries closed in the United States from 1964 to 1984.[21]

The Claretians' new strategy was to seek more mature vocations, of college age or older.[22] New kinds of formation programs opened. The eastern province studied at St. Louis University where seminarians had a much more open experience, but few remained in formation with the Claretians.[23] The western province gathered its men at the Adult Vocation Educational Center, known as AVE, in San Francisco in 1967. The AVEmen took classes at the University of San Francisco (later Graduate Theological Union). With full sideburns and some with beards, they wore jeans, t-shirts, and sandals, so blending into the larger student body. A visitor might catch one of these new-styled seminarians, perched on a windowsill, book on his lap—the roofs and cityscape behind him. At one point, an India-print bedspread decorated the chapel. These adult vocations, ages twenty-one and older, interacted with other religious and a wide range of students. As then-novice Robert Bishop laid it out, "Claretians, modern followers of a modern Saint, prepare to minister to a changing world."[24]

Provocative vocation ads ran in *U.S. Catholic*. A photo of a brick centered one, beckoning "Join our protest movement. Our upstart congregation is too young and too small to identify with the status quo." Playing on the anti-establishment vibe, another ad invited readers to "Send for our job opportunity brochure. Earn only a few dollars a year, without much spare time," further touting their work in the "inner city, in the missions of Guatemala, on secular campuses, in journalism and publishing." "We'd even dig an archaeologist" led another ad. In Los Angeles, a billboard announced, "Serve as a Claretian priest or brother. Dial: (213) s-e-r-v-i-n-g)." Desperate for vocations, they even poured money into vocation ads in *Time*, *TV Guide*, and *Car & Driver* in the early 1970s. The Claretian Visitor General from Rome observed in 1980 that "the

Join our protest movement.

Our upstart congregation is too young and too small to
identify with the status quo. Founded in 1849, we have
only 6,000 members world-wide. Perhaps that is why,
responding to the needs of the changing times, we find it
easy to move out to where the action is. Among our favorite
assignments are the inner city and missions in Latin
America, where there's no shortage of injustice to confront.
We believe that Christianity, in the tradition of the early
martyrs, must be somewhat anti-Establishment in every
age. We don't lock up our zealous young men for taking
this idea seriously. If you agree, we invite you to march
with us. Put down your brick and contact our vocations
director, Father Lawrence Hoge. Phone (312) 236-7782.

The Claretians

221 W. Madison St., Chicago, Ill. 60606

Figure 5.3 Vocation ad, *U.S. Catholic*, 1969. Source: Claretian Missionaries Archives USA-Canada.

great fear for the future is the lack of personnel." More positively he noticed "fraternal life in all houses was considered good to excellent" and, tellingly, "when you talk about ministries everybody vibrates."[25]

A Real Sense of Church and of Ecumenism

The US provinces had indeed created an array of new ministries from 1965 on. The western province took on new communities, employing a team ministry approach, in English-speaking Arvada, Colorado, and among Spanish-speaking migrants in central Oregon. They sent men to Nigeria and the Philippines. They eventually supported the United Farm Workers (UFW) and, in time, the Mexican American Catholic College (initially called the Mexican American Cultural Center, hereafter, MACC). The eastern province had fewer personnel, but tended to act more quickly. In Guatemala, they made good use of teams including sisters, lay volunteers, and local catechists. They moved into campus ministry in Baton Rouge and Long Island. Their vision was most evident in Chicago. In addition to administering three Latino parishes, the St. Jude Shrine, and the publications, the Claretians performed what might be termed social work. They set up a medical center and housing initiatives to serve and stabilize the largely Brown and Black South Chicago neighborhood. The Claret Center in Hyde Park offered counseling services, with a staff of psychotherapists and spiritual directors.[26] The eastern province channeled the gains from the 1970 sale of St. Jude Seminary into the Claretian Social Development Fund, which provided grants to social justice projects nationally. For example, the Claretians funded the Detroit Fast Food Organizing Project and the Workers' Rights Project in Greenville, South Carolina. They provided financial backing to UNO (United Neighborhood Organization) in South Chicago. The Claretians played a leading role in the Eighth Day Center for Justice, which brought together twenty religious orders, male and female, to work for a better, more just world. These eastern province ventures projected "a real sense of Church and of ecumenism."[27]

Ministry at Louisiana State University (1965–79) exemplified the Claretians' commitment to renewal as they helped students and other parishioners find meaningful ways "to be Church." Campus ministry was new to the Claretians, beyond some brief stints at Texas State University and East Los Angeles City College. But that apostolate appealed to many men when the eastern province sought input about possible new ministries. Fr. Grainer offered his personnel to various bishops across the eastern United States and Bishop Robert Tracy of Baton Rouge took them up on it. Working at a public university that enrolled many Catholics intrigued the Claretians. In August 1965, three youngish, bespectacled priests (all St. Jude Seminary graduates) headed south. Fr. Michael Cody, a Chicagoan, reported, "We're dealing, primarily, with cultural Catholics. It's part of being Louisianan." The Newman Center, part of Christ the King parish, became a lively place of guitar Masses and informal meetings with students at all hours. The LSU students took a shine to the Claretians with whom they enjoyed baseball games. The Claretians left unsaid any local tensions over the federal court mandate for LSU's full integration in 1964. Perhaps at Cody's urging, Newman Center students ventured into Black Baton Rouge, going door to door, to gather info for Medicare. In doing so, Cody commented, these (white) students were "finding out how other people live."[28] Fr. Joseph Peplansky (1933–2011) arrived in 1969 and recalled it as an "exciting time for campus ministry" given the vital issues of the Vietnam War, racial justice, and ideals of liberation, including women, as well as the emerging hippie culture.[29] Things hummed along at the Claretian-run Newman Center for four years. Then one September Sunday in 1969, Fr. Cody walked off the altar, mid-Mass, in protest.

Michael Cody was a model Claretian in many respects. From a comfortable South Side Chicago family, he quickly advanced to superior and rector at St. Jude Seminary. He also exhibited a progressive spirit prior to Vatican II. He resigned from the Seminary's leadership and joined the small team of diocesan priests who comprised the Cardinal's Committee for the Spanish Speaking in Chicago. In the early 1960s, he actively advocated on the behalf of striking Hispanic workers. He dressed in a manner that earned a warning from the provincial to "keep uniformity in dress." In 1963, Cody preached missions at rural churches in Arkansas. He wanted to serve as a military chaplain; he twice applied to serve in the Peace Corps (without his superior's knowledge). Cody applied to serve in the new missions in Guatemala (but was not selected). He then requested permission to do cursillo work in Tanganyika with the Maryknolls. At the 1969 provincial chapter, it was Cody and Fr. Ed Ryan who suggested living as worker-priests. Cody then asked Grainer about taking law classes while continuing the ministry at LSU (again turned down). Cody was, in sum, an idealistic, restless spirit. When he learned of the police killing of three Negro youths in Baton Rouge in the summer of 1969 and the diocese's complacency vis-à-vis racial justice, Cody took his stand at the 11 am Mass.

His action confused and stunned parishioners, awaiting communion, and his fellow priests. Cody prepared a statement and took interviews with journalists. He accused the Diocese of Baton Rouge of "excessive concern over robes, offices, and dignities," while failing to address racial justice. "God has left the Church, and I for one am going to look for him."[30] The parish council supported him. Moreover, both the Claretian superior in Baton Rouge and the provincial in Chicago backed Cody. He remained at LSU, but would not celebrate Mass. Two months after his action, he wrote frankly to Grainer, "I can't feel any great enthusiasm for it all. Even the good news from Rome seems too little and too late." Cody struggled with his sense of loyalty to the Church, but fretted that it "just seems that we don't want to take the Gospel seriously. Perhaps I'm too idealistic and demanding." Cody felt the absence of "proclaiming the Gospel—and that's my bag! But I am in limbo and feeling more and more alienated from the Center." In winter 1970, on a leave of absence granted from the Claretians, Cody enrolled in law school in Chicago; in 1971 he requested (and received) laicization.[31]

The Claretians continued at LSU and Christ the King parish. They celebrated nine Masses each Sunday. They hosted student hootenannies and meetings of the Married Women's Club. They experimented with intimate liturgies with students kneeling in a circle. The mission aimed to awaken a sense of being Christian. This progressive, Vatican II–style apostolate could have carried on to our times. But in 1979 controversy arose over a scheduled lecture by Fr. Charles E. Curran, theology professor at the Catholic University. In light of Curran's 1969 statement of dissent on the papal encyclical, *Humanae Vitae*, regarding birth control, the bishop cancelled Curran's talk. The Claretians opposed the bishop. While the students, families, and many diocesan priests supported the Claretians' steadfast advocacy of freedom of speech, the conservative bishop prevailed. As the Claretians packed their bags in summer 1979, local Catholics wished them the best: "Y'all take care, Claretians, we'll miss y'all much."³² Fifteen years at LSU did yield two Claretian vocations, Frs. Len Brown and Carl Quebedeaux, who carried on this legacy of passionate, ideal-driven ministry.

The province of the West, meanwhile, embedded themselves in a new parish: St. Anne's in Arvada, a growing city just northwest of Denver, Colorado, in 1971. The highly functioning, middle-class parish seemed an odd place for a *missionary* congregation. Twenty-seven hundred people attended Sunday Masses. About 15 percent of St. Anne's parishioners had Spanish surnames, but all services were in English. The goals were twofold: to bring St. Anne's into the spirit of renewal, and, for the Claretians and the parishioners, to experiment with team ministry.³³

When three Claretian priests assumed administration of St. Anne's on Ash Wednesday, 1971, the parish had already enacted liturgical changes that arose out of Vatican II. The pastor faced the congregation as he celebrated the Mass in English, not the Latin of many centuries. Women no longer covered their hair and both women and men served as lectors. St. Anne's took part in ecumenical worship events. The parish council met regularly.³⁴ The Claretians introduced more changes. They chose to concelebrate the Mass as much as possible, not just on feast days. The Claretians soon inaugurated mini-parishes: creating seventy-one groups of about forty families. (One mini-parish brought together ten "Spanish-Mexican American families.") The parish directory explained, "since everyone cannot go to the same Mass Sunday after Sunday, parishioners see many new faces every time they come to church and often feel like strangers." These small faith communities aimed to foster meaningful connections in a large, growing suburban parish. A year after arrival, the diocesan newspaper reported that team ministry at St. Anne's "puts Christianity into practice," quoting Fr. Robert Villanueva. Villanueva (1936–84), a priest from San Antonio, Texas—Rome educated—further described a model of concentric circles, with the archbishop at the center, encircled by the parish team and full-time staff, surrounded by the laity, then the community at large. "We are building community through liturgy and action," in the words of team member Fr. John Martens (1937–95).³⁵

The St. Anne's worship committee circa 1973 used the model of concentric circles, but notably did not position the archbishop in the center, instead using "Christ in Action." Rendered in pink, turquoise, and purple, the model placed priests as merely part of the team, just a slice in the circle. (The diocese was left out altogether.) The laity, staff, and clergy team members engaged in ongoing conversations to envision the possibilities of being Catholic.

By 1972 Fr. Villanueva, sporting sideburns, requested transfer to a "Chicano parish." In 1974 the parish team wrote their provincial superior, "The parish is built up in regards to lay participation and pastoral concerns . . . What more can the Claretians do but keep it going?" The Claretians were ready to turn over direction of the parish to others. After years of questioning their mission in Arvada, the team finally left in 1980. "We feel we have brought the parish to a point of VII development, lay participation."[36]

The laity in Arvada may have seen the decade of renewal differently. The well-researched history of St. Anne's published in 1995 remembers the Claretians fondly, but offers little on their innovations. This parish history presents the 1970s as a time of parochial school crisis (as costs exceeded tuition) and the acquisition of a new organ; a place of spaghetti suppers, church plays and musicals. When the team and the parish council opted to move the statue of St. Anne to the sanctuary's rear, some parishioners were deeply upset. The mini-parishes had moderate success, with some groups still meeting decades later.[37]

From 1971 to 1980, sixteen Claretian priests and deacons served at St. Anne's—about 20 percent of the province's active personnel. Team ministry at Arvada became a topic of conversation, in essence a model, for the province as a whole. Reflecting on the St. Anne's experiment, Fr. Ralph Berg (1935–) stressed the critical importance of frequent community-building activities and meetings among the team. Acting as a team took time and required members' willingness to share, not to allow members to "take over" or to avoid participation.[38] The eastern province also upheld the concepts of team and collaboration. Team ministry was essential to the missions in Guatemala. As Fr. Marty Kirk (1938–96) declared, "Claretian ministry is done in community." As opposed to individual ministries, he added, "Team ministry is an especially appropriate style for Claretians." Kirk, a dynamic Chicagoan with a twinkle in his eye, was a programmatic and theological leader for the Claretians, if not much involved with Hispanic ministry.[39]

In contrast to a comfortable suburban parish, the western province ventured to rural Oregon. With makeshift worship spaces and a scattered migrant population, the work in Oregon brings to mind the Claretians' ministry in the 1910s and 1920s. Once again, they were following the migrants. But the Oregon missions drew from the 1970s playbook by using team ministry and in nurturing lay leadership. Hispanics, mostly Mexican, comprised 30 percent of rural Catholics, but few clergy there spoke Spanish or seemed willing to attend to their needs. The western province agreed to staff the new mission in the central Willamette Valley. Fr. Joseph Gamm (1920–2012) arrived in February 1978, to get the lay of the land. By summer, four Claretians lived in a small home in Dallas, Oregon, and Misión Claret emerged.[40]

Oregon was terra incognita for the California-based province. Hand-drawn maps of Oregon, annotated with the towns served by the Claretians, proliferated in this correspondence. The maps aimed to stress the mission's immense size. Here the missionary could expect to spend many hours behind the wheel. Some burned out from the expectations placed upon them. One map also listed the area's *problems*: from social injustice to farmworkers, the undocumented, to episcopal ignorance and apathy. The *needs* included "pastoral help on all levels, social services, moral awareness/'conscience-i-zation.'" That last term echoed ideas flowing north from Latin America.

In June 1978, Fr. Rosendo Urrabazo headed north for his first assignment following his ordination in Texas. Central Oregon's green fields and orchards greeted him. His most recent work had been in a state hospital in Austin, a highly institutionalized place. Hispanic ministry in Oregon, he realized, had virtually no structures. Urrabazo mostly tagged along with Fr. Gamm or Br. Modesto León and took note of the size of the Spanish-speaking population in five towns and the extant structures for them, of which there were few.[41] The missionaries lacked contact with many small clusters of farmworkers.

Urrabazo strongly recalls the hostility of local, Euro-American laity and how rural clergy hesitated to incorporate newcomers into the existing parishes. As the young priest reported to his provincial in Los Angeles, "Of all the activities we've started, the most important in my mind is that there is *presence* in the valley. The presence is first as ourselves then as ministers at the service of God's people." Urrabazo signed off his report, "*En Cristo*."[42]

Clergy assigned to Oregon needed to speak Spanish. Hispanic clergy predominated over the years, from young Urrabazo to the seasoned Fr. Henry Herrera and Br. Modesto León (who was Cuban). Fr. Gamm, another veteran missionary, was born in Istria, on the Adriatic Sea. He grew up in Los Angeles, where he learned Spanish by playing on the streets. Gamm spent most of his career in predominantly Spanish-speaking parishes such as St. John's in San Marcos and Soledad in Los Angeles. At fifty-eight, he took on the challenge of migrant ministry in Oregon with a mix of pragmatism and idealism.[43]

Gamm confronted both Anglos and Spanish speakers at Oregon churches. These rural parishes balked at integration. Faced with a growing Mexican presence, Euro-American priests and laity stalled the newcomers' use of the church. With excuses from "their kids are too noisy" to "they take too much altar wine," everywhere it was a fight just to use the church facilities. In 1978, Gamm called a parish meeting in which the Mexican and Anglo laity sat on opposite sides of the sanctuary. The priest reminded all of their shared Catholic identity; they formed a single Church. "You need to be Catholic," Gamm cajoled, "You need to be open to other people, to strangers, to foreigners." With his persistence, the tone changed and barriers eased. At monthly picnics with Spanish speakers and on home visits, Gamm made connections with people. When he told people, in Spanish, "I chose to be Mexican" ("Yo escogí ser mexicano"), he successfully communicated his solidarity with the Mexicans and Tejanos who worked in Oregon's fields.[44] He wrote to Los Angeles, requesting boxes of Guadalupe prayer cards (printed at the behest of recently deceased Fr. Thomas Matin). Vatican II or not, people always wanted *la guadalupana*. After two years of living and working in community, Gamm accepted the invitation to establish Hispanic ministry several hours north in the Hood River area. Gamm remained there for four years, a lone Claretian presence, collaborating with clergy in the Diocese of Baker.

Fr. Henry Herrera arrived at Misión Claret at age sixty-three and he served as superior from 1981 to 1984. After decades in varied roles—from principal at San Gabriel Mission High School to two demanding stints in the Philippines—Herrera seemed comfortable living in community in Dallas, Oregon, where he shared a house with two other Claretians. The semi-rural setting, with its wheat fields and farm animals, fascinated him. His photos captured the yard's apple and walnut trees and the pink azaleas blooming in the spring. A light snow carpeted the area some winter days. Inside, the modest house was classic seventies style, with knotty pine paneling; the cook and her grandson preparing food in the kitchen, a can of Folgers coffee on the counter. The living room, carpeted in moss green shag, offered a cozy spot in December, with a Christmas tree, the fireplace burning, and the mantel covered in holiday cards. Tigre Junior and Princess, the cats, perched on windowsills. Herrera filled his shelves with mementos from the Philippines, stuffed animals, diplomas, and Virgin of Guadalupe icons. The missionaries gathered around the kitchen table for simple birthday parties, with a cake, smiles, and some cans of Budweiser.

Snapshots included Sister Antona Schedlo, FSPA (1936–), who joined the Oregon team in September 1981, after a decade of mission work in El Salvador.[45] At team meetings, the Claretians, Sr. Antona, and an occasional lay employee discussed local needs, divvied up responsibilities for cursillos, youth encuentros, leadership training, Bible classes, jail visits, and translator duties. The team also walked in Guadalupe processions at St. Joseph's in Salem, thirty-five miles away. Schedlo and Br. León made the effort to visit the migrant camps, where they showed film strips to teach about the sacraments. Team minutes show less evidence of priests doing this work.[46] Their pastoral plan stressed training "Hispanics to be Christian leaders in their communities and to help integrate them in the life of their territorial parish." Someone present might raise the strategy of "See, Judge, Act," watchwords of Catholic Social Action and the Latin American liberationists. Schedlo clearly brought Catholic perspectives from Central America and Mexico (where she spent summers studying pastoral theology). She regularly gave talks in Oregon about US influence in El Salvador; the Claretian team members respected her social justice activism.[47]

In theory, Misión Claret covered five counties. In practice, the team focused on four places: Salem, the state capital, and the towns of Jefferson, Independence, and Dayton. Dayton, with about 1,500 residents, proved the most engaged community with efforts predating the Claretian presence. The Mexican-origin Catholics purchased an old garage to use as a worship space in 1973. Eighty people came regularly for Sunday Mass, making do in the dirty, cold facility with cement floors. The laity next raised funds to buy a movie theater which they began, as funds allowed, to rehab into *their* church, St. Martin de Porres.[48] Parishioners raised twenty-six thousand dollars through food sales and queen contests, but needed more. The Claretians assembled a funding request to the Catholic Extension Society in Chicago for thirty-six thousand dollars to complete the conversion to a proper church. The grant was approved. The church was dedicated on November 1, 1980. The day began with a soccer game and a parade. The archbishop of Portland presided at the dedication, followed by cultural presentations and a pig roast. St. Martin's became "the first Hispanic Catholic church in the Northwest region," a title the parish proudly upholds today.[49]

Misión Claret's impact on católicos in the region was limited beyond St. Martin's. Living in Dallas was misguided as the town had few Mexican residents. Every worship site was at least thirty minutes away. The Claretian reports and letters mentioned few laypeople by name. The team did not take on the distinct needs of migrants and farmworkers, for example, mounting ongoing efforts to uphold workers' rights or to provide access to legal or health services. The Claretians did lay the groundwork for the Archdiocese of Portland to seek more Spanish-speaking clergy and to acknowledge the growing numbers of Spanish-speaking Catholics who came seasonally and increasingly settled out. The Archdiocese relied on the Claretians and its Vicariate San Salvador to cover Spanish speakers. Yet staffing remained inadequate. Diocesan clergy and parishes everywhere needed to assume more responsibility. Misión Claret staffing likewise was insufficient given the needs and did not engage lay volunteers in its efforts.[50] Herrera closed a report by reiterating episcopal ignorance and apathy. He quoted Fr. Urrabazo's impressions from six years earlier regarding the need for presence to support the Catholic newcomers.[51] When the Claretians took leave of the little white house in 1984, after seven years, rural Catholic Oregon had not improved much for Spanish speakers.

Old Parishes, New Challenges

The Claretians have long debated whether parish administration fit with their missionary calling. Fr. Luis Olivares asserted, "I favored parishes because they worked." While the Claretians sought new apostolates and experiments from campus ministry to migrant outreach, they maintained their decades-old commitments to parishes across the country.[52] But even the familiar inner-city parishes experienced new challenges in the 1960s and 1970s. How to respond to the threat of highway construction? What was a priest's responsibility with rising numbers of undocumented parishioners?

New highways and urban renewal projects (often dubbed blight removal) throughout the nation threatened parishes in older, working poor areas. In San Antonio, Interstate 10 literally cut off Immaculate Heart of Mary from its neighborhood to the west—cars and trucks loudly speeding by just a block from the church's front door.[53] In East Los Angeles, construction and opening of the 710 freeway likewise hampered connection to the parishioners who lived west of Our Lady of Solitude Church; fortunately, the church and school did not face the freeway. In El Paso the future dimmed in 1969 for San Francisco Xavier Church (Claretian administered since 1942); highway construction would isolate the parish, literally constricted by three highways. By year's end, the El Paso Claretians reported that their parishes were "decimated by new freeways."[54] In Perth Amboy, the small house-church on Lawrence Street, woefully inadequate in space, finally met its demise in the mid-1960s with the construction of Route 440 (that connected drivers to the Outerbridge Crossing into Staten Island). This forced the Claretians, the diocese, and Our Lady of Fatima parishioners to build a new church in a different neighborhood.

In Chicago, expressway construction first chipped away at the largest Mexican colonia surrounding St. Francis of Assisi Church, a Claretian parish. Then, in 1961, officials announced the neighborhood as the site of the future campus of the University of Illinois in Chicago. The Claretian province moved its residence from St. Francis to a large house ten miles west in Oak Park in 1962. Bulldozers and wrecking balls arrived the next year and ground breaking began for the campus. Residential blocks were erased, forcing mass relocation. St. Francis School closed in 1964. Only a few dozen parishioners remained in walking distance to *la catedral mexicana*. The parish's future was in doubt—many longtime parishioners feared "the end of St. Francis" ("el fin de San Francisco").[55]

Fr. Peter Rodríguez (1931–2004) arrived at St. Francis in 1961 when its future was in doubt. The Spanish-born Rodríguez came to the United States in his twenties to learn English in order to join Claretian missions in Japan. Instead, the soft-spoken, scholarly Spaniard was ordained in Chicago, taught briefly at St. Jude Seminary, before devoting the rest of his life to Spanish-speaking ministry in Chicago. Assigned to St. Francis, he initially lacked the confidence to preach. Rodríguez commented decades later that "I didn't like pastoral work because my field of expertise was literature and education. Little by little, I found my identity as a priest and a human being. The Mexicans and Puerto Ricans who attended St. Francis of Assisi helped me much more than I helped them."[56] He would serve at St. Francis for seventeen years. He grew into a voice for the voiceless there and, more broadly, for Chicago Latinos.

Rodríguez's Spanish roots did not hamper his relationships with Latin American parishioners. He connected with people over coffee and *pan dulce* in church halls after Mass, listened at the well-attended meetings of the JOC (Young Catholic Workers), or directed a choir. Spanish speakers throughout the city knew the priest through his columns in various Spanish-language papers, radio programs, and finally on television.[57] St. Francis was located near the city's center. Latino people, especially immigrants, took the el trains and buses from their homes across the city and even the suburbs to St. Francis. To many Mexicans in Chicago, he was "a cool priest," or in a Mexican play on words, "un padre muy padre." St. Francis, even without its neighborhood, thrived in the 1960s. I talked with many new arrivals from Mexico who arrived at St. Francis and felt welcomed. As one man put it, "como si estaba yo en mi pueblo" (as if I was in my village). Smiling, they often brought up Padre Pedro in these conversations.[58]

For Rodríguez the priesthood was not just celebrating Mass on Sundays, but creating Church everywhere a priest went. He spoke out during his homilies, but further urged action standing with people in front of the churches where he served. Early in his time at St. Francis and before Vatican II, Rodríguez took on social justice causes. He accompanied striking workers on the picket lines at Chicago's Zenith factories, nationally known for manufacturing radio and television sets. He castigated the Immigration and Naturalization Services (INS) for actions in which agents racially targeted people at bus stops, in supermercados, and in St. Francis's foyer.[59] Photography was Rodríguez's hobby, but he also turned it into a tool for justice. In the early 1970s, Rodriguez was arrested for taking photos during an INS raid on a factory. At his trial, Rodriguez kept in mind, "'Whatever I do for the least of these, I do for Christ,' Christ was an undocumented person in Egypt. He didn't have any papers." The judge dismissed the charges.[60]

Rodríguez, a collaborator with the Archdiocese, served as its director of Hispanic Ministry in 1979–82. He was a mover for the inauguration in 1985 of the archdiocesan Spanish-language paper, *Chicago Católico*.[61] He did not shy away from chastising the hierarchy to do more for the ever-expanding Latino laity. He warned "The church is deceiving themselves—*cumplamiento* [complying]" is not enough. He urged the Archdiocese to provide "true services for Spanish-speaking people."[62] While always serving at Claretian parishes, Rodríguez found his professional network in the wider Archdiocese of Chicago. He did not serve in the Claretian provincial government, but stood out as an advocate and activist for Hispanic people in Chicago.

The numbers of undocumented people surged as the bracero program ended in 1964 and the 1965 Immigration and Nationality Act established a quota of visas available for people in the Americas. Mexican visa-seekers exceeded the number of available slots. Fr. Rodríguez became one of the most public voices for the undocumented in Chicago. He testified before Congress and used the pulpit and the media to condemn the climate of fear for these Chicagoans.

On the west coast, Fr. Luis Olivares (1934–93) was an outspoken Claretian who spearheaded the sanctuary movement in Los Angeles. Historian Mario García explores Olivares's winding path to priest-as-activist. A vocation from San Antonio, Olivares upon ordination dedicated nearly a decade to administrative duties for the Claretians. In the 1960s, as the world changed around him, Olivares retained "a pre-Vatican II mindset about being a priest." He did not identify as a Chicano. He liked nice cars and Gucci clothes. Younger Claretian seminarians often identified with Vatican II and they questioned Olivares as a "company man" with his flashy lifestyle.[63] When the Los Angeles activist group Católicos por La Raza protested at the cardinal's midnight Christmas Mass in 1969, demanding more for Mexican Americans from the Church, neither Olivares, nor any Claretians, were involved.[64]

Olivares entered these struggles a bit late, when in 1974 he assumed his first parish ministry at Our Lady of Solitude (or, Soledad) in East Los Angeles. The parish became an organizing hub to support the UFW, and there Olivares met Cesar Chavez. From then on, he became an activist priest, for whom no contradiction existed between baptizing babies, celebrating Masses, and "speaking at a rally or picketing stores. He was now a converted priest."[65] Contact with Chavez further restored his ethnic identity. Long known as "Louis," Olivares reclaimed his birth name "Luis." He came to hold tremendous sway in Los Angeles with a large following among Latino Catholics and wide ecumenical ties. His fearless, often renegade stance attracted much media coverage in the 1980s.[66] For a decade or so, Olivares's and Rodríguez's advocacy for the immigrant and the poor overlapped. Because they worked in the largely separate provinces of the East and the West, these two Claretians barely intersected.

Somos Iglesia: The Claretians and the Chicano Challenge

Reclaiming Spanish names was just a small part of the high-volume dialogue between the Chicano movement and Catholic Church. "El *movimiento* unleashed a fury of demands for more social action by the church," evokes historian Roberto Treviño. In 1968 the organization PADRES (*Padres Asociados para Derechos Religiosos, Educativos, y Sociales* or "Priests Associated for Religious, Education, and Social Rights") brought together Mexican American priests. PADRES founders, mostly diocesan clergy from the Southwest and California, took a confrontational stance that owed more to the Brown Power movement than to Vatican II. Richard Martínez interviewed early leaders who detailed their treatment as "second-class priests by a church that treated their ethnic kin like second-class Catholics." Anglo pastors often denied Mexican American assistants the chance to use Spanish for the homily or hearing confessions. The Church saw Mexican laypeople as "incompetent, dependent, ignorant." PADRES laid bare disturbing numbers. In 1970, the US Catholic Church counted two hundred Mexican American clergymen (of fifty-four thousand) or a mere 0.37 percent. "Typically angry and confrontational" in their early years, PADRES members pushed for the naming of Mexican American bishops, mobile team ministry, and the inculturated ("Raza controlled") education which emerged as MACC in San Antonio.[67]

PADRES raised awareness of the second-class status of Latino Catholics and this, in turn, instigated new conversations among the Claretians about their apostolate. In chapter meetings and the more free-flowing assemblies, these debates dovetailed with the Claretians' post-conciliar renewal discussions about their charism, identity, and historic and modern mission. Examining word and action, the Claretians struggled in the 1970s over whether to focus their ministry on Hispanic people. The debate hung in the air, if unresolved.

The Claretians' direct involvement with PADRES was minimal at first. The eastern province sent two representatives to the first meetings in San Antonio and Arizona: Frs. Severino Lopez and Peter Rodríguez. The eastern province took the activist organization seriously. Following the first PADRES gathering in 1969, the newsletter reported that the group "bears the stamp of the Brown Power movement now fermenting in the Southwest." Grainer sent a note of support to PADRES, hoping they would influence bishops. He encouraged Mexican American Claretians and others involved in Spanish-speaking apostolate to participate and "give it their active interest and cooperation."[68] PADRES evolved as an exclusionary organization and therefore provincials like Eugene Grainer and Patrick McPolin did not have a place at the table; nor would Spaniards like Pedro Rodríguez, despite his outsized advocacy with Chicago Latinos.

The western province seemed to ignore PADRES entirely. It went unmentioned in their newsletters and chapter meetings. Given that the Claretians devoted themselves to Spanish-speaking people since arriving in 1902, their limited involvement with the upstart PADRES is surprising. The Claretians' significant percentage of Mexican American vocations also would seem to presage their involvement with the group.

As PADRES took off, conversations among the Claretians about Latino ministry became more explicit. For example, the eastern province affirmed in 1968 that "while historically the Congregation in the US entered the apostolate to the Spanish-speaking by reason of circumstance, the Chapter reaffirms the Province's dedication to this work by choice, in view of the apostolic demands in this area. This is an apostolate which complies with the mandate of St. Anthony Claret . . . that we give preference in our apostolates to the poor."[69] The leadership's reaffirmation to Spanish-speaking people seems half-hearted. Was it an apostolate to the poor? Or an apostolate to the Spanish-speaking? In practice, it was both.

All the while the eastern province sent a flotilla of personnel to Guatemala and staffed parishes in New Jersey and Chicago, overflowing with new arrivals from Mexico and Puerto Rico who needed Spanish-speaking clergy. The East however did nothing systematic to support language training. The province worked on instinct as opposed to intercultural training.[70] While reaffirming in word their apostolates to Spanish-speaking people and the poor, the province also took on ministry in middle-class Fairfax, Virginia, and campus ministry at Louisiana State and several universities on Long Island.

The western province largely let the Chicano movement pass by during its most confrontational years. Notwithstanding the Claretians' historic anchors in Mexican San Antonio, Arizona, and Los Angeles, and the fact that Mexican Americans made up about 20 percent of its members, the province sent no representatives to PADRES and ignored its existence. The provincial newsletter failed to mention the Católicos por La Raza's action at St. Basil's in 1969. It ignored the 1970 Chicano Moratorium, an infamous anti-war gathering that took place near their Soledad parish. Only in 1971 did the province leadership directly address their apostolate to Hispanics. A committee on the apostolate laid out the numbers of Spanish-speaking Catholics in the west, adding "this group constitutes an oppressed minority." Because the US bishops "are putting strong emphasis on the apostolate of the Spanish-speaking" and "we have been committed to this apostolate from the beginning," the leadership agreed to continue this emphasis, while acknowledging that certain individuals were drawn to other ministries.[71] As in the East, there was no clear-cut plan for apt cultural and linguistic training.

Looking back two decades later, Luis Olivares felt the congregation missed an opportunity to build upon their history of Hispanic ministry. Instead, the western province acted on the notion of "we've got to be all things to all men, that we don't want to develop a specific identity as being exclusively devoted to Hispanic ministry."[72] Olivares captured the Claretians' long-term and fundamental ambivalence about its identity.

The ambivalence was unmistakable in the 1970s when the western province actively sought vocations in Ireland and took on majority white, middle-class parishes in Arvada, Colorado, and Bellevue, Washington.

Personal encounters with Cesar Chavez and the UFW eventually sparked culturally relevant change in the western province. Richard Estrada, a seminarian from East Los Angeles, proposed to organize support for the UFW at Soledad parish for a summer internship in 1974. Olivares oversaw the project and Soledad's basement hall became the site for planning the UFW boycott. When Olivares himself joined the meetings, he met Cesar Chavez and so began a deep collaboration.[73] Ten people from the UFW "crashed" at the AVE Center in 1976; the next morning television cameras awaited Chavez who spoke to reporters, flanked by Estrada, distinctive with his afro. Months later, Chavez stayed at the Provincial House in Los Angeles. He publicly thanked the Claretians for "helping us build a Union for farm workers in this State and eventually across the nation." When Chavez came to Chicago, he visited the Claretian parishes to further support for the UFW.[74] Only in the mid-1970s did the western provincial council begin to promote a Vatican II vision of missionaries out in the world versus parish-bound priests.[75]

Priests suddenly began to don stoles with colorful bands, evoking Mexican serapes. Seminarians at AVE sent an extended position paper, unbidden, to the National Conference of Catholic Bishops demanding that the Church support UFW boycotts, question the "entire American business ethic," and reconsider its stance on homosexuality.[76] The province approved study at MACC, the epicenter of Chicano theology, in 1976; seminarians Richard Estrada and Rosendo Urrabazo immersed themselves in culturally relevant study there, a change from the Claretian curriculum that gave only cursory attention to Hispanic culture. As Urrabazo recalled, "At MACC, I found my place in history. A lot of the feelings I had, feelings of alienation, of being different, of not being accepted, were not just my feelings, but those of a whole group of people."[77] From this point on, the spirit of the Council and the language and actions of the Chicano movement colored the Claretians' work. In 1978 the western province committed personnel to initiate Misión Claret, the migrant ministry in Oregon.

Claretians in both provinces continued to serve Latino Catholics across these turbulent decades. Most historic parishes did not transform

Figure 5.4 Henry Hererra drawing, n.d. Source: Herrera personal papers, Claretian Missionaries Archives USA-Canada.

much in these years. The Santo Nombre and the guadalupanas persisted, perhaps joined by cursillistas.[78] The fiestas and kermesses retained a timeless feel, perhaps with a Chicano rock band joining the entertainment lineup. Some Claretian pastors assumed a more political and activist stance, even on the altar, but most did not. That persistent tension between the Claretians' hard-fought efforts to achieve American status (versus "backward Spaniards" as discussed earlier) and work in Mexican parishes still colored some attitudes. Fr. Henry Herrera, who had seen it all, laid bare that thread of detachment and disdain toward Hispanic ministry in an acerbic cartoon he drew at a chapter meeting in the 1980s. Obviously exaggerated, Herrera noted his province's hypocrisy.

* * *

The impact of Vatican II on the Claretians and their ministries is complicated. Work that embodied the Council's spirit emerged. The LSU campus ministry and parish, Guatemalan missions, and the AVE Center stand out. Yet meaningful renewal took a decade or more to unfurl, especially in the West, in addition to delayed engagement with the Chicano movement. For the US leadership, renewal often took a back seat to the immediate concerns of plummeting vocations and personnel defections. Vatican II's influence on Hispanic laity was limited or at least diffuse. Quietly counter to the Council's spirit, their parishes continued to cherish Marian and eucharistic devotions. Fr. Joseph Peplansky found that little changed in the mid-1960s at Our Lady of Guadalupe in Chicago. It remained a place of "novenas, medals, house blessings," and the annual parish carnival. Social action was limited to Christmas drives for the poor.[79] The national *Encuentros* of Hispanic Catholics that began in the 1970s seem more impactful. The Encuentros promoted greater pastoral planning, encouraged integration into the US Catholic Church, without assimilation.[80] While the Claretians had engaged in this work since 1902, their direct involvement with these national meetings was minimal. Whether facing the Chicano movement, the anti-war movement, or the spirit of the Council, most Claretians simply did the day-to-day business of keeping their church communities going, while welcoming ongoing arrivals from Latin America. As Leslie Woodcock Tentler puts it, "Like most Americans, most priests watched the period's political battles from the sidelines."[81] Among Claretians, Michael Cody, Luis Olivares, and Peter Rodríguez conspicuously spoke their truths.

Most histories of Vatican II end with Pope Paul VI's death and the start of John Paul II's papacy in 1978. The ideals of renewal and dialogue have persisted much longer among the US Claretians. The global congregation pushed questions of mission and charism, asking confreres in 1987, "How do you live your Cordimarian spirituality?"[82] St. John the Evangelist Church, in San Marcos, Texas, offers a vivid example of how Vatican II spirit lived on. St. John's, the longtime Claretian-administered parish, moved into a brand-new structure in 1970 that had a modern Vatican II feel, physically at least. St. John's was an ethnically mixed but largely ethnic Mexican parish. The new church featured ten thousand square feet of air-conditioned space on the main floor, all modern lines, exposed brick walls, barrel vault ceiling painted white, and little ornamentation. Tall, narrow windows let in natural light. The new sanctuary had no stained glass. "Contemporary" summed up the

Figure 5.5 St. Anthony Mary Claret, St. John the Evangelist Church, San Marcos, Texas. Photo by Anthony Head.

new St. John's, "its style is derived from the needs, techniques, and economics of our day."[83] Here, parishioners, friends, Claretians, and family gathered for the first ever ordination at St. John's: the 1978 ordination of Rosendo Urrabazo. The new priest would soon find himself in the fledgling mission in Oregon.

Twenty years later, Fr. Brian Culley, St. John's pastor in 1996–2002, heard people say that the modern sanctuary was "cold." Updating the parish complex usually meant funds went to necessary changes behind the scenes: new air conditioning, computers, repairing a leaking roof on the hall, or fixing plumbing. Culley envisioned adding warmth to the sanctuary with stained glass panels. The parish council loved the idea. He suggested iconography, sought funds, and contacted the Cavallini glass company in San Antonio. Six panels replaced the plain windows in 2000. Images of St. John the Evangelist, St. Francis of Assisi, and St. Therese Lisieux, all historically popular devotions, took up three windows. The middle panels embodied a Claretian spirituality: on the right, an approachable St. Anthony Mary Claret carries a cross and a holy book, its open pages emblazoned in Spanish "Anunciar las buenas noticias a los pobres" ("To announce the good news to the poor"). Across the sanctuary, the middle window showcases the Immaculate Heart of Mary, who bears a resemblance to depictions of the Virgin of Guadalupe. Facing her in the next window: Pope John XXIII, cloaked in warm red robes, the convener and visionary behind the Second Vatican Council. Culley chuckles as he describes the glassmakers' reaction to including this image. "But he's not a saint!" they protested. Culley insisted that the window show John with a halo, feeling that the late pope merited such recognition. Parishioners loved the windows.[84] The Texas sun shines through, bringing color and warmth into their church. St. John's, today a diocesan parish, bears the marks of late twentieth-century Claretian charism: rooted in Claret's missionary zeal, with a great passion for Mary, attuned to the Vatican II spirit, and attentive to Spanish-speaking Catholics.

Conclusion

> We are missionaries. We followed the migration of Mexicans to Texas, California, to New Jersey. We were following, ministering to Mexicans—and we were the only ones who accompanied them. Think *acompañamiento*, as Pope Francis urges. We are witnesses, witnesses to persecutions. We developed Hispanic ministry and handed it to the larger Church.
> —Bishop Plácido Rodríguez (2022)

> How are we accomplishing our mission today as a Province, is there unity in our diversity?
> —Fr. Beauplan Derilus (2022)

The pioneering missionaries who barnstormed southern Texas in 1902 would be pleased that the Claretians today work in four states, as well as at the Mexican border and in two Canadian provinces. Leaders who pushed for training American vocations a century ago would be gratified that 56 percent of Claretian priests here were born in the United States. But imagine their astonishment upon meeting the 22 percent of their confreres who hail from India and Africa. The fact that every Claretian parish in the United States celebrates *misa en español* and English would fit their plans; the Vietnamese Masses at San Gabriel might surprise them. The National Shrine of St. Jude still graces Our Lady of Guadalupe Church in Chicago. Jude's devotees today are more likely to watch a live-streamed novena and to donate digitally. The Claretians' use of the press to strengthen faith continues with the award-winning magazine *U.S. Catholic*, but also in the form of radio, podcasts, and vlogs in Spanish and English. The midcentury advocates for Perth Amboy's embryonic Spanish-speaking parish would be stunned by the modern Our Lady of Fatima Church in downtown Perth Amboy, now a majority-Latino city.

This closing chapter explores the changing landscapes and cultures of contemporary Claretian missions, along with the evolution of the province itself looking to the future. The two US provinces—East and West—merged and consolidated resources in 2011. The Canadian Vice Province became part of the United States Province in 2014: now the Claretian United States–Canadian Province. The leadership aims to bring the province together in meaningful ways, especially as they incorporate an increasingly international membership. The Claretians' shifting sense of mission unfolds in a time of uncertainty for the wider Catholic Church. As Fr. James Martin SJ puts it, "the whole church—the big, contentious, worldwide, supremely messy, post-Vatican II church that struggles to find its way in the modern world."[1] News of the clergy sexual abuse of minors roils the supremely messy Catholic world, including the Claretians. Throughout all the ferment the Claretians remain, in their words, dedicated to "bringing the Word of God to all people as companions on their journey through life."[2]

I have argued throughout this book that what distinguishes the Claretians is their accompaniment of Latino Catholics. This commitment makes them distinct in American Catholic history. The Claretians followed the migrations of misunderstood, vulnerable, and often maligned Spanish-speaking people. When the rest of America barely recognized the Latino people who worked the lowest paid jobs in the fields, mines, or steel mills and raised families in shacks and boxcars, the Claretians maintained a steady, supportive presence. Bishop Plácido Rodríguez shares, "we were following, ministering to Mexicans—and we were the only ones who accompanied them. Think *acompañamiento*, as Pope Francis urges." He further reflected that as Claretians, "we developed Hispanic ministry and handed it to the larger Church."[3] When many dioceses ignored the católicos in their midst, Claretians accompanied them wherever possible.

Mexican and Puerto Rican people brought their faith and devotions in tattered suitcases and in their hearts and the Claretians nurtured these attachments to the Sacred Heart, the Virgin of Guadalupe, Our Lady of Divine Providence, and memories of the martyred Cristeros. Long before "inculturation" had a name and a theology,[4] many Claretian clergy met the people halfway, be it with native dancers (*matachines*) on some feast days or supporting the teaching of catechism to children in Spanish. The Oblates in Texas and the occasional Jesuit understood these approaches in the early twentieth century. Today multiple religious congregations and many dioceses offer culturally sensitive ministry with Spanish speakers and their families. The Claretians did it first and in multiple regions of the country. The Hispanic Ministry Resource Center, founded in 1990, melded the province's expertise in both publishing and Hispanic ministry, to share Spanish-language, culturally relevant material in print, on the web, or podcasts.

The Claretians long worked the fringes of US Catholic society—with mexicanos and puertoriqueños. Today the fringes are becoming the center. Latinos and Latin Americans comprise the majority of Catholic laypeople in the United States. Yet too many bishops and parishes still struggle to understand people who are hardly strangers in our midst. Too often clergy fail to acknowledge the needs and diversity of católicos.[5] Not all pastors understand the ways católicos want to connect with the Church and parish. Imagine the hurt caused by diocesan pastors refusing to celebrate December 12, to honor the Virgin of Guadalupe, in parishes with climbing numbers of Mexican laity. Or, a pastor quipping to Mexican American parishioners after the Mass, "I know two Spanish words: Hallelujah and Amen." Lisa, a college-educated, second-generation Chicagoan (her parents were married at a Claretian parish) feels this sting from her young pastor. Her nearby parish simply does not feel like home. Such remarks would not come out of a Claretian-run parish, historically or today. Whether in parish or campus ministry, it is not simply a matter of translation. As Fr. Francisco Javier Reyes asserts, "it is about listening and accompanying people where they are and embracing the value that people already bring to their campus ministry."[6] Being present, listening, and accompanying has been central to the Claretian mission since they began their work in the United States and remains so.

The Church Is the People: Parishes Today

Scattered throughout the country are nearly one hundred churches or schools initiated by the Claretians, often administered by them for decades. The formerly Claretian-administered parish, Immaculate Heart of Mary Church in Martindale, Texas, had an inexplicable pull on me. My visit was compelled by the century-old descriptions and photos of this small, vibrant Catholic community (*un pueblo católico de corazón*), with laity who balanced the cotton fields with their desire to express faith in community. I drove to Martindale for the Sunday 8 am Spanish Mass in May 2022. Turning off the state highway at the town's only stoplight, there stood the white church, gleaming in the sun and remarkably unchanged from 1920s photos. The pews filled, guitar music accompanied the Mass, and parishioners sang with gusto. Some people wore scapularies the size of a playing card. Padre Rafael, a diocesan priest from Mexico, preached about living with love and letting go of past grudges. "Alabaré alabaré . . . a mi Señor," people sang joyfully, praising the Lord, and clapping in time. An image of the Immaculate Heart of Mary graced the altar. Up in the choir loft, a bit forgotten, stood an image of St. Anthony Mary Claret.

After Mass, the guadalupanas sold coffee, *champurrado*, and tamales. Some elders described Immaculate Heart as "my second home." One recalled her mother telling her about a Padre Inocencio [Martín]. Several members of the Archconfraternity of the Immaculate Heart of Mary asked me about getting pins to distribute to members. But no one seemed to know about the Claretian connection to the devotion for whom their church had been named. As the breakfast crowd scattered, climbing into their pickups, I explored the grounds, with Stations of the Cross and ample space for the annual kermess with music, burgers, tacos, and lotería on a warm summer weekend. Walking through Martindale's two-block downtown, few signs existed of the Mexican people who had sustained the local economy. The historic Martindale cemetery, also downtown, marked the resting spot of Anglo residents only. The Claretians, who worked in tandem with the Cordi-Marian Sisters, nurtured the Mexican Catholic community at Martindale for over eighty years. Claret may stand forgotten in the choir loft, but the Claretians' sustained mission has left a vigorous legacy.

Parishes with formative Claretian histories exist in Ft. Worth and El Paso, Yuma and Phoenix, Chicago, Los Angeles, and elsewhere. Reminders of their work vary greatly: from misspellings on websites to carefully researched parish histories, from a clearly etched cornerstone to active sodalities that evoke Claret and his charism. Claret is handsomely portrayed in a stained-glass panel at St. John's in San Marcos, Texas, but without an identifying label or a Claretian, each year fewer parishioners recognize Claret and the Claretians' legacy.

Let's drop in on two current Claretian-run parishes. I visited St. Anthony Mary Claret Church in Fresno in November 2022. Built by the Claretians and parishioners in 1951, the mid-sized sanctuary is made of cinder blocks, painted white.[7] There is no stained-glass, just clear, pebbled glass windows. This is a house of worship for people of limited financial means, but of great devotion. Flanking the altar, a statue of Claret on the left, the Virgin of Guadalupe and Juan Diego on the right. For Day of the Dead that week, below Guadalupe, parishioners created a four-tier altar that commemorates departed loved ones, *los muertos*. Many dozens of framed photos jostled for space with *pan de muertos*, apples and pomegranates. Bright orange marigolds (*cempasúchil*, the Nahuatl word used in Mexico and its diaspora) adorned the altar, shaped into delicate arches and in exuberant bunches, straight from someone's garden. Over the past week people had filled a basket with handwritten notes that name their loved ones. The Mass concluded, many people made their way to the multiple devotional spaces outdoors: to pray or to light a candle. The parish has extensive grounds, with outbuildings for catechism classes, Stations of the Cross, signage and stands stored until the parish harvest festival comes each fall. People waited in line to purchase breakfast in the spacious, high-ceilinged parish hall. Highly organized teams of men and women took orders for menudo, sopes, champurrado, and the like. The Virgin of Guadalupe hangs high above the parishioners, who sat at long tables with folding chairs. It was the first indoor Sunday meal at St. Anthony Claret since the pandemic's start. People radiated happiness to work together once again in the kitchen or to linger over a cafecito, greeting friends and acquaintances.

While Fresno is a majority-Latino city, this church, tucked away on the city's southeastern edge, holds a special place for the local community. For generations the parish has welcomed people drawn to the San Joaquin Valley for seasonal work on its farms. Four (of five) Sunday Masses are celebrated in Spanish. The sons and daughters of migrant laborers serve as lectors, eucharistic ministers, catechists, and youth group leaders. Others get involved in prayer groups or play in a church band. The parish maintains an active farmworker ministry, in which Claretians and lay volunteers travel to seven outlying towns and camps to celebrate Mass, distribute coats, teach catechism, or play soccer with kids. People may have journeyed alone to Fresno from Texas or Oaxaca, but at St. Anthony's many walk together, making connections, as they share Catholic rituals.[8] Fr. Art Gramaje (1962–) describes the parish as an "oasis" or second home for its members; at St. Anthony Claret, "the church is the people."[9]

On the opposite side of the country I visited Our Lady of Fatima Church in Perth Amboy, New Jersey. On downtown Smith Street, the modern architecture did not automatically signal a Catholic church. Inside, the roomy sanctuary draws one in with its warm, varied tones of golden brown, brick and wood; diffused light streams in through multicolored windows. On my September 2022 visit, the sanctuary felt welcoming. So did the people. Men greeted each other with abrazos. All the lectors and servers were named before each Mass. The 9 am misa en español nearly filled the pews. With tambourine, bongos, conga, guira, and guitar, the musicians accompanied the Mass with lively music with strong hints of the Dominican Republic and Puerto Rico. The laity clapped in time and sang with passion. Before closing, the parish celebrated birthdays with blessings and the up-tempo swell of "Happy Birthday," sung by the parishioners.

At Fatima, the parish is more than Sunday Mass. On Saturday morning, cars filled the parking lot behind the church hall. In the gym (that doubles as a hall), women completed setup for a wedding party that afternoon in the social center. A block away, a line formed outside of the Claret Center: parents waiting to enroll their children in CCD classes. In a spacious hall, catechists and other volunteers spoke Spanish, registering the children. The Center is a recently refurbished commercial building dating to the turn of the last century. Its cleanly painted, refloored offices and classrooms offer dignified, updated spaces for classes, lay society meetings, the parish food pantry, and even a quiet, well-landscaped garden for parish use. A conference room on the second floor, with a long set of windows, overlooks Smith Street. Diocesan officials request use of the room for meetings in Perth Amboy. Overall, Our Lady of Fatima is a remarkable place: a vibrant, inclusive pan-Latino parish, unusually strong in the wake of the COVID pandemic.[10]

In the United States the Claretians currently administer parishes in San Antonio, South Chicago, Fresno and San Gabriel, California, and Perth Amboy and Jersey City, New Jersey. They also direct the Newman Center at California State University, Fresno. In summer 2024, the province made the decision to leave longtime parishes in Stone Mountain, Georgia, Springfield, Missouri, and Prescott, Arizona. The province also encompasses several parishes in Québec and Vancouver. Albergue San Óscar Romero, a joint US-Mexico ministry, shelters and supports refugees in Ciudad Juárez.

The Claretians' relative devotion to parish service versus other missionary apostolates deserves reflection. Almost all these parishes benefit from the congregation's emphasis on community life. A Claretian parish has two to four priests in residence. Compared to many diocesan parishes, staffing is more constant and knowledge of the parish community is stronger. Claretian parishes focus on the poor and immigrants, if not exclusively. The US parishes all offer Spanish-language liturgies. Most host food pantries. The churches tend to be inculturative: recognizing and incorporating diverse devotional traditions of the laity. At Perth Amboy's Our Lady of Fatima, for example, the parish celebrates special Masses and novenas for La Providencia (November 19), the Virgin of Altagracia (January 21), and in December, la Guadalupana, in addition to the fiesta of Fatima, the parish patroness, in May. The inherently global nature of the Claretian Missionaries means that the US province draws on a wealth of provinces for its staffing. At San Gabriel in 2022, for example, the community included priests from Mexico, Nigeria, the United States, and Vietnam. Linguistic and cultural knowledge within the resident group enables apt staffing for that parish's diverse laity. In some cases, the existence of a Claretian parish speaks to the congregation's history and commitment to a specific geography and population. Our Lady of Guadalupe in South Chicago and Immaculate Heart of Mary in San Antonio both manifest Claretians' stalwart defense of a place and its people in the face of deindustrialization, urban renewal, and depopulation.

Clergy Sex Abuse: Moving Beyond Silence and Euphemisms

The multiple spasms of news, accusations, disbelief, lawsuits, and mistrust about the clergy sexual abuse of minors has been afloat since the 1990s. I suspected my research would reveal cases of priests and brothers accused of sexual abuse. And it did. Silences and euphemisms appear in historic documents, like a whisper that raises questions, but no answers, about individual Claretians. For example, the provincial wrote to a priest about a confrere in 1967, "yes, I'm afraid he's gone. It was a very difficult decision for me, but eventually I had to ask him to leave. He had so many fine qualities that I overextended myself several times by making allowances for his unacceptable behavior and attitudes." The letter promised "a more detailed explanation when I see you later." I flagged this opaque reference upon first read, but now realize that concerns about this person might have nothing to do with sexual abuse.[11] The circumstances that led Fr. Andrew Roy to leave the Claretians in the 1950s are similarly obscure (see chapter 3). Sometimes, an individual was sent to a treatment program, for a reason that went unsaid: alcohol, mental illness, or sex abuse? Occasionally, a Claretian might suddenly appear from Mexico or might be sent to the Mexican province.

The Claretians are part and parcel of the scandal in the Catholic Church. Bishopaccountability.org lists accused clergy from 116 male religious orders. That Database of the Accused names twenty-three Claretian priests and brothers accused of sexual abuse, including cases that resulted in six settlements and one conviction. (One of the accusations has been deemed not credible.)[12] Like other religious orders and the dioceses, the Claretian leaders reassigned problematic clergy, sent some for treatment, but until recent decades seldom removed them from ministry. Claretians who carried on relationships with adult women were tolerated in the mid-twentieth century, their broken vow of celibacy known by many. The "bonded masculinity" or fraternalism of the priesthood has allowed many clergymen to look the other way regarding immoral behavior.[13] Alumni of the Claretian junior seminaries, long closed, hold veiled memories of inappropriate touching by a deceased prefect, but suppress any public accusations.[14] "Holy orders are not so holy," remarks priest and scholar Joseph Chinnici, OFM.[15]

The *Chicago Sun-Times* in 2021 published Robert Herguth's scathing exposé of the Claretians' history of sexual abuse of minors, underlining the six accused men who had ministered at Our Lady of Guadalupe Church at some point. The article did not provide any breaking news, but it singled out the Claretian leadership for their lack of transparency and communication about the history of abuse in the province. Herguth criticized the province's failure to update its website to post public lists of Claretians with credible accusations of child sexual abuse.[16] Today, three years after the article's publication, the provincial website outlines protocols and encourages reporting of abuse (see the Safe Environment tab). Nevertheless, the absence of a published list of those accused of sexual abuse on their website presents a worrisome lack of transparency.[17]

Susan Bigelow Reynolds writes persuasively about patterns of clerical sex abuse among Latinos, with diocesan leadership keeping known abusers "in active ministry, shuffled from parish to parish." These placements were common in inner city parishes and places with vulnerable Latino laity due to their undocumented status, poverty, or limited English.[18] Perhaps past Claretian provincials thought that the majority Mexican laity in South Chicago would not complain about problematic clerical behavior.[19] I found no evidence of this, but neither was I looking for such information. The province should look more squarely at their history, "the injuries done and the penances required."[20]

Nurturing an Intercultural Province

In June 2022, the Claretian Missionaries of the USA-Canada Province met at their province-wide assembly at St. Mary of the Lake University outside of Chicago. Eighty people gathered for their first assembly since the start of the COVID-19 pandemic. I visited for a day and met dozens of priests and brothers at meals and in informal chats. The priests, brothers, and students wore a casual array of checked shirts, polos, an occasional t-shirt, and a tunic of West African colors and design. Their dress signaled their many languages and personalities. The encounters instilled a new sense of purpose in completing this book. My readers, I understood, would include dozens of younger confreres who hail from Sri Lanka, Haiti, or Cameroon.

For the 5 pm Mass in the conference center chapel, a portrait of the Founder was propped at the pulpit's foot. Five Claretians in white con-celebrated the English-language Mass. The first celebrant, a Spaniard with British-tinged English, remarked that we were celebrating the So-lemnity of St. Anthony Mary Claret, admitting with a touch of humor that it was not Claret's day, "but we can do what we want."

The homilist, Fr. Beauplan Derilus, was younger than most and spoke English with a slight lilt—he is a native speaker of Haitian Creole. Derilus declared,

> We are united in mission even if we don't look exactly alike or we don't do things in the exact same way. We are united in mission, but we remain distinct to each other and do things differently. God celebrates and en-courages our uniqueness and our diversity of gifts and talents. Our dif-ferences are a grace for our vocation and mission. We are one in mission even when we remain different to each other in mission.

He asked his confreres: "How are we accomplishing our mission today as a Province, is there unity in our diversity? Do our missions coincide with the unity that Jesus speaks of? What do people see when they look at our missions? What do they see when they look at our charism?" He then explored *listening*. "Do we listen?" Does Putin listen to Ukrainian fami-lies? . . . Do Haitian politicians listen to the people? Does the Catholic hierarchy listen to LGBT people?" Back to this assembly, he pointedly questioned, "In our Province, do we always listen effectively and objec-tively to each other? Maybe yes, maybe not." Derilus closed, "Let us pray to Him to help us step out of our zone of comfort and learn how to listen more attentively to one another. Let us not work to look exactly alike in our mission, but different. Let us be very different, always different, but one in Christ and one in our vocation and mission. May we always cel-ebrate our differences and the diversity of our gifts."[21] My research until then had focused on the pioneering Spaniards and the emergence of an American province. This homily alerted me to the complexity of work in the internationally diverse community.

After the provocative homily, a co-celebrant from Africa read a list, the necrologium, of the Claretians who had died on that date. He recited the year, name, and place of death of a dozen Claretians. The day's list went back to the early twentieth century. Most of those remembered were españoles of whom half had died in Spain. The list also included the missionaries who died far from home, such as in Equatorial Guinea and Sweetwater, Texas. Reading aloud and listening, together, underlined the place of history, remembrance, community, and the global missions that connected everyone present with seminaries and residences past and present, around the world. Claretians in America have always formed just a piece of a global congregation.

Starting with a small band of Catalan followers in the 1850s, today the Claretians work in seventy countries with about three thousand members. Fr. Mathew Vattamattam, a native of Kerala, India, is serving his second term as Superior General of the Congregation of the Claretian Missionaries. Of seventy-three priests in the United States and Canada in 2020, a scant majority were born in this country. Mexico and India are the most common home countries of Claretians here; Canada, Nigeria, Peru, and Spain are represented by a few as well. Members of the US-Canada province also come from Cameroon, Colombia, Brazil, Congo, Cuba, Ecuador, El Salvador, Guatemala, Haiti, Honduras, Panama, and Vietnam. The Claretians celebrate the international composition of this province.

Working optimally with the international membership of the Claretians in the United States remains a test. From the 1920s through 1960s, American Claretians shared a bond of seminary and novitiate experiences. Today a Claretian working in the United States might complete his training in Colombia, India, or the Philippines. Arriving here means learning or improving English (and usually Spanish), but also growing to understand the diversity of US culture and among the Claretians. When I visited Perth Amboy, the rectory was home to Claretians from Cameroon, India, Mexico, and the United States. In San Gabriel, I sat down to lunch with Claretians from the United States, Vietnam, Nigeria, and Mexico. The array of available condiments was astounding, but group conversations did not always flow easily.

Imagine the trials a recently arrived priest from South Asia or West Africa might face. Most will be directed to accent reduction training for their spoken English. The province will send some men to learn Spanish—to Puerto Rico or MACC in Texas—for their upcoming parish assignments. For the first time in his life, many young Claretians will need to use a credit card and a bank account. Living in small communities here, they will need to seek their own medical care and obtain winter clothing. The older American Claretians likely relax by watching football or baseball, but cricket or soccer may not hold their attention. Can you interest your new confreres in the celebration of Pongal, a Tamil harvest festival? When February arrives, will the priests in your residence care about the Gunadala Mary Matha festival, a staple of your Catholic life in southern India? The internet brings news of elections and violent upheaval from home, but few people surrounding you are aware of any of this.

Meanwhile, it can be puzzling to differentiate between your parishioners from Mexico and those from El Salvador or Venezuela—and they all talk a bit differently from the phrases you learned in the Spanish course. If you come from the Caribbean or Africa, most Americans simply see you as "black" and you will need to negotiate the norms of race in this country. Every day brings with it the need to cross a variety of borders: of nation, language, race, and of lived religion. The provincial provided a couple weeks to acclimate to life in the United States but, honestly, there is too much to absorb. No boot camp can prepare you to be a Catholic missionary in the United States. That was true for the Spaniards in the early twentieth century. Working as a missionary means displacement and requires self-sacrifice. Then and now, it is simply a challenge.

Retreats and assemblies, on hold for more than two years due to the pandemic, are crucial for building connections across the province, aiming for cohesion and community across languages, nationality, and age. With opportunities for prayer, dialogue, and unstructured conversations, these multi-day gatherings remain essential opportunities to build cohesion. These periodic gatherings may have a special importance for Claretians in the more geographically isolated locations, such as Texas and Vancouver.[22] As Fr. Derilus posed the question to his confreres at the assembly: "How are we accomplishing our mission today as a Province, is there unity in our diversity?" Claretians need to discuss these vital questions now and in the future. Wherever possible, crossing borders of nation and culture—in person or virtually, in word and in action—seems ideal to nurture interculturalism within the local communities as well as the larger province.

The work of running parishes, seeking and training new vocations, writing reports and homilies continues. When communities do not work as well as they might, some Claretians murmur the mantra "Aramos con los bueyes que tenemos" ("We plow with the oxen we have"). Fr. Teodomiro "Theo" Fuentes (1927–2018) repeated the phrase, recalling rural Spain in earlier times. He meant that sometimes people are not as helpful as expected, but you have to work with what you have.

A through line in this book has focused on the transition from an entirely Spanish membership before 1930 to an American majority and leadership circa 1960. Today the province stands at another demographic shift. In the next decade or so, no national group will dominate. With membership hovering around eighty priests and brothers, the province was last this small in the 1930s. As the province ages and members pass away, it becomes more reliant on the global congregation for its membership. The majority of younger and mid-career Claretians grew up outside of the United States. The seven students living in the Claretian formation house in Chicago in 2023 came from China, the Philippines, Vietnam, the Congo, India, and one from California. The congregation and its parishes are experiencing "mission in reverse." Journalist John Allen writes appreciatively about the influx of foreign-born clergy in the United States, "the Church here would come grinding to a halt without them. They help keep our parishes, schools, hospitals and other Catholic institutions not only afloat, but dynamic and vital. Beyond that, they're also ambassadors of the other 94 percent of the Catholic world in our midst."[23] Catholic clergy from Latin America, South and Southeast Asia, and Africa will sustain and impact American parishes, including the Latino-majority parishes where Claretians have accompanied people since 1902.

ACKNOWLEDGMENTS

I came to Claretian history because of their century of work in Chicago. The Claretians' track record for accompaniment of Latino Catholics impressed me. My friend and colleague Malachy McCarthy, then archivist for the Claretians, urged me to take on a history of the US province. Fr. Rosendo Urrabazo, CMF, also encouraged me to consider the project. No book-length history documented the Claretians' history and legacy. As I realized the extent of the Claretian footprint in Latino ministry on a national level, I grew more intrigued. The Claretian Missionaries founded missions and parishes in marginalized communities whose histories deserved telling. Uncovering and telling these US Latino stories has been a gratifying adventure for this historian.

The archivists at the Claretian Missionaries Archives have supported this project from start to finish. Malachy McCarthy's tireless work in cataloguing the splendid photo collection helped me to outline the book before visiting the archive. He retired from the archive about a year into my research, but remains at the ready to discuss all things Claretian history. Doris Cardenas, head archivist since 2022, has been a great support. Her keen eye and exhibit on the Claretian presence in Panama grabbed my attention and planted the seed for the Central American chapter. Poring over the odd piece of ephemera in person or with an email query sparked conversations with Doris and Kristen Melkonyan that have sustained me when much of the research and writing process has been a solo experience. Thanks also to Jessie Koontz and Ron Stua. The CMAC team made me feel at home throughout many visits to Chicago. Spending time at 205 W. Monroe is always better for the kindness of Jerice Barrios, Rebecca Goss, Ken Medina, Kathi Gormley, and Newland Smith.

The Claretian Missionaries entrusted me to tell their history. Fr. Rosendo Urrabazo, then provincial superior, opened the door and then let me be. I treasure the few conversations we had about the congregation's history and hope for more. Fr. Brian Culley avidly supported the research and provided vital information when I asked about Perth Amboy, Chicago, San Marcos, Soledad, or Fresno. I had crucial, candid exchanges with Claretians Benjamin Arrieta Romero, Mark Brummel, Edgar Colocho, Beauplan Derilus, Art Gramaje, Paul Keller, Thomas Mallavarapu, Bibin Mathew, Tom McGann, Steve Niskanen, Gilles Njobam, John Raab, Francisco Javier Reyes, Plácido Rodríguez, Alberto Ruiz, Gabriel Ruiz, and José Sanchez. Thanks also to María Contreras, Gail Peters, Coni Schneider, and Sandy Trevino.

The Claretian Alumni Association kindly let me tag along to their reunions online and in Momence and shared many stories. Pat Reardon, seasoned writer, SJS alum, and friend, has been a wonderful sounding board. When I was feeling shy about doing interviews, he urged me to "invite yourself. Be courteously pushy, like a reporter." Olga Cordero Kilmer always shares her unique Claretian history from Chicago, Springfield, and Panama.

A generous scholarly community encouraged my work. I am especially grateful for conversations with Mario García, Tim Matovina, Robert Wright OMI, and Julia Young. I build on their model of engaged scholarship and true collegiality. For their interest and comments on my drafts, thanks to Emiliano Aguilar, Selena Aleman, Peter Alter, Matthew Butler, Ismael Cuevas, Susan Behrens-Fitzpatrick, Kristine Ashton Gunnell, Brett Hendrickson, Michael Innis-Jiménez, Ann Durkin Keating, Jim Krippner, Polly Lauer, Maggie McGuinness, Terry McKiernan, Jerry Poyo, Patrick Reardon, and David Sandell. I received input as well from Fr. David Endres, Jojo Galvan, Patrick Hayes, Matt Hinojosa, Aura Jirau Arroyo, Eileen Markey, Gavin Moulton, Ramón Alonso Pérez Escutia, Michael Pfeifer, Diego Ramírez, Thomas Rzeznik, and John Theils. Christine Doran, editor of her father's diaries, earns special mention. Access to Brian Doran's book enriched my understanding of daily life in the Guatemala missions. Fr. Anton Grech, a priest in Izabal and social media enthusiast, allowed me to follow the current-day parishes where the Claretians worked decades ago. His tireless work to publicize the history of the Izabal *mártires* deserves a special *grazzi*.

I presented portions of the book at the American Catholic Historical Association, the Newberry Library Seminar in Religion and Culture, the Oblate School of Theology, Vernacular Architecture Forum, the

Conference on Carlos E. Castañeda's "Catholic" Texas, and with Historians of Catholic Mexico (gracias Ricardo Álvarez-Pimentel and Nathan Ellstrand).

These people eased my entry to Texas history: Kenneth Hafertepe, Donna Guerra, Margaret Leeds, Mercedes Formolo, Lisa Martinez, John McKiernan-Gonzalez, María Elena Urrutia, and Bob Wright. In San Gabriel, I was welcomed by the Cagigas family and Mary Camarenna; in Fresno by the Gutierrez family and Connie Vargas.

Archivists and librarians across the country offered help and corrections: Dan Fitzpatrick, US Army Chaplain Corps Historian; Meg Romero Hall, Director of Archives and Records Center, Archdiocese of Chicago; Kathleen Jarvis, Jerome Public Library; Sharon Kabel, creator of the Periti of Vatican II project; Elvira Sanchez Kisser, Catholic Archdiocese of San Antonio Archives; Vilma Novak, Perth Amboy Free Public Library; Arro Smith, San Marcos Public Library; and Tim Wenzl, Archivist Emeritus, Catholic Diocese of Dodge City.

Incisive comments from readers at New York University Press pushed me to write a better book. Jennifer Hammer has been an advocate for this book. She and Brianna Jean guided me through the publication process as true professionals. Cartographer Molly O'Halloran improved on my original ideas for the maps. Many thanks to copy editor Karen Verde and indexer Heather Dubnick for their thoughtful attention to detail. When I needed a last-minute photo from San Marcos, Anthony Head came through for me.

Dan Freidus, my dear partner in life, cheerfully put up with my absences and my often-distracted state for the past three years. His engagement with my work never ceases to amaze me. Thank you, Dan, for building me a desk . . . and for the tofu lasagna.

APPENDIX

Claretian-Administered Mission Churches by County in South Central Texas, ca. 1903–20

Atascosa County
  Charlotte
  Christine
  Jourdanton
  Lytle
  Pleasanton
  Poteet
  Rossville
Bandera County
  Bandera
  Medina
Bastrop County
  Elgin
  Red Rock
  Smithville
Bexar County (San Antonio)
  Atascosa
  Bexar
  El Carmen
  Elmendorf
  Graytown
  Helotes
  Honey Creek
  Macdona
  San Antonio
  San Francisco de la Espada
  San José

San Juan Capistrano
Somerset
Von Ormy
Caldwell County
  Cedar Creek
  Fentress
  Luling
  Lockhart
  Martindale
  Maxwell
  Uhland
Colorado County
  Weimar
Comal County
  New Braunfels
DeWitt County
  Cuero
  Garfield (or Travis County)
  Yoakum
Edwards County
  Rocksprings
Frio County
  Bigfoot
  Derby
  Dilley
  Moore
  Pearsall

Gonzales County
  Gonzales
Guadalupe County
  New Berlin
  Seguin
  Staples
Hays County (San Marcos)
  Buda
  Kyle
  San Marcos
Karnes County
  Helena
  Hobson
  Karnes City
  Kenedy
  Runge
Kendall County
  Boerne
  Waring
Kerr County
  Kerrville
La Salle County
  Cotulla
  Encinal
  Fowlerton
  Los Angeles
  Millet
Lavaca County
  Shiner
McMullen County
  Tilden

Medina County
  Castroville
  Devine
Travis County
  Creedmoor
  Manor
Victoria County
  Victoria
Wilson County
  Cañada Verde
  Floresville
  Saspamco
Mission locations unknown
  Chilipitin
  El Picoso
  Hansey
  Las Calaveras
  Las Gallinas
  La Mota Seca
  Los Vasquez
  Menchaca
  Miner Ranch
  Privilegio
  Rancho Brown
  Rancho Hugo
  Rancho Leal
  Rancho Perez
  Rancho Walsh
  San Agustín
  Santa Rosa

NOTE ON SOURCES

Few sustained histories of the Claretians' work in the United States exist. The Claretians occasionally compiled albums to mark calendrical milestones, often for fundraising. In 1952 they self-published a substantial English-language overview, with a gold cover and many photos that showcased their many foundations, to mark their fiftieth anniversary in the United States. Some individuals wrote press releases and magazine articles that highlighted Claretian projects, for example, chronicling the development of the St. Jude Police League or a new seminary, often published in Claretian publications such as *The Voice of St. Jude*. Fr. Camilo Torrente wrote autobiographical sketches and Fr. Severino Lopez penned a thoughtful memoir, but these personal reflections remain the exception in US Claretian writing. Necrologies, obituaries written by a fellow Claretian, vary greatly in content and quality; these life sketches tend to be laudatory and must be read against other sources about the individual. The writing of necrologies, once a great art and service to the congregation, became less common after 1960. In November 1940, the *Provincial Bulletin* coaxed Claretians to send in news to the bulletin: "The history of this new Province of ours is in the making, and, unless we, poor mortals write down the achievements of today, whether they seem big or small to us, they will be forgotten." Presciently, the editor added that these submissions would "let us alleviate and speed up the work of future historians."

In 1941–44, Fr. Camilo Torrente, one of the US pioneers, took on the task of writing a comprehensive history of the US province. (He began writing some of this history in 1921, as directed by Fr. Zaldívar.) The elderly priest visited Claretian houses and gathered documents. He drafted most of a lengthy volume (the first of a projected two), but his sight worsened and his mental faculties declined. Fr. Joseph Berengueras took up the draft and assembled an almost complete manuscript of the Claretians through 1947. He based chapters by geography and foundations, starting with early missions and parishes in Texas and California; in these he retained much of Torrente's engaging, first-person accounts. Berengueras began each chapter with a chronological narrative of the founding years, described offshoot missions (some in places that no longer exist), and ended each with a jumble of stories, lists of foundation staff, and necrologies. My favorite chapter is "Tentativas Pasajeras," an accounting of attempted ministries in places from Utah to Brooklyn, Saginaw to Wichita. The author shared draft chapters with Claretians at each named foundation, seeking corrections and additions. Some people responded—resulting in marginal notes. In November 1945, the province sent Torrente's writing to Claretian residences for corrections; only four responded. (Six months later, the *Bulletin* reported in May 1946, "Due to lack of cooperation, the work has stopped.") Berengueras did this work ca. 1944–47, in Los Angeles, while suffering from tuberculosis and other health problems. The ailing priest returned to Panama in 1948, leaving bundle upon bundle of typed manuscript in Spanish, but none were ever fully edited. (Berengueras passed away in Barcelona in 1951 at age 49.) The ambitious history of the province remained not quite complete and was never published. The goal likely was to complete the history for publication to commemorate the centennial of the congregation's founding in 1849. The Berengueras manuscript exceeds five hundred pages (in varying states of editing) and fills several boxes in the CMAC. Overall, this manuscript contains a treasure trove of anecdotes that generally celebrate the Claretians' triumphs and persistence. Yet, for someone unfamiliar with the Claretians' trajectory, it presents a challenging read. Torrente and Berengueras both seemed to relish writing with some very local, old-fashioned peninsular Spanish phrases.

Fr. Joseph Daries (1930–2016) completed an English-language "Historical Sketch, The Claretians in the U.S.A. 1902–1977" to mark the seventy-fifth anniversary of the congregation's arrival in this country. This unpublished, typescript history is just forty-one pages. It glosses over many stories and places, but offers a reasonable chronology of key events and an overview of change for the province, especially of change in formation structure after Vatican II. At times Daries relied on generalization and overblown language, depicting his confreres as heroic. Following Claretian sources, he tended to mark their history by the twenty-five-year epochs that were so celebrated by Catholic leaders but often irrelevant to demonstrating change. Overall, the Daries history offered a reader-friendly survey, if scant on analysis.

Claretians in America: A Pictorial History, 1902–2012, edited by Malachy McCarthy and Daniel Magner, offers an engaging outline of the US Claretians' remarkably wide-ranging ministry. Each page features one or two photos and a succinct explanation of the place, people, and activity shown. Presented chronologically, the book offers a taste of the CMAC's rich photography collection. Some one thousand photos are available (and searchable) at https://claretianmissionariesarchives.org/digital-collections/.

To readers in search of a research project, many rich sources await further attention. Someone should examine the Claretians' work across Arizona. A story remains to be written about Fr. Thomas Matin, the people of Palo Verde, La Loma, and Bishop, and their beloved Santo Niño Church, buried under the blue of Dodgers Stadium. The US Claretian missions in the Philippines, Japan, and Nigeria should be studied. The female religious who worked in tandem with the Claretian Missionaries merit more attention.

The Claretian Missionaries Archives USA-Canada in Chicago is a work in progress. The collection generally lacked finding guides while I worked there, and many collections were unprocessed. The record number system in use will likely change. It appears that some documentation pertaining to the western province remains in California. While the provincial approved my access to requested personnel files, dossiers deemed more sensitive remained beyond my reach.

NOTES

INTRODUCTION

1 Various Catholic News Service accounts, May, 1950; *La Esperanza*, Claretian-published weekly, available on the Catholic News Archive, https://thecatholic newsarchive.org/.

2 "A Picture Pilgrimage," *The Voice of St. Jude* (hereafter, VSJ), July 1950; De Prada necrology; Joaquín De Prada personal papers, Claretian Missionaries Archives USA-Canada, Chicago, Illinois (hereafter, CMAC).

3 Photos from Claret canonization, CMAC.

4 McDannell, *Material Christianity*, 39–41.

5 Thompson, "Cordimarian Spirituality," 341–43.

6 Claret, *Autobiography*, 132. Fr. Josep Xifré oversaw the Claretians' tremendous growth as Superior General in 1858–99.

7 Claret, *Autobiography*, 101, 57.

8 Claret, *Colección de los opúsculos*.

9 McGreevy, *American Jesuits*, 107–08, on the Catholic press in the mid-nineteenth century.

10 Claret, *Autobiography*, 205.

11 Claret, *Autobiography*, 141, 155–56.

12 Sargent, *Assignments*, 168.

13 Fr. Jaime Clotet quoted in Alonso, *Misioneros claretianos*.

14 Claret, *Autobiography*, 133.

15 *Bulletin of USA Province* (hereafter, PB), 1947, 188–95. Quote here from a later translation to English.

16 Sargent, *Assignments*. Among many Claretian-authored biographies of Claret, see Lozano, *Mystic and Man of Action*.

17 "Catholic Book Club Archives," *America*, January 30, 2015, www.americamaga-zine.org; Cummings, *Saint of Our Own*, 99.

18 NBC recording, CMAC; *PB*, April–May 1950.

19 *La Esperanza*, May 21, 1950. *La Voz*, San Antonio's Catholic weekly, printed similar expressions of gratitude to Claret during the season of his canonization. Catholic Archdiocese of San Antonio Archives (hereafter, ARCHSA).

20 Moses, "Afire with the Itinerant Spirit," 217.

21 Bishop Granjon quoted in *Claretians in America*, 106.

22 The two-hundred-page book devoted two pages to laypeople who supported the Claretians' efforts. Female religious, present in nearly every Claretian parish, did not receive their due.

23 O'Toole, *Faithful*, 3.

24 M. García, *Father Luis Olivares*; Kanter, *Chicago Católico*; Macias, "Spanish Myths and Mexican Realities"; Matovina, *Guadalupe and Her Faithful*; McCarthy, "Which Christ Came to Chicago"; Orsi, *Thank You, Saint Jude*.

25 González, *Strangers No Longer*; Reynolds, *People Get Ready*; Hinojosa, Elmore, and González, *Faith and Power*; Hendrickson, *Mexican American Religions*; Young, *Mexican Exodus*; Matovina, *Latino Catholicism*; M. García, *Católicos*; Badillo, *Latinos and the New Immigrant Church*; Treviño, *Church in the Barrio*; Dolan and Hinojosa, *Mexican Americans and the Catholic Church*.

26 Berengueras ms., CMAC.

CHAPTER 1. FOLLOWING THE MEXICANS

1 Moses, "Afire with the Itinerant Spirit," 217.

2 Martin, *Songs My Mother Sang*, xv.

3 Berengueras ms., CMAC; *Anales de la Congregación* (hereafter, *Anales*); Cabré Rufatt, *Historia de los Misioneros Claretianos en México*; *Bodas De Diamante*.

4 Butler, *Popular Piety*, 105, 143. Wright-Rios, *Revolutions in Mexican Catholicism*.

5 *Anales*, 1910.

6 *Anales*, August 1902.

7 The *Miserere* is a prayer for repentance that draws from Psalm 51.

8 *Anales*, September 1902. On annual missions that targeted native villagers, see Butler, *Popular Piety*, 124.

9 *Anales*, August 1902.

10 *The Claretian Star*, April–July 1939, CMAC. Torrente shared his recollections with readers, especially American seminarians, in "My Bag of Stories."

11 Both quotations, *Anales*, August 1908.

12 *Anales*, 1910.

13 *Anales*, 1903.

14 *Anales*, 1910.

15 Berengueras ms., CMAC. Verdaguer first contacted the Claretians in 1901. When they agreed to visit, he urged them to read about French missions in Texas, likely referring to Fr. Emmanuel Domenech.

16 Berengueras ms., CMAC.

17 Berengueras ms., CMAC.

18 Wright, "Mexican-Descent Catholics."

19 This mode of parish mission involved "an intense course of sermons, preached by a visiting missionary, that aimed at stirring sorrow for sin and fear of its punishment." Tentler, *American Catholics*, 84.

20 Chapter 1, Berengueras ms., CMAC.

21 G. Hinojosa, "Mexican-American Faith Communities," 31, 39. Wright, "Mexican-Descent Catholics," spotlights underrecognized efforts to serve Mexican Catholics in Texas ca. 1880–1910.

22 Letter from San Antonio, October 13, 1902. *Anales*, 19.

23 Valerio Jiménez, *River of Hope*, 279; Foley, *White Scourge*, 42.

24 Montejano, *Anglos and Mexicans*, 222.

25 Muñoz Martinez, *Injustice Never Leaves You*; Johnson, *Revolution in Texas*.

26 Davis, *Sueños y recuerdos*, 77–78. Fr. Eugene Sugrañes, age 28, was the first superior. Br. José Justo Hormachea (1888–1965) accompanied him, but left the Claretians when he married a local, apparently Mexican woman and opened "Joe the Tailor Shop" in San Marcos.

27 Muñoz Martinez, *Injustice Never Leaves You*, 21; Johnson, *Revolution in Texas*.

28 Chronicle, St. John the Evangelist Church, San Marcos, CMAC; *Anales*, 1917.

29 Chapter 3, Berengueras ms., CMAC.

30 Foley, *White Scourge*, 49–51, 62. Foley describes racial tensions and the cotton economy in Caldwell County.

31 Scott E. Wagner, "Martindale, TX," *Handbook of Texas Online*, accessed August 12, 2024, www.tshaonline.org. The Texas State Historical Handbook ignores Martindale's Mexican population, only mentioning its black-white divide.

32 Esparza, *Raza Schools*, 28. Churches sponsored many early Mexican schools in Del Rio.

33 Chapter 3, Berengueras ms., CMAC. The vague accusation of a renegade Mexican suggests anti-clericalism among some mexicanos, but my research on Martindale did not find this.

34 Badillo, *Latinos and the New Immigrant Church*, 26–28.

35 Chronicle for 1920, St. John the Evangelist Church, San Marcos; rededication program 1987, Immaculate Heart of Mary Church, Martindale, CMAC. Falbo and Deodati, a San Antonio–based firm, oversaw the 1919 addition of a tower for $1,000.

36 Davis, *Sueños y recuerdos*, 36. The First Hispanic Baptist Church in Martindale existed in 1915, but with a fleeting presence.

37 Annual report on Missions and Stations, 1917, St. John the Evangelist Church, San Marcos, CMAC. The Archcofradia of the Immaculate Heart of Mary and the Society of Cristo Rey drew the most members.

38 Chronicle, St. John the Evangelist Church, San Marcos, 1920, CMAC. In fall 1920, the parish school in San Marcos was staffed by "Maestra Directora" Anastacia Martinez, who taught in Spanish. Señorita Concha Martinez taught in English and served as *cantora* at St. John's.

39 Chronicle, St. John the Evangelist Church, San Marcos, 1920, CMAC.

40 Rededication program 1987, Immaculate Heart of Mary Church, Martindale, CMAC.

41 *La Esperanza*, August 28, 1938.

42 Barragán Goetz, *Reading, Writing, and Revolution*, 124; Esparza, *Raza Schools*, 27.

43 Caro, *Years of Lyndon Johnson*, 166–69.

44 Iglesia Del Carmen, Colectas 1903–1919, Immaculate Heart of Mary–San Antonio papers (hereafter, IHM), CMAC. These activities recorded in Losoya in February 1916.

45 *PB*, March 1947.

46 Meeks, *Border Citizens*; Benton-Cohen, *Borderline Americans*.

47 Young, *Mexican Exodus*, 23; Butler, *Popular Piety*, 48.

48 Daries ms., 6; 1914 reports, *Anales*, 607, 613. The reported numbers of exiled Claretians vary. Some came north by land, others arrived by boat to New Orleans. Some went to temporary residences in Martindale, Pearsall, and other Texas towns.

49 The Claretians administered parishes in Yuma and Phoenix, and many small towns from those centers. They opened Mt. Claret Center near Phoenix for cursillo and other retreats in 1963.

50 Many details from Roberto Rabago's memoir-in-stories, *Rich Town, Poor Town*.

51 Chapter 9, Berengueras ms., CMAC.

52 Rabago, *Rich Town, Poor Town*, xv, 40, 47.

53 YWCA-sponsored International Institutes across the country offered educational and recreational opportunities for foreign-born women and their children.

54 Brogdon, "History of Jerome," 86, 136.

55 Chapter 9, Berengueras ms., CMAC.

56 *Anales*, June 1918.

57 Chapter 9, Berengueras ms., CMAC. In September 1918, United Verde managers accused several Mexican men of murdering a company watchman and claimed to find a suitcase carrying grenades. Brogdon, "History of Jerome," 73.

58 Clements, *After the Boom*. Vyto Starinskas, "Splash of Jerome's Racist History Now Worth $225,000," *The Verde Independent*, March 2, 2019; Chapter 9, Berengueras ms., CMAC; Brogdon, "History of Jerome," 26.

59 The Claretians ministered across Yavapai County to Clarkdale, Clemenceau, and Cottonwood. By the mid-1920s they established churches in Mayer, Crown King, Bagdad, and Drake.

60 1933 entries, Chronicle, Holy Family Church, Jerome, CMAC.

61 Chronicle, Holy Family Church, Jerome, CMAC. "Tantos mexicanos son incultas y papagoya."

62 Garcilazo, *Traqueros*.

63 Fr. John Handly, quoted in the *Dodge City Journal*, April 29, 1929. Cited in "A City within a City Dodge City's Mexican Village—Dodge City, Kansas," Kansas Historical Markers, April 10, 2018, www.waymarking.com.

64 Wenzl, *Dodge City's Mexican Village*. Former residents warmly recall the Mexican Village.

65 R. Serrano to Felix Cepeda, October 9, 1913. Dodge City, Kansas papers, CMAC.

66 Wenzl, *Dodge City's Mexican Village*; Loyola University Chicago Archives & Special Collections. Catholic Church Extension Society Records. Subgroup 4: Chapel Car, Series 2: Chapel Car Logs, 1907–1955.

67 Dodge City, Kansas papers, CMAC; Wenzl, *Dodge City's Mexican Village*. Claretian correspondence reveals a plan to employ three Sisters of St. Joseph at the Mexican school in 1915; the teachers never appear in the archived correspondence.

68 Lujano, "Social History." In Hutchison, St. Teresa Church did not welcome Mexicans. Our Lady of Guadalupe mission opened in 1927 by an exiled priest from Mexico.

69 Bishop Hennessy again invited the Claretians to his diocese in 1930; they declined.

70 See photos "Old Hickory 'Mexican Village' and 'Virginia Mess No. 3,'" Tennessee Virtual Archive, https://teva.contentdm.oclc.org.

71 "Tentativas Pasajeras" chapter, Berengueras ms., CMAC; Kyriakoudes, *Social Origins*, 99; "Mexican Village Interesting Feature of Old Hickory," Tennessee Virtual Archive, https://teva.contentdm.oclc.org.

72 *Old Hickory News*, as transcribed on the Old Hickory History Facebook page, March 14, 2018.

73 Copeland, *Plague in Paradise*, discusses Brualla's work.

74 León Monasterio necrology, *PB*, 1945.

75 Chapter 1, Berengueras ms., CMAC.

76 Berengueras in chapter "Tentativas Pasajeras" describes brief ministries including Santa Fe (1911–12), Salt Lake City (1929), San Diego, Texas (1921), Port Elizabeth, New Jersey (1931), and Saginaw, Michigan (1941–43).

77 The Claretians received similar requests from the bishop of Salt Lake City and the archbishop of New Orleans in the early twentieth century, but declined.

78 G. Hinojosa, "Mexican-American Faith Communities," 31. On Mexican laity and the Oblate missionaries, see Valerio Jiménez, *River of Hope*, 198–202.

79 Letter from San Antonio, September 25, 1902. *Anales*, 1902. "Hablan tan estropeadamente nuestro bello idioma, como estropeadamente practican nuestra fe."

CHAPTER 2. BUILDING URBAN PARISHES

1 Photo, Dedication of Immaculate Heart of Mary School, San Antonio, Texas. September 26, 1926, CMAC; announcement, September 19, 1926, Libro de advertencias, IHM.

2 Kanter, "Faith and Family." The 1927 entry comes from material later shared with me by a Barroso family member.

3 Exemplary studies on parishes in different regions include Endres, *Many Tongues*; Pfeifer, *Making of American Catholicism*.

4 Matovina, *Guadalupe and Her Faithful*, examines San Fernando's history; Badillo, *Latinos and the New Immigrant Church*, chapter 2, focuses on early twentieth-century San Antonio.

5 Perez, *Laredito*; Miller, *West Side Rising*. "San Antonio—Parroquia de Corazón de María" chapter, Berengueras ms., CMAC. Laredito was largely demolished by 1970.

6 Parish annual reports, Immaculate Heart of Mary papers, ARCHSA. *Archdiocese of San Antonio Diamond Jubilee*, 242, 274. The Claretians administered Immacu-

late Heart of Mary Church in Poteet during 1912–31 and El Carmen in Losoya during 1903–44, among other places.

7   *The Claretian 1902–1927*, CMAC. The school's design and construction cost $75,000.

8   G. Hinojosa, "Mexican-American Faith Communities," 41–42; R. Garcia, *Rise of the Mexican American*, 152, 157–79. Angela Tarango, "The Gym, La Trinidad United Methodist Church, San Antonio, Texas." American Religion, accessed August 12, 2024, www.american-religion.org/empty-places/latrinidad. La Trinidad Methodist church was founded in 1876. Catholic leaders in San Antonio often expressed fears of Protestant proselytizing in the barrios.

9   Young, *Mexican Exodus*.

10 M. García, *Father Luis Olivares*, 33, 35–36, 48; March 1923 entry, Congregación de San Luis Gonzaga ledger, IHM.

11 Apostolado del Corazón de Jesús ledger, 1915–53, IHM. Del Arenal Fenochio, "Una devoción mariana francesa." The Sacred Heart devotion began in mid-nineteenth-century France and took hold in Mexico in the 1870s.

12 Matovina, "Natives and Newcomers"; G. Hinojosa, "Mexican-American Faith Communities," 62.

13 M. García, *Father Luis Olivares*, 44.

14 Montejano, *Anglos and Mexicans*, 222.

15 Young, *Mexican Exodus*, 131. On Corpus Christi, all parish associations joined in a solemn evening procession. Corpus processions in Los Angeles signaled support of the Cristeros.

16 Announcement for May 31, 1937, Libro de advertencias, IHM. Perez, *Laredito*.

17 Orozco, *Pioneer of Mexican-American Civil Rights*. Perales, a devout Catholic, was a member of San Fernando Cathedral parish.

18 Various ephemera on 1948 procession, "Cartas y Memorias para el archivo," IHM. Matovina, *Guadalupe and Her Faithful*, 123, discusses processions, gender separation, and order.

19 García was not a Claretian.

20 Chapter 12, Berengueras ms.; Crónica, Our Lady of Guadalupe Church, Chicago, papers (hereafter, OLG), CMAC; Ripero, "Origen de Fundación de Chicago" 1946, OLG. McCarthy, "Which Christ Came to Chicago," 203–04.

21 Innis-Jiménez, *Steel Barrio*, 67, 84; Martínez-Serros, *Last Laugh*; Jirasek and Tortolero, *Mexican Chicago*.

22 "Chicago—Guadalupe" chapter, Berengueras ms., CMAC.

23 Ripero, "Origen de Fundación de Chicago," 1946, OLG.

24 Tort to Cardinal Mundelein, December 21, 1932, James Tort personnel file, CMAC. The Claretians shared their situation with the exiled archbishop of Guadalajara José Francisco Orozco y Jiménez. He intervened on their behalf with the Extension Society which then assisted their projects in Chicago.

25 Kuenster, *How Saint Jude Came to Chicago*, 34–25. Census 1924–25, OLG. Innis-Jiménez, *Steel Barrio*, 62–63; McCarthy, "Which Christ Came to Chicago," 206.

26 Kanter, *Chicago Católico*, 24–26.

27 Announcement Book 1924–27, OLG.

28 Tentler, *American Catholics*, 182.

29 Announcement Book 1924–27, OLG. "tomaron ice cream y cakes . . . resultando la fiesta."

30 Young, *Mexican Exodus*, 41. On Claretian-sponsored actions in Texas and Chicago to support the Cristeros' struggle, see pp. 73–74.

31 Announcement Book 1924–27, OLG. The Jacona novenas were held in 1926–27 with visiting priest Amando J. de Alba (1881–1942).

32 Young, *Mexican Exodus*, 40.

33 September 30, 1928 entry, Crónica, OLG; McCarthy, "Which Christ Came to Chicago," 214.

34 Sophenisba P. Breckinridge and Edith Abbott's 1911 report, quoted in Innis-Jiménez, *Steel Barrio*, 58.

35 Crónica, OLG.

36 Innis-Jiménez, *Steel Barrio*, 148–49; McCoyer, "Darkness of a Different Color," 194–95; Balderrama and Rodríguez, *Decade of Betrayal*, 150–51. Federal deportations minimally affected Mexican Chicago in the 1930s.

37 Leonard Cuellar letter, December 31, 1937, Henry Herrera personnel file, CMAC.

38 Kanter, *Chicago Católico*, chapter 3, on Mexican American youth at St. Francis of Assisi.

39 Booklet, "Solemn Blessing and Dedication, Stain of Glass Windows," OLG.

40 Fr. Daube's Mission Club underwrote the tribute to the two missionary saints. Albert Daube, a Claretian from Chicago, died in 1949 (see chapter 3).

41 McGinnis, *History of Perth Amboy*, chapter 8. Bishop Griffin, October 21, 1943, OLF.

42 OLF papers; James Tort personnel file, CMAC.

43 Souvenir of the Dedication, Immaculate Heart of Mary Mission, November 6, 1949, OLF.

44 Rev. Robert J. Wister, "The Archdiocese of Newark and Immigration." accessed August 12, 2024, https://blogs.shu.edu/archdiocese-immigration/. The history of Latin American Catholics in New Jersey, currently five dioceses, needs attention. Perth Amboy was in the Diocese of Newark, but is now part of the Diocese of Metuchen. On Puerto Rican Catholics in New York, see Díaz-Stevens, *Oxcart Catholicism*; A. Garcia, *Kingdom Began in Puerto Rico*; Badillo, *Latinos and the New Immigrant Church*, 73–83.

45 Roy, *Live, Learn, Love*. Roy served in Perth Amboy in 1948–56 and Matin, circa 1955–60. An older Slovak priest, Fr. Rura, welcomed Roy.

46 Roy to Bishop Griffin, December 21, 1948; Roy to Griffin, July 27, 1953, OLF.

47 The Claretians suddenly removed Roy from Perth Amboy in 1956. Circumstances suggest malfeasance in his work, perhaps of a financial or sexual nature. The Claretians ordered him to the Philippines, which he refused. He left the congregation and took a position in the Diocese of Richmond, Virginia. Years later Roy was accused of sexual abuse in Virginia.

48 Roy, report on Puerto Rico trip, August 31, 1954, OLF. Roy received the flag just months after Puerto Rican nationalists mounted an armed attack in the US Capital.

49 "Perth Amboy Aids Its Puerto Ricans," *New York Times*, March 1, 1953.

50 On Matin's work in Chicago, see Kanter, *Chicago Católico*, 39–41, 52–53.

51 Bishop Ahr to Matin, June 10, 1958, CMAC.

52 Circa 1958, Fr. Matin brought four Mexican sisters to Perth Amboy: Catechists of the Most Sacred Hearts of Jesus and Mary. Tenth Anniversary book, OLF.

53 "Que Hago? Adonde Voy?" brochure, OLF. "Así iras por el camino de la verdadera Felicidad, del bien y de la justicia. Y todas las demás cosas se te darán por añadidura."

54 Details from obituaries of people who migrated from Guayanilla to Perth Amboy. These death notices suggest a more positive history than Pedro Pietri's 1973 poem "Puerto Rican Obituary."

55 1966 Hall Ave Riot folder, Perth Amboy Free Public Library (hereafter, PAFPL). Puerto Rican youths threw rocks and bottles in the streets for four consecutive nights, July 30 to August 2, 1966. David Rodríguez Arce's arrest for loitering may have been the trigger. Hard facts on the 1966 uprising are few beyond newspaper clippings.

56 *Evening News*, August 2, 1966, 1966 Hall Ave Riot folder, PAFPL.

57 *New York Times*, August 2, 1966.

58 Orengo to Bishop Ahr, August 6, 1966, OLF.

59 Program, 1969 Latin American Heritage Banquet and Show, OLF. See photos in D. Kanter, "Celebrating Latin American Heritage in 1960s Perth Amboy," September 5, 2023, https://claretianmissionariesarchives.org.

60 Program, 1969 Latin American Heritage Banquet and Show, OLF.

61 ZPA or *Zjednoczenie Polakow w Ameryce* (Unity of Poles in America).

62 Osborne, *American Catholics*, 164.

63 Liturgical artist Adé Bethune, quoted in Osborne, *American Catholics*, 198; "Perth Amboy Church's Dream Now a Reality," *News Tribune*, September 20, 1971. Our Lady of Fatima folder, PAFPL. Osborne, *American Catholics*, 191. The Trenton firm Kramer, Hirsch and Carchidi designed the church.

64 Luis Turon CMF, "Our Lady of Fatima: Sociological Study of the Parish," unpublished paper, 1972, OLF. Sixty percent of Perth Amboy's Spanish-speaking high school graduates in 1971 planned to attend college.

65 Tort cited in M. Garcia, *Católicos*, 126–27.

66 Powers, *Morte D'Urban*, 13. The 1962 novel chronicles the Clementines, a fictitious Catholic order.

CHAPTER 3. COMMUNICATING IN TWO LANGUAGES

1 Lopez, *El Poche*, 29–37.

2 For decades Claretian postulants were expected to follow *The Mirror of the Postulant*, a pocket-size book featuring twenty-five pages of regulations and sixty-three pages of prayers.

3 Lopez, *El Poche*, 40. The Spaniards' rigor, he opined, stemmed from their "Jansenistic piety." G. Alonso, *Misioneros claretianos* (35–37) stresses the austerity and seriousness of the pre–Vatican II seminary training in Spain.

4 Lopez, *El Poche*, 40–41. Emphasis mine.

5 Lopez, *El Poche*, 40–41. The correct spelling is *güero*. Perhaps Lopez picked up the less common *el poche* from the El Poche Café, a popular restaurant near San Gabriel Mission.

6 Lopez, *El Poche*, 5, 5–56.

7 *La Esperanza*, April 1, 1953. "Para los Padres Claretianos la segregación es algo repugnante que ellos conceptúan como una arbitrariedad, completamente contraria a la doctrina y a las enseñanzas de Nuestro Señor Jesucristo."

8 Granjon quoted in *Claretians in America 1902–1952*, 106.

9 Chapter 3, Berengueras ms., CMAC.

10 December 1904 report from San Antonio, *Anales*, vol. 10.

11 Brown, "Theory and Practice of Language," 57.

12 Daries ms., 4, CMAC. In 1904 the Claretians in San Antonio became American citizens.

13 Chronicle, St. John the Evangelist Church, San Marcos, CMAC.

14 Sugrañes necrology, *PB*, April 1946. On Sugrañes as promoter of Spanish fantasy heritage, see Macias, "Spanish Myths and Mexican Realities," 178, 202. *The San Antonio Express* published Sugrañes's history of the city's floods in 1921. Miller, *West Side Rising*, 22–23.

15 Zaldívar necrology, *PB*, July 1946. Some Claretians studied at the Marianists' Chaminade College in Missouri.

16 The House of Studies closed and the building was sold in 1973.

17 McCarthy and Magner, *Claretians in America*, 25; Kanter, *Chicago Católico*, 23. Mother Frances Xavier Cabrini, Superior of the Missionary Sisters of the Sacred Heart of Jesus, knew Zaldívar and encouraged him to contact Mundelein.

18 *VSJ*, March 1935. Tort described the anticlerical persecution and his exile.

19 Tort necrology, *PB-E*, November 1958; Kuenster, *How Saint Jude Came to Chicago*, 34–36.

20 Kanter, *Chicago Católico*, 51; Matovina, *Guadalupe and Her Faithful*, 123.

21 Kuenster, *How Saint Jude Came to Chicago*, 52–59; Orsi, *Thank You, St. Jude*, 7–8, 28. Tort claimed to find a St. Jude prayer card in a church pew in Prescott, Arizona several years earlier, perhaps left by a Chilean miner. I surmise his global Claretian network influenced him, given the popular St. Jude church run by the Claretians in Santiago.

22 Tort necrology, *PB-E*, November 1958. On the St. Jude League's activities among Chicago's overwhelmingly Catholic police officers, see Adams, "Patrolmen's Revolt," 6–9.

23 Tentler, *American Catholics*, 226. Novenas were very popular events in the mid-century.

24 Orsi, *Thank You, St Jude*, 18. Orsi writes, "there were no more exuberant devotional promoters than Father Tort and his successors at the National Shrine of St. Jude."

25 Thomas, with Davidson, *Make Room for Danny*, 34, 77, 13.

26 Marlo Thomas, Danny's daughter, volunteered as a young adult with the Claretians in Los Angeles.

27 *The Voice of St. Jude* subscribers were clustered in midwestern and northeastern states.

28 Tort to Provincial Resa, December 27, 1931. James Tort personnel file, CMAC. Emphasis mine.

29 Tort, report on Our Lady of Guadalupe, First Provincial Chapter USA 1929, CMAC.

30 Sanz to Provincial Sedano, September 28, 1937. Foundation Correspondence 1931–39, St. Jude Seminary papers (hereafter, SJS), CMAC. "Ya llegó el tiempo de que los Claretians sean algo por estas tierras."

31 Report on St. Jude Seminary, Second Provincial Chapter USA 1935, CMAC. Mundelein conceded only "If a piece of ground could be obtained in the extreme southern portion of the diocese he might agree."

32 Chronicle 1933–45, SJS.

33 Mischke and McPolin celebrated their First Mass for the St. Jude Police League at Our Lady of Guadalupe Church on May 23, 1943.

34 Chronicle 1933–45, SJS.

35 Chronicle 1933–45, SJS. One faculty member commented, "I'm teaching four classes, including Spanish. A lot of effort for few students."

36 Report on St. Jude Seminary, Second Provincial Chapter USA 1935, CMAC.

37 Puigi to Provincial Sedano, March 21, 1936. Foundation Correspondence 1931–39, SJS.

38 Ellacuria to Provincial Sedano, January 7, 1937. Foundation Correspondence 1931–39, SJS.

39 Purchasing the land ($5,850) was a gamble given the low enrollment. The new seminary needed to be designed and built at a much higher cost.

40 García Hernández, *Crónica Martirial*; Alonso, *Misioneros claretianos*, 27, notes the post–Civil War increase of professed men in Spain.

41 Fall 1936 entries, Chronicle 1933–45, SJS; Jaime Tort, *Resumen de Martirio y Novena de los Misioneros martirizados en Barbastro en el mes agosto del año 1936*, 1949. Tort personal papers, CMAC. An English-language version was published in 1939. The work of Tort and other memorialists would lead to the beatification of the Claretian Martyrs of Barbastro in 1992. Severino Lopez, a novice in 1936, recalls how the Spanish Civil War polarized the Claretians in the US. *El Poche*, 46.

42 Second Provincial Chapter USA 1935, CMAC.

43 Adams, "Patrolmen's Revolt," 8.

44 Chronicle 1933–45, SJS.

45 1958 clipping, St. Jude Seminary newspaper clippings, SJS.

46 Adams, "Patrolmen's Revolt," 9. The Police Branch of the St. Jude League selected the police chaplain until 1960. This high-profile position had a number of perks.

47 Patrick Reardon, email to author, January 21, 2022.

48 Second Provincial Chapter USA 1935, CMAC.

49 Ribera, *On the Threshold.* Fr. Manuel Milagro (v) was pleased this "real gem of Claretian literature" was translated for use in "our American province."

50 Lopez, *El Poche,* 44; *Stepping Stone,* September–October 1960, CMAC.

51 A 1975 CARA study clarified the factors in the poor retention rates of junior seminaries. Brandewie, *In the Light of the Word,* 99, 104–06.

52 Lopez, *El Poche,* 41.

53 Second Provincial Chapter USA 1935, CMAC.

54 Casaldáliga, *I Believe in Justice and Hope,* 15. Of his seminary training in 1950s Spain, the missionary recalls that Claretian students renounced languages other than Castilian to further unity in the congregation.

55 M. García, *Father Luis Olivares,* 81.

56 M. García, *Father Luis Olivares,* 53, 59–60.

57 M. García, *Father Luis Olivares,* 79–81. Gomez, *Memoirs of a Seminarian.* Gomez's frank memoir of Del Amo in the late 1940s mentions no discomfort over race and language.

58 Kristen Melkonyan, "'A thousand and one things have happened': Letters from a WWII Chaplain." November 10, 2023, https://claretianmissionariesarchives.org. Crosby, *Battlefield Chaplains.* Catholic chaplains served men of all denominations.

59 Ribera, *On the Threshold,* 241.

60 Fr. Henry Herrera personal papers, CMAC.

61 Herrera is included on the Diocese of Fort Worth's list of priests who had "allegations with a semblance of truth made against them regarding sexual misconduct with minors." He worked in the diocese in 1975–79. www.Bishop-accountability.org.

62 Patrick Reardon, email to author, February 16, 2022.

63 Bishop Plácido Rodríguez CMF, interview, Oak Park, IL, July, 20, 2022. Rodríguez, "Cristero Witness," describes his family's Cristero history which led to migration to the US.

64 Bishop Plácido Rodríguez CMF, interview, Oak Park, IL, July, 20, 2022.

65 Patrick Hayes, personal communication, August 26, 2022. Brandewie, *In the Light of the Word,* 133. The SVDs required five years of German for their men in formation.

66 Albert Daube CMP, "St. Jude Seminary," *VSJ,* October 1, 1937.

67 The *PB* published Daube's detailed letters from Latin America.

68 Daube's death made the front page of *La Prensa. La Voz,* the Catholic paper, reprinted that coverage, April 24, 1949, ARCHSA.

69 *PB,* May 1949; January–February, 1951.

70 *PB,* March–April 1941.

71 Minutes, Fifth Provincial Chapter, *PB,* April 1953.

CHAPTER 4. WORKING IN THE SHADOWS OF EMPIRE

1 Cited in "25 Años de misión Padres Claretianos, 1966–1991," Guatemala files, CMAC. "En América hay un campo muy grande y muy feraz y con el tiempo

saldrán más almas para el cielo de América que de Europa. Esta parte del mundo [Europa] es como una viña vieja, que no da mucho fruto, y América es viña joven."

2 Dries, "American Catholics in a Global Context," 239. Forty Catholic mission magazines were published in the US in the 1930s. Br. Rene Lepage (1939–) was drawn to missionary life upon reading about the Maryknolls' work. As a Claretian, he served in the Philippines, India, Nigeria, and Cameroon. Cardenas, Diaz, and Urrabazo, *Missionary Lens of Brother Rene LePage*.

3 Albert Daube, "St. Jude Seminary," *VSJ*, October 1937.

4 "World-wide Claretian Missions" map, in *Claretians in America 1902–1952*. *PB*, January 1950. Todd, *VSJ*, October 1954. The three-day fair "A World to Win" took place in October 1949.

5 Strauss, "Missionary Empire," 6.

6 Fitzpatrick-Behrens, *The Maryknoll Catholic Mission*, 40. 1,060 foreign clergy worked in Central and South America in 1956. The number rose to 3,400 in 1968.

7 Guna is now the default spelling for the people historically labeled "Kuna" in Panama.

8 *VSJ*, August 1935.

9 *VSJ*, December 1937.

10 *Claretians in America 1902–1952*, 174. La Placita's Infant of Prague Society donated the funds for the Parroquia Niño Jesús De Praga circa 1952.

11 Pablo Neruda, "The United Fruit Co.," accessed August 13, 2024, https://allpoetry.com.

12 A. Martínez, "Relatos visuales."

13 Howe, *Chiefs, Scribes, and Ethnographers*, 175–78. Howe examines the linguistic and ethnographic scholarship of José Berengueras, Jesús Erice, and Manuel Puig.

14 *Claretians in America 1902–1952*, 175. Br. Pascual Gómez also drowned in Panama.

15 Berengueras, *El auxiliar del misionero*. Quotations from 1946 edition.

16 Strauss, "Missionary Empire," 9. Jesuits in Belize projected a "missionary as hero" archetype.

17 Berengueras necrology, *PB*, January–April 1952. Manuel Puig, fellow missionary in Panama, wrote the twenty-two-page tribute.

18 Benet necrology, *PB*, May 1947. The five-page tribute was lengthy for a brother.

19 Berengueras, *El auxiliar del misionero*, 62–63.

20 Román to Provincial Emaldia, November 10, 1945; Serrano to Provincial Emaldia, July 18, 1944, Panama files, CMAC.

21 Erice to Provincial Emaldia, May 20, 1942, Panama files, CMAC. "Estoy predicando en indio todos los domingos."

22 Howe, *Chiefs, Scribes, and Ethnographers*, 25–26, 40.

23 Erice to Provincial Emaldia, May 12, 1942, Panama files, CMAC.

24 Erice to Provincial Emaldia, May 5, 1946; Erice to Berengueras, September 17, 1946; clipping, "Cuatro indígenas de San Blas van a estudiar a los Estados Unidos," n.d., Panama files, CMAC.

25 Erice to Berengueras, February 1, 1947, Panama files, CMAC.

26 Yearbook, Del Amo Junior Seminary, 1950, CMAC.

27 US-trained Claretians from Panama include Raphael Chen, Juan Correa, Leslie Delgado, and William Figueroa. Fr. Ibelele Nikktiginya Davies CMF (also known as Fr. Juan Jose Davies) may have studied at Dominguez in 1945, before completing his studies in Spain. He is reputedly the first Guna priest.

28 Correa to Provincial Emaldia, April 23, 1947, Panama files, CMAC.

29 *Juventud Sanblaseña*, October 19, 1947, CMAC.

30 Puig, *Indios cunas*. Puig wrote a Guna grammar text and dictionary, also published in the 1940s.

31 Defense Technical Information Center, "A Brief Review of Selected Aspects of the San Blas Cuna Indians."

32 "Missionary Academic of Dominguez Seminary Exhibit, 1949," photo, Claretian Missionaries Digital Archives.

33 Various photos, Richard Todd CMF with catechists, Parroquia de Santo Tomás de Castilla, Guatemala, Claretian Missionaries Digital Archives.

34 In 1953, the Claretians divided the US Province. The Province of the East, Chicago-based, included all Claretians east of the Mississippi. The distinct character of the two provinces revealed itself in the 1960s and 1970s.

35 Hurteau, *Worldwide Heart*, 136, 181. Considine, a Maryknoll Father, may have ghostwritten the papal calls.

36 Mahon with Davis, *Fire under My Feet*; Hurteau, *Worldwide Heart*.

37 Grainer to Superior General, August 15, 1964, Grainer correspondence, Guatemala files, CMAC.

38 Grainer did not mention the CICOP gathering in this memo. Chicago again hosted CICOP in 1965 and 1966. Hurteau, *Worldwide Heart*, 182.

39 Hurteau, *Worldwide Heart*.

40 "Mission Survey," *Claretian*, Fall 1965, CMAC.

41 Hernández Sandoval, *Guatemala's Catholic Revolution*; Fitzpatrick-Behrens, "Maya Catholic Cooperative Spirit"; Strauss, "Missionary Empire." Local reforms were underway by the Catholic church in Guatemala. The Maryknolls had worked in highlands Guatemala since the 1940s.

42 Memorandum, Grainer to Provincial Council, June 16, 1965, Grainer correspondence, Guatemala files, CMAC.

43 "Address at Departure Ceremonies," St. Jude Seminary, January 9, 1966, Grainer correspondence, Guatemala files, CMAC.

44 Zimmerman to Grainer, January 13, 1966, Grainer correspondence, Guatemala files, CMAC.

45 The Claretian sources ignored the Garífunas' distinctive linguistic and cultural aspects. Today, Garífuna language and worship styles are commonly acknowledged in the Catholic parish in Labuga (as local people call Livingston). These differences were unmistakable in the funeral Mass in Esquipulas in 2024 for Fr. Milton Álvarez, Claretian and the first Garífuna priest.

46 Fitzpatrick-Behrens, "Maya Catholic Cooperative Spirit." The Izabal co-ops failed compared to similar ventures in the highlands.

47 Fitzpatrick-Behrens, *Maryknoll Catholic Mission*, 20.

48 Zimmerman to Grainer, June 24, 1966, Grainer correspondence, Guatemala files, CMAC. The orthography of Guatemalan native languages has evolved greatly. Q'eqchi' is now the default spelling used in Izabal.

49 Fitzpatrick-Behrens, *Maryknoll Catholic Mission*, 20; Moses, "Afire with the Itinerant Spirit," 223.

50 Briskey to Grainer, January 3, 1967; Zimmerman to Grainer, September 1 [n.d., likely 1966], Grainer correspondence, Guatemala files, CMAC.

51 A clinic in El Estor bears Marie T. Egan's name. She served thirty-two years in Guatemala.

52 Fitzpatrick-Behrens, *Maryknoll Catholic Mission*, 134; Moses, "Afire with the Itinerant Spirit," 216.

53 González (1941–2020) was born in Amarillo, Texas. She served as the president of the Mexican American Catholic College in San Antonio.

54 Hernández Sandoval, *Guatemala's Catholic Revolution*, 1. The Guatemalan government expelled four Maryknoll missionaries in December 1967, fearing their radicalism would spark revolution.

55 Todd trained at CIDOC in Cuernavaca. Founded by Ivan Illich, the center was a hotbed of critical thinking and "de-Yankeefication."

56 Mahon with Davis, *Fire under My Feet*, 37, 45. See online photo exhibit "San Miguelito," Archdiocese of Chicago Archives and Records Center.

57 Todd to Grainer, March 20, 1970, Grainer correspondence, Guatemala files, CMAC; Chomsky, *Central America's Forgotten History*, 57–58. Fr. Pedro Arrupe, SJ, first used the phrase "preferential option for the poor" in 1968.

58 Leatham (1940–82), an Irish Claretian, served in Guatemala circa 1968–70. He entered diocesan service in the Diocese of Lubbock, Texas. He was later named a monsignor.

59 "ACHTUS Citation—Edgard Beltrán," V Encuentro, June 4, 2019, http:// vencuentro.org.

60 Todd to Grainer, December 15, 1969, Grainer correspondence, Guatemala files, CMAC.

61 The plan accompanied letter, Todd to Grainer, March 21, 1971, Grainer correspondence, Guatemala files, CMAC.

62 Doran, *Carpenter Wanted*, 120. The compound replaced Campo Dos (Field Two) soccer field, giving rise to its popular name, Campo de Dios (Field of God).

63 Todd to Grainer, November 21, 1970, Grainer correspondence, Guatemala files, CMAC.

64 Chomsky, *Central America's Forgotten History*, 84.

65 "Memo from Guatemala," May 28, 1970; Todd to Grainer, November 21, 1970, Grainer correspondence, Guatemala files, CMAC.

66 Mischke to Grainer, March 9, 1971, Grainer correspondence, Guatemala files, CMAC. Walter Mischke critiqued the El Estor parish where "we have only main-

tained a 'status-quo'—if that much." Richard Wilson, *Maya Resurgence*, 15. This anthropologist stresses native catechists as promotors of "orthodox" Catholicism.

67 Project summary, Santo Tomás pastoral team, March 1971, Grainer correspondence, Guatemala files, CMAC.

68 Jerson Xitumal Morales, "Mama Leya la comadrona del pueblo," *Prensa Comunitaria KM169*, November 15, 2017, https://prensacomunitar.medium.com.

69 Todd to Grainer, March 17, 1971, Grainer correspondence, Guatemala files, CMAC.

70 Chomsky, *Central America's Forgotten History*, 81; "Nickle Project Set in Guatemala," *New York Times*, March 16, 1974, 42. A Canadian mining company initially developed the mine, despite local concerns.

71 Guatemala report to Chapter, 1974. Eastern Province: Provincial Chapters, CMAC.

72 Dries, "American Catholics in a Global Context," 244; Markey, *Radical Faith*. Eleven American Catholic missionaries were killed in Central America between 1959 and 1990.

73 Fray Claudio Bratti OFM and Fr. Anton Grech, "Biografía de los mártires del Vicariato de Izabal," unpublished report, 2020. Bac's family maintains that he was killed for being a catechist and for defending land in his aldea.

74 Area team meeting, February 10, 1981, Guatemala files, CMAC.

75 Maruzzo and Navarro were beatified in 2018.

76 Bratti and Grech, "Biografía de los mártires del Vicariato de Izabal."

77 Area team meetings, February, March, 1981, Guatemala files, CMAC.

78 Area team meeting, March 2–3, 1981, Guatemala files, CMAC.

79 Bratti and Grech, "Biografía de los mártires del Vicariato de Izabal."

80 Report, "Personas desaparecidas en el Estor y aldeas desde el 14 de octubre de 1982," Guatemala files, CMAC.

81 Bratti and Grech, "Biografía de los mártires del Vicariato de Izabal." Two years earlier, the equipo pastoral discussed ways to minimize danger to Felipe. Team meeting, February 10–12, 1981, Guatemala files, CMAC.

82 Grandin, *Empire's Workshop*, 64.

83 Grandin, *Empire's Workshop*, 121. Grandin underlines explicit US support of the Guatemalan government and military.

84 Chomsky, *Central America's Forgotten History*, 96.

85 Andrés to la Coordinara de El Estor n.d., Guatemala files, CMAC. Fr. Andrés took over El Estor when Fr. Moran departed after thirteen years. He questioned authorities about the imprisonment and torture of sixteen-year-old Jesús Caal Tení in December 1983.

86 "Oración del Centenario," November 2, 1990. Edmund Andrés personal papers, CMAC. "La tarea ha sido y será siempre de todos crear un pueblo unido." "Vencer la ignorancia, curar dolencias, trazar y abrir nuevos caminos, liberar al que es esclavo, dar a todos un justo señorio."

87 Memorandum, Dick Farrell, November 12, 1991; typed comments by Santiago and Chavarría [in Spanish]. Guatemala files, CMAC.

88 Cited in Strauss, "Missionary Empire," 17. Hartch, "Ivan Illich and Leo Mahon."

89 Strauss, "Missionary Empire," 8, 22. By contrast, thirty-five American Jesuits worked in Belize in 1951. One hundred Maryknoll clergy worked in Guatemala in 1967.

CHAPTER 5. RE-IMAGINING MISSION

1 Rosendo Urrabazo personal papers, CMAC.

2 O'Malley, *What Happened*, 11, 49–50, 307; McDannell, *Spirit of Vatican II*, 135, 176.

3 The Claretians sponsored cursillos at their parishes in the 1960s. In 1963 they developed a national cursillo/retreat center in Phoenix, the Mt. Claret Center. Nabhan-Warren, *Cursillo Movement in America* offers a good overview of cursillo.

4 The Claretians divided the US Province in 1953. The Province of the West included all houses and schools west of the Mississippi River, with leadership in Los Angeles. The Chicago-based Province of the East included Claretians east of the Mississippi. The two provinces merged and consolidated resources in 2011.

5 F. Hinojosa, *Apostles of Change*; San Miguel, *In the Midst of Radicalism*, 46.

6 Frison, a Spaniard, did little parish work in the US. He spent 1960–69 in Rome. In his later years, he wrote Larraona's biography. Casaldáliga recalls how Vatican II created divides among Claretians in Spain. *I Believe in Justice and Hope*, 23.

7 *PB-E*, March–April 1963, 640–41.

8 Based on my survey of print issues held at CMAC. For question-raising essays, see Burns, *Best of US Catholic*. I recommend John Kuenster, "A Parish Mourns Its Dead Servicemen," about the eleven men from Our Lady of Guadalupe in Chicago. *US Catholic*, October 1970.

9 Rzeznik, "That '70s Catholicism."

10 Many pamphlets went into reprints. Many titles were originally published as articles in the Claretian magazines *US Catholic*, *Jubilee*, and *Today*. Kristen Melkonyan, archivist, proved indispensable in documenting and parsing the pamphlet collection.

11 *PB-E* 1966.

12 *PB-E*, January–February 1963, 629–30.

13 Interview, Fr. Mark Brummel CMF, Oak Park, IL, July 20, 2022.

14 Interview, Bishop Plácido Rodríguez CMF, Oak Park, IL, July 20, 2022.

15 *PB-E* 1965.

16 Report on Government, Eastern Province: Third Provincial Chapter, 1968, CMAC.

17 All perpetually professed members could vote. Grainer was reelected as Provincial.

18 Minutes, April 8–10, 1969, Eastern Province Assembly, CMAC.

19 Lernoux, Jones, and Ellsberg, *Hearts on Fire*, 141; Tentler, *American Catholics*, 314–17; McDannell, *Spirit of Vatican II*, 200; Brandewie, *In the Light of the Word*, 105; Rippinger, *Benedictine Order in the United States*, 248.

20 Olivares interview, Heyck, *Barrios and Borderlands*, 220.

21 Fisher, *Communion of Immigrants*, 143.

22 Claretian leaders cited Pope Pius XII's *Menti Nostrae* regarding adult vocations' potential as men "often equipped with greater and more solid virtue." AVE Center papers, CMAC.

23 Edmund Andrés oral history, January 26, 1977, CMAC. At the Claretville theologate (Calabasas, California) in 1964–66, students protested traditional discipline and their superiors pushed back.

24 Robert Bishop, CMF, "Claretians in Campus," *St. Ignatius Bulletin*, February 1969, AVE Center papers, CMAC.

25 Eastern Province: Provincial Chapters, June 1980, CMAC.

26 The Claret Center was established in 1979 by Fr. Marty Kirk and Sr. Mary Ellen Moore, SH. Cirone, *Shared Mission*, 19–21.

27 Claretian Social Development Fund report, Third Provincial Chapter, Eastern Province: Provincial Chapters, June 1980, CMAC; Román Ángel Moreno, General Visitation Report, April 25, 1980, Eastern Province: Provincial Chapter, June 1980, CMAC.

28 "The Newman Apostolate at L.S.U.," *US Catholic*, October 1966.

29 Joseph Peplansky oral history, January 12, 1977, CMAC.

30 *Catholic Commentator*, September 26, 1969, Baton Rouge papers, CMAC.

31 Michael Cody personnel file, CMAC.

32 Louisiana State University Catholic Center, Baton Rouge papers, CMAC.

33 On archdiocesan support for renewal in Denver parishes, see McDannell, *Spirit of Vatican II*, 162–66. John Hencier CMF examined St. Anne's team ministry in his dissertation, "New Form of Parish Team Ministry," chapter 7.

34 Lindstrom, *Shrine of St. Anne*, 83.

35 Hencier, "New Form of Parish Team Ministry," 110; "Team Ministry Is Building Community," *Denver Catholic Register*, October 12, 1972.

36 St. Anne team to O'Connor, October 18, 1974; O'Connor to Superior General, February 27, 1980, Shrine of St. Anne, Arvada papers, CMAC.

37 Lindstrom, *Shrine of St. Anne*.

38 Ralph Berg, report "Arvada Team Ministry Experience, 1971–81," June 2016, Shrine of St. Anne, Arvada papers, CMAC.

39 Program for Renewal, Third Provincial Chapter, Eastern Province: Provincial Chapters, 1980, CMAC; Patrick T. Reardon, "A Tribute for Marty Kirk, C.M.F.," August 27, 2022, https://patricktreardon.com/; Cirone, *Shared Mission*.

40 Six Year House Report, February 22, 1983, Oregon Missions papers, CMAC. The Archdiocese of Portland began discussions with the Claretians in 1977. Gamm lived with diocesan priest Fr. Francis Kennard in Dallas, Oregon. The Claretians took over the house.

41 Rosendo Urrabazo, personal communication to author, February 28, 2023.

42 Urrabazo to O'Connor, July 23, 1978, Oregon Missions papers, CMAC.

43 After ordination, Gamm threw himself into missionary work including saying Mass in a school auditorium in Goodyear, Arizona, in 1946, and serving seven years in England.

44 Rosendo Urrabazo, personal communication to author, February 28, 2023.

45 Schedlo briefly recounts her Oregon work in Dahlke, *Memoir of a Gringa Mission-ary*. The team first included Sr. Marcia Sims SSS.

46 Phone interview, Sr. Antona Schedlo FSPA, June 1, 2023. Schedlo aimed for four home visits each week, in addition to other pastoral responsibilities.

47 Oregon Missions papers, CMAC.

48 Miriam Corona and Flora Maciel Garibay, "Oral History of San Martín de Porres Catholic Church" (2013). *2013 Projects*, https://digitalcommons.linfield.edu.

49 Team meeting minutes, November 1980, Oregon Missions papers, CMAC.

50 The eastern province in this era worked closely with volunteers in Guatemala and in 1983 expanded these programs in Chicago, Missouri, and New Jersey.

51 Six Year House Report, February 22, 1983, Oregon Missions papers, CMAC.

52 Olivares interview, Heyck, *Barrios and Borderlands*, 220.

53 Immaculate Heart of Mary files 1911–71, ARCHSA; Meghan McCarthy, "A History of Urban Renewal in San Antonio." *Planning Forum*, accessed August 13, 2024, https://sites.utexas.edu/planningforum.

54 *TIPS*, 1969, CMAC. In 1968, the western province renamed its bulletin *TIPS* (Timely Information for the Province and Service). Claretians administered Guardian Angel since 1932 and St. Francis Xavier since 1942, plus smaller mission churches.

55 Kanter, *Chicago Católico*, 86–87.

56 Quotation, from newspaper *Chicago Católico*, n.d., Peter Rodríguez personal papers, CMAC.

57 Rodríguez began on the radio in 1962. His weekly column "Meditaciones" ran in *Prensa Libre* ca. 1965–66 and in *El Informador* ca. 1969–71.

58 Bishop John Manz, quoted in paper *Chicago Católico*, April 2004; Kanter, *Chicago Católico*, 103, 135.

59 Eastwood, *Near West Side Stories*, 268, 306.

60 On the INS actions, see his "Reflexiones," *New World*, April 6, 1973; Claretian-authored obituary-press release, March 17, 2004. Peter Rodríguez personal papers, CMAC.

61 Rodríguez wrote monthly columns for *Chicago Católico* from 1985–1990, mostly on pastoral topics. He also addressed more secular themes, including immigration.

62 Peter Rodríguez oral history, January 20, 1977, CMAC.

63 M. García, *Father Luis Olivares*, 148, 150.

64 M. García, *Father Luis Olivares*, 182. F. Hinojosa, *Apostles of Change*, chapter 2.

65 M. García, *Father Luis Olivares*, 161, 177.

66 Pfeifer, *Making of American Catholicism*, 122–29.

67 Treviño, *Church in the Barrio*, 176; R. Martínez, *PADRES*, 41, 7, 33, 10, 84.

68 *PB-E*, November 1969.

69 Report on Government, Eastern Province: Third Provincial Chapter, 1968, CMAC.

70 Román Ángel Moreno, General Visitation Report, April 25, 1980, Eastern Province: Provincial Chapter, 1980, CMAC.

71 "Recommendations Submitted by the Capitular Commission on the Apostolate," Western Province: Eighth Provincial Chapter, 1971, CMAC.

72 Heyck, *Barrios and Borderlands*, 221.

73 M. Garcia, *Father Luis Olivares*, 158–60. Beyond a brief mention of Chavez's work in a 1966 provincial bulletin, provincial leadership seemed oblivious to the UFW until 1974. Pawel, *Crusades of Cesar Chavez*, details his contacts with Catholic clergy, but mentions neither Olivares nor the Claretians.

74 *TIPS*, 1976, CMAC. Eastwood, *Near West Side Stories*, 305.

75 The western province initiated its Social Concerns Committee in 1975.

76 Gerald T. Floyd, CMF, "Changing Moral Values in a Changing Society," 1975, AVE Center papers, CMAC.

77 Quoted in *San Antonio Light*, June 21, 1987. Urrabazo maintained a Chicano focus. He completed his dissertation on "Machismo: Mexican American Male Self-Concept" at the Graduate Theological Union in 1986. He served as MACC's second president in 1987–93.

78 Dolan and Hinojosa, eds., *Mexican Americans and the Catholic Church*, 107, 116. Gilberto Hinojosa credits cursillos in Texas as reviving "the spiritual life of the entire parish."

79 Deck, *Second Wave: Hispanic Ministry*, 77; Joseph Peplansky oral history, January 12, 1977, CMAC.

80 Paredes, *History of the National Encuentros*. It seems that a single Claretian addressed an Encuentro gathering: Bishop Plácido Rodríguez in 1984.

81 Tentler, *American Catholics*, 315.

82 Thompson, "Cordimarian Spirituality," 355–56. "Como vives tu espiritualidad cordimariano?"

83 Dedication booklet, November 22, 1970, St. John the Evangelist Church, San Marcos, CMAC.

84 Brian Culley, personal communication to author, May 1, 2023. Beatified in 2000, John XXIII was canonized in 2014.

CONCLUSION

1 James Martin SJ, "The Problem with Mother Angelica and EWTN." *America Magazine*, August 12, 1995, www.americamagazine.org.

2 "Our Mission," Claretian Missionaries United States-Canadian Province, www.claretiansusa.org.

3 Interview, Bishop Plácido Rodríguez CMF, Oak Park, IL, July, 20, 2022.

4 Sison, *Deep Inculturation*; McGreevy, *American Jesuits*, 219.

5 Hosffman Ospino, "Is the U.S. Church's Hispanic Catholic Hope Slipping Away?" *The Boston Pilot*, September 26, 2023, www.thebostonpilot.com. Ospino is an incisive voice on the relationship between Latinos and the future of the American church.

6 Fr. Francisco Javier Reyes quoted in Maria Benevento, "Campus Ministers: The Future Is Here, Listen to College-Age Latinos." *National Catholic Reporter*, November 21, 2018, www.ncronline.org.

7 Sandell, *Open Your Heart*, 41–42. The Fresno Claretians also administer the smaller Cristo Rey Church in nearby Malaga, built in 1935.

8 Sandell, *Open Your Heart* is based on research at St. Anthony Mary Claret Church in 2000–01.

9 Interview, Art Gramaje, November 16, 2022. Gramaje served as St. Anthony Mary Claret's pastor circa 2005–08 and 2014–17.

10 When I visited Latino parishes elsewhere in the country during 2021–23, Claretian or other, pews were seldom full. Pastors often excused the attendance as a symptom of the COVID era.

11 Grainer to G. Zimmerman, February 2, 1967, Grainer correspondence, Guatemala files, CMAC.

12 In addition to Bishopaccountability.org, additional accusations and documentation should be examined in the online Clergy Files Produced by Archdiocese of Los Angeles, other dioceses where Claretians served, and the report of the Illinois Attorney General.

13 Seitz, "Stoic Brothers," 15–21.

14 Estrada, *UnHoly Communion*. By contrast this former adult seminarian openly shares his experience with the Claretians.

15 Chinnici, *When Values Collide*, 157. 4.2% of diocesan clergy were accused and 2.7% of religious priests.

16 Robert Herguth, "Hear No Evil. Speak No Evil. See No Evil," *Chicago Sun Times*, June 20, 2021.

17 Examples of better transparency and admission of responsibility include the websites of the Jesuits Midwest or the Society of the Divine Word.

18 Reynolds, "I Will Surely Have You Deported." On the role of "criminally derelict" bishops, see Tentler, *American Catholics*, 333.

19 J. D. Long-García, "Is There a Sexual Abuse Reckoning Coming for the Latino Church?," *America*, August 3, 2018. In this essay Hosffman Ospino commented that Latino Catholics responded differently to the revelations of abuse in Boston. Their "cultural Catholicism somehow invites responses that also involve prayer, forgiveness and reconciliation."

20 Chinnici, *When Values Collide*, 189.

21 Fr. Beauplan Derilus CMF, homily, June 2, 2022.

22 Chicago and Los Angeles both have three Claretian residences. Their members have the chance to socialize on feast days and similar occasions.

23 John L. Allen, Jr., "Foreign Nuns, Priests Embody Historic Opportunity for U.S. Church," *Angelus*, March 8, 2017, http://angelusnews.com; McDannell, *Spirit of Vatican II*, 222.

SELECTED BIBLIOGRAPHY

INTERVIEWS

Edmund Andrés CMF, interview with Brian Dillon, January 26, 1977, CMAC.
Mark Brummel CMF, interview with the author, Oak Park, IL, July 20, 2022.
Art Gramaje CMF, phone interview with the author, November 16, 2022.
Joseph Peplansky CMF, interview with Brian Dillon, January 12, 1977, CMAC.
Peter Rodríguez CMF, interview with Brian Dillon, January 20, 1977, CMAC.
Plácido Rodríguez CMF, interview with the author, Oak Park, IL, July 20, 2022.
Antona Schedlo FSPA, phone interview with the author, June 1, 2023.

WORKS CITED

Adams, Megan Marie. "The Patrolmen's Revolt: Chicago Police and the Labor and Urban Crises of the Late Twentieth Century." PhD diss., University of California Berkeley, 2012.
Alonso, CMF, Gustavo. *Misioneros claretianos III: La renovación conciliar*. Editorial Claretiana, 2007.
Andes, Stephen J. C., and Julia G. Young, eds. *Local Church, Global Church: Catholic Activism in Latin America from Rerum Novarum to Vatican II*. Catholic University of America Press, 2016.
Archdiocese of San Antonio Diamond Jubilee 1874–1949. Archdiocese of San Antonio, 1949.
Badillo, David. *Latinos and the New Immigrant Church*. Johns Hopkins University Press, 2006.
Balderrama, Francisco E., and Raymond Rodríguez. *Decade of Betrayal: Mexican Repatriation in the 1930s*. Rev. ed. University of New Mexico Press, 2006.
Barragán Goetz, Philis. *Reading, Writing, and Revolution: Escuelitas and the Emergence of a Mexican American Identity in Texas*. University of Texas Press, 2020.
Benton-Cohen, Katherine. *Borderline Americans: Racial Division and Labor War in the Arizona Borderlands*. Harvard University Press, 2011.
Berengueras, CMF, José María. *El auxiliar del misionero de Darien*. Imprenta Claret, 1936. Reprinted in 1946.
Bodas De Diamante, 1884 1959 Mexico. Claretian publication, n.d.
Brandewie, Ernest. *In the Light of the Word: Divine Word Missionaries of North America*. Orbis Books, 2000.
Brogdon, John Carl. "The History of Jerome, Arizona." MA thesis, University of Arizona, 1952.

Brown, Mary Elizabeth. "The Theory and Practice of Language in Scalabrinian Parishes for Italian Immigrants in the United States, 1887–1933." *U.S. Catholic Historian* 33, no. 3 (Summer 2015): 51–68.

Brummel, CMF, Mark Joseph. "A Bibliography of the Writings By and About the Claretian Fathers in the United States, 1902–1962." Master's diss., Catholic University of America, 1964.

Burns, Robert E. ed. *The Best of US Catholic*. Thomas More Press, 1984.

Butler, Matthew. *Popular Piety and Political Identity in Mexico's Cristero Rebellion: Michoacán, 1927–29*. Oxford University Press, 2004.

Cabré Rufatt, CMF, Agustín. *Historia de los Misioneros Claretianos en México*. ECCLA Ediciones, 2014.

Cardenas, Doris, Manuel Antonio Diaz, CMF, and Rosendo Urrabazo, CMF, eds. *Missionary Lens of Brother Rene LePage, CMF*. Claretian Missionaries, 2022.

Caro, Robert A. *The Years of Lyndon Johnson: The Path to Power*. Vintage, 1990.

Casaldáliga, CMF, Pedro. *I Believe in Justice and Hope*. Fides/Claretian, 1978.

Chinnici. Joseph P. *When Values Collide: The Catholic Church Sexual Abuse and the Challenges of Leadership*. Orbis Books, 2010.

Chomsky, Aviva. *Central America's Forgotten History: Revolution, Violence, and the Roots of Migration*. Beacon Press, 2021.

Cirone, CMF, Ted. *Shared Mission: Marty Kirk, C.M.F.* Claretian Missionaries, 2012.

Claret, Anthony Mary. *Colección de los opúscolos*. Imprenta de la H. de la V. Pla, 1849.

Claret, Anthony Mary. *The Autobiography of St. Anthony Mary Claret*. Tan Books, 1985. 1st English ed. 1945.

Claretians in America 1902–1952. Privately published, 1952.

Clements, Eric L. *After the Boom in Tombstone and Jerome, Arizona: Decline in Western Resource Towns*. University of Nevada Press, 2003.

Copeland, Jeffrey S. *Plague in Paradise: The Black Death in Los Angeles, 1924*. Paragon House, 2018.

Crosby, SJ, Donald F. *Battlefield Chaplains: Catholic Priests in World War II*. University of Kansas Press, 1994.

Cummings, Kathleen Sprows. *A Saint of Our Own: How the Quest for a Holy Hero Helped Catholics Become American*. University of North Carolina Press, 2019.

Dahlke, Mary K. *Memoir of a Gringa Missionary: A Dream Fulfilled*. Unpublished, 2018.

Daries, CMF, Joseph, and Ronald Stua. *The Claretian Missionaries Chronological History, USA-Canada Province: 1902–2017*. Privately published, 2022.

Davis, Steve, ed. *Sueños y recuerdos del pasado, Dreams and Memories of the Past: a Community History of Mexican Americans in San Marcos*. Hays County Historical Committee, 2000.

Deck, Allan Figueroa. *The Second Wave: Hispanic Ministry and the Evangelization of Cultures in the United States*. Paulist Press, 1989.

Del Arenal Fenochio, Jaime. "Una devoción mariana francesa en México: Nuestra Señora del Sagrado Corazón." *Relaciones* 19, no. 76 (Otoño 1998): 161–194.

Díaz-Stevens, Ana María. *Oxcart Catholicism on Fifth Avenue: The Impact of the Puerto Rican Migration upon the Archdiocese of New York.* University of Notre Dame Press, 1993.

Dolan, Jay P., and Gilberto M. Hinojosa, eds. *Mexican Americans and the Catholic Church, 1900–1964.* University of Notre Dame Press, 1994.

Domenech, Emmanuel. *Missionary Adventures in Texas and Mexico.* Longman, Brown, Green, Longmans, and Roberts, 1858.

Doran, Brian. *Carpenter Wanted: Two Years in Guatemala.* Edited by Christine Doran. Self-published, 2020.

Dries, OSF, Angelyn. "American Catholics in a Global Context." In *The Cambridge Companion to American Catholicism,* edited by Margaret M. McGuinness and Thomas F. Rzeznik. Cambridge University Press, 2021.

Eastwood, Carolyn. *Near West Side Stories: Struggles for Community in Chicago's Maxwell Street Neighborhood.* Lake Claremont Press, 2002.

Endres, David J. *Many Tongues, One Faith: A History of Franciscan Parish Life in the United States.* Academy of American Franciscan History, 2018.

Esparza, Jesús Jesse. *Raza Schools: The Fight for Latino Educational Autonomy in a West Texas Borderlands Town.* University of Oklahoma Press, 2023.

Estrada, Hank. *UnHoly Communion: Lessons Learned from Life among Pedophiles, Predators, and Priests: Expanded Edition.* Red Rabbit Press, 2021.

Fisher, James T. *Communion of Immigrants: A History of Catholics in America.* Oxford University Press, 2002.

Fitzpatrick-Behrens, Susan. *The Maryknoll Catholic Mission in Peru, 1943–1989: Transnational Faith and Transformation.* University of Notre Dame Press, 2012.

Fitzpatrick-Behrens, Susan. "The Maya Catholic Cooperative Spirit of Capitalism in Guatemala: Civil-Religious Collaborations, 1943–1966." In *Local Church, Global Church: Catholic Activism in Latin America from Rerum Novarum to Vatican II,* edited by Stephen J. C. Andes and Julia G. Young. Catholic University of America Press, 2016.

Foley, Neil. *The White Scourge: Mexicans, Blacks, and Poor Whites in Texas Cotton Culture.* University of California Press, 1997.

Garcia, Angel. *The Kingdom Began in Puerto Rico: Neil Connolly's Priesthood in the South Bronx.* Fordham University Press, 2020.

García, Mario T. *Católicos: Resistance and Affirmation in Chicano Catholic History.* University of Texas Press, 2008.

García, Mario T. *Father Luis Olivares: A Biography.* University of North Carolina Press, 2018.

García Hernández, CMF, Pedro. *Crónica martirial: 271 Misioneros Claretianos Mártires 1936–39.* Publicaciones Claretianos, 2000.

Garcia, Richard A. *Rise of the Mexican American Middle Class: San Antonio, 1929–1941.* Texas A&M University Press, 1991.

Garcilazo, Jeffrey Marcos. *Traqueros: Mexican Railroad Workers in the United States 1870 to 1930.* University of North Texas Press, 2012.

Gomez, Pete. *Memoirs of a Seminarian*. Self-published, 2022.

González, Sergio M. *Strangers No Longer: Latino Belonging and Faith in Twentieth-Century Wisconsin*. University of Illinois Press, 2024.

Grandin, Greg. *Empire's Workshop: Latin America, the United States, and the Rise of the New Imperialism*, rev. ed. Picador, 2021.

Hartch, Todd. "Ivan Illich and Leo Mahon: Folk Religion and Catechesis in Latin America." *International Bulletin of Missionary Research* 36, no. 4 (2012): 185–188.

Hencier, John J. "A New Form of Parish Team Ministry in the Roman Catholic Church." PhD diss., San Francisco Theological Seminary, 1975.

Hendrickson, Brett. *Mexican American Religions: An Introduction*. Routledge, 2021.

Hernández Sandoval, Bonar. *Guatemala's Catholic Revolution: A History of Religious and Social Reform, 1920–1968*. University of Notre Dame Press, 2018.

Heyck, Denis Lynn Daly, ed. *Barrios and Borderlands: Cultures of Latinos and Latinas in the United States*. Routledge, 1994.

Hinojosa, Felipe. *Apostles of Change: Latino Radical Politics, Church Occupations, and the Fight to Save the Barrio*. University of Texas Press, 2021.

Hinojosa, Felipe, Maggie Elmore, and Sergio M. González. *Faith and Power: Latino Religious Politics Since 1945*. New York University Press, 2022.

Hinojosa, Gilberto. "Mexican-American Faith Communities in Texas and the Southwest." In *Mexican Americans and the Catholic Church, 1900–1964*, edited by Jay P. Dolan and Gilberto M. Hinojosa. University of Notre Dame Press, 1994.

Howe, James. *Chiefs, Scribes, and Ethnographers: Kuna Culture from Inside and Out*. University of Texas Press, 2009.

Hurteau, Robert. *A Worldwide Heart: The Life of Maryknoll Father John J. Considine*. Orbis Books, 2013.

Innis-Jiménez, Michael. *Steel Barrio: The Great Mexican Migration to South Chicago, 1915–1940*. New York University Press, 2013.

Jirasek, Rita Arias and Carlos Tortolero. *Mexican Chicago*. Arcadia, 2001.

Johnson, Benjamin Heber. *Revolution in Texas: How a Forgotten Rebellion and Its Bloody Suppression Turned Mexicans into Americans*. Yale University Press, 2005.

Kanter, Deborah E. "Faith and Family for Early Mexican Immigrants to Chicago: The Diary of Elidia Barroso." *Diálogo* 16, no. 1 (Spring 2013): 21–34.

Kanter, Deborah E. *Chicago Católico: Making Catholic Parishes Mexican*. University of Illinois Press, 2020.

Kuenster, John. *How Saint Jude Came to Chicago: The Story of Enduring Devotion to the Patron Saint of People Seeking Hope and Solace*. Claretian Publications, 2004.

Kyriakoudes, Louis M. *The Social Origins of the Urban South: Race, Gender, and Migration in Nashville and Middle Tennessee, 1890–1930*. University of North Carolina Press, 2003.

Lernoux, Penny, Arthur Jones, and Robert Ellsberg. *Hearts on Fire: The Story of the Maryknoll Sisters*. Centenary ed. Orbis Books, 2012.

Lindstrom, Lois Cunniff. *Shrine of St. Anne: A History, 1920–1995*. Published by the shrine, 1995.

Lopez, CMF, Severino. *El Poche: Memoirs of a Mexican American Padre*. Claretian Missionaries, 2004.

Lozano, Juan Maria. *Mystic and Man of Action, Saint Anthony Mary Claret: A Study in the Development of His Spiritual Experience and Doctrine*. Claretian Publications, 1977.

Lujano, John D. "A Social History of the Mexican-American Community of Hutchinson, Kansas." MA thesis, Emporia State University, 1996.

Macias Jr., John Joseph. "Of Spanish Myths and Mexican Realities: Social and Racial Development in San Gabriel, California, 1771–1971." PhD diss., Claremont Graduate University, 2012.

Magner, CMF, Dan. *Missionary Brothers: Anecdotal Stories from the Archives of the United States-Canada Province of the Claretian Missionaries*. Claretian Missionaries, 2023.

Mahon, Leo, with Nancy Davis. *Fire under My Feet: A Memoir of God's Power in Panama*. Orbis Books, 2007.

Markey, Eileen. *A Radical Faith: The Assassination of Sister Maura*. Nation Books, 2016.

Martin, Patricia Preciado. *Songs My Mother Sang to Me: An Oral History of Mexican American Women*. University of Arizona Press, 1992.

Martínez, Alexandra. "Relatos visuales misionales de los cuerpos indígenas: vergüenza y civilización en Chocó, Colombia 1909–1930." *Memoria y Sociedad* 21, no. 43 (2017): 66–85.

Martínez, Richard Edward. *PADRES: The National Chicano Priest Movement*. University of Texas Press, 2005.

Martínez-Serros, Hugo. *The Last Laugh and Other Stories*. Arte Público Press, 1988.

Matovina, Timothy. *Guadalupe and Her Faithful: Latino Catholics in San Antonio, from Colonial Origins to the Present*. Johns Hopkins University Press, 2005.

Matovina, Timothy. *Latino Catholicism: Transformation in America's Largest Church*. Princeton University Press, 2012.

Matovina, Timothy. "Natives and Newcomers: Ethnic Mexican Religious Convergences in 1920s San Antonio, Texas." *US Catholic Historian* 37 (Summer 2019): 1–18.

McCarthy, Malachy R. "Which Christ Came to Chicago: Catholic and Protestant Programs to Evangelize, Socialize, and Americanize the Mexican Immigrant, 1900–1940." PhD diss., Loyola University Chicago, 2002.

McCarthy, Malachy R., and Daniel E. Magner. *Claretians in America: A Pictorial History, 1902–2012*. Claretian Missionaries, 2015.

McCoyer, Michael. "Darkness of a Different Color: Mexicans and Racial Formation in Greater Chicago, 1916–1960." PhD diss., Northwestern University, 2007.

McDannell, Colleen. *Material Christianity: Religion and Popular Culture in America*. Yale University Press, 1995.

McDannell, Colleen. *The Spirit of Vatican II: A History of Catholic Reform in America*. Basic Books, 2011.

McGinnis, William C. *History of Perth Amboy New Jersey 1651–1958*. American Publishing Company, 1958.

McGreevy, John T. *American Jesuits and the World: How an Embattled Religious Order Made Modern Catholicism Global*. Princeton University Press, 2016.

McGuinness, Margaret M. and Jeffrey M. Burns, eds. *Preaching with Their Lives: Dominicans on Mission in the United States after 1850*. Fordham University Press, 2020.

McGuinness, Margaret M., and Thomas F. Rzeznik, eds. *The Cambridge Companion to American Catholicism*. Cambridge University Press, 2021.

Meeks, Eric V. *Border Citizens: The Making of Indians, Mexicans, and Anglos in Arizona*. University of Texas Press, 2007.

Miller, Char. *West Side Rising: How San Antonio's 1921 Flood Devastated a City and Sparked a Latino Environmental Justice Movement*. Trinity University Press, 2021.

Mirror of the Postulant. Missionary Sons of Immaculate Heart of Mary, 1926.

Montejano, David. *Anglos and Mexicans in the Making of Texas, 1836–1986*. University of Texas Press, 1987.

Moses, OP Donna Maria. "Afire with the Itinerant Spirit: Paradigm Shifts in the Foreign Missions." In *Preaching with Their Lives: Dominicans on Mission in the United States after 1850*, edited by Margaret M. McGuinness and Jeffrey M. Burns. Fordham University Press, 2020.

Muñoz Martinez, Monica. *The Injustice Never Leaves You: Anti-Mexican Violence in Texas*. Harvard University Press, 2018.

Nabhan-Warren, Kristy. *The Cursillo Movement in America: Catholics, Protestants, and Fourth-Day Spirituality*. University of North Carolina Press, 2013.

O'Malley, John W. *What Happened at Vatican II*. Harvard University Press, 2008.

Orozco, Cynthia E. *Pioneer of Mexican-American Civil Rights: Alonso S. Perales*. Arte Público Press, 2020.

Orsi, Robert A. *Thank You, Saint Jude: Women's Devotion to the Patron Saint of Hopeless Cases*. Yale University Press, 1998.

Osborne, Catherine R. *American Catholics and the Church of Tomorrow: Building Churches for the Future*. University of Chicago Press, 2018.

O'Toole, James M. *The Faithful: A History of Catholics in America*. Harvard University Press, 2008.

Paredes, Mario. *The History of the National Encuentros: Hispanic Americans in the One Catholic Church*. Paulist Press, 2014.

Pawel, Mariam. *The Crusades of Cesar Chavez: A Biography*. Bloomsbury Press, 2014.

Perez, Rueben M. *Laredito, the Forgotten Neighborhood West of San Pedro Creek/Laredito, El West Barrio Olvidado De San Pedro Creek*. Self-published, 2013.

Pfeifer, Michael J. *The Making of American Catholicism: Regional Culture and the Catholic Experience*. New York University Press, 2021.

Powers, J. F. *Morte D'Urban*. New York Review of Books, 2000.

Puig, Manuel María. *Los indios cunas de San Blas: su origen, tradiciónes, costumbres, organización social, cultura, y religión*. N.p., 1948.

Rabago, Roberto. *Rich Town, Poor Town: Ghosts of Copper's Past*. Copper Star, 2011.

Reynolds, Susan Bigelow. *People Get Ready: Ritual Solidarity and Lived Ecclesiology in Catholic Roxbury*. Fordham University Press, 2023.

Reynolds, Susan Bigelow. "'I Will Surely Have You Deported': Undocumenting Clergy Sexual Abuse in an Immigrant Community." *Religion and American Culture* 33, no. 1 (2023): 1–34.

Ribera, CMF, Raymond. *On the Threshold of the Religious Life: A Guide for Novices*, trans. Charles Fabing CMF. Claretian Major Seminary, 1938.

Rippinger, OSB, Joel. *The Benedictine Order in the United States: An Interpretive History*. The Order of St. Benedict, 1990.

Rodríguez, CMF, Plácido. "Cristero Witness, Emigrant, Claretian Bishop: Invited Remarks at the 2018 Annual Meeting of the Texas Catholic Historical Society." *Catholic Southwest* 29 (2018): 58–68.

Roy, Andy. *Live, Learn, Love: Experiences of My Life*. Lewis Printing Company, 1986.

Rzeznik, Thomas. "That '70s Catholicism: The View from Philadelphia." *American Catholic Studies* 134, no. 2 (Summer 2023): 77–94.

Sandell, David P. *Open Your Heart: Religion and Cultural Poetics of Greater Mexico*. University of Notre Dame Press, 2015.

San Miguel, Guadalupe. *In the Midst of Radicalism: Mexican American Moderates during the Chicano Movement 1960–1978*. University of Oklahoma Press, 2022.

Sargent, Daniel. *The Assignments of Antonio Claret*. Declan X. McMullen Company, 1948.

Seitz, John C. "Stoic Brothers and Feeling Men: Contemporary Clerical Masculinities in the United States." *American Catholic Studies* 132, no. 2 (Summer 2021): 15–21.

Sison, Antonio D., ed. *Deep Inculturation: Global Voices on Christian Faith and Indigenous Genius*. Orbis Books, 2024.

Strauss, Charles T. "Missionary Empire: American Catholics in Belize and Guatemala, 1941–1961." *American Catholic Studies* 130, no. 3 (Fall 2019): 1–36.

Tentler, Leslie Woodcock. *American Catholics: A History*. Yale University Press, 2020.

Thomas, Danny, with Bill Davidson. *Make Room for Danny*. G. P. Putnam's Sons, 1991.

Thompson, Thomas A. "The Cordimarian Spirituality of St. Anthony Mary Claret and the Claretians." *Marian Studies* 67, article 11 (2016): 337–358.

Treviño, Robert R. *The Church in the Barrio: Mexican American Ethno-Catholicism in Houston*. University of North Carolina Press, 2006.

Valerio Jiménez, Omar S. *River of Hope: Forging Identity and Nation in the Rio Grande Borderlands*. Duke University Press, 2013.

Wenzl, Tim. *Dodge City's Mexican Village: A Place in Time 1906–1956*. Self-published, 2022.

Wilson, Richard A. *Maya Resurgence in Guatemala: Q'eqchi' Experiences*. University of Oklahoma Press, 1995.

Wright-Rios, Edward. *Revolutions in Mexican Catholicism: Reform and Revelation in Oaxaca, 1887–1934*. Duke University Press, 2009.

Wright, Robert E. "Pioneer Religious Congregations of Men in Texas before 1900." *Journal of Texas Catholic History and Culture* 5 (1994): 65–90.

Wright, Robert E. "Mexican-Descent Catholics and the U.S. Church, 1880–1910: Moving Beyond Chicano Assumptions." *U.S. Catholic Historian* 28, no. 4 (2010): 73–97.

Young, Julia G. *Mexican Exodus: Emigrants, Exiles, and Refugees of the Cristero War*. Oxford University Press, 2015.

INDEX

Page numbers in italics indicate figures.

accompaniment, 46, 79, 132, 162, 163, 173
Adult Vocation Educational Center (AVE), 138, 155, 157
Adveniat and Catholic Relief, 121
Africa, 2, 13, 19, 22, 173
African Americans, 58, 94, 97
Afro-Garífuna people, 17, 116
Afro-Guatemalans, 116
Afro-Panamanians, 104–5
aggiornamento (updating), 17, *131*, 135–36
Aguiar, Victoriana, 52
Albergue San Óscar Romero, 167
Albuquerque, New Mexico, 37
Alcaria Santiago, María, 126
Allen, John, 172
Alliance for Progress, 128
altar boys, 48, 54, 76, 84
Alvarado, Robert, 48–49, 50, 51, 55–57, *56*, 79, 96, 109, 111, 128
Álvarez, Isabel, 1
Álvarez, Milton, 124, 197n45
American vocations, nuturing, 87–93
Americanization, 16, 38, 39, 50
Anales, 19
Andrés, Edmundo, 125–26, 127–28, *127*, 201n23
Anglo Catholics, 16–17, 30, 40, 59, 62–63, 65, 79, 98–99, 155; privileges of, 38–39, 95; racism and, 78, 152–53; recruitment of, 97; segregation and, 30; at seminaries, 95; St. Jude and, 86–87. *See also* Euro-American Catholics
Anglo-Irish province, 120
anti-Catholic attitudes, 15–16, 29–30, 31
anti-clerical movement, 26, 60–61, 83
anti-Mexican attitudes, 15–16, 29–30, 31

anti-war movement, 141, 157
Apostolate of Prayer (Apostolado de la Oración), 39, 52–53, 55, 69, 72, 73, 74
Aransas Pass, 27
Archconfraternity of the Immaculate Heart of Mary, 38, 53, 65
Archdiocesan Office for the Spanish Speaking, 99
Arizona, 21, 25, 36–42, 57, 81, 82, 90, 96–98, 153, 154, 164, 167, 183. *See also specific locations*
Arroyo Navarro, Luis Obdulio, 124
Arvada, Colorado, 140, 143–44, 155
Asia, 101, 173
Asians, 94
Asociación de Apostolados, 69, 72
Asunción Church (Perth Amboy, New Jersey), 68, 71
Atlixco, Mexico, 25
Atucha, John, 42
Austin, Texas, diocese of, 36

Bac, Pablo, 123–24
Barbastro, Spain, seminary at, 90, 194n41
Barcelona, Spain, 22
Barroso, Elidia, 49, 50, 57, 59
Bartlett, Richard, 97
Bartlett, Roger, 114, 116, 117–18, *117*, 119
Baton Rouge, Louisiana, 140, 141, 142
Bellevue, Washington, 155
Beltrán, Edgar, 120
Benet, José, 107–8
Berengueras, Joseph, 19, 21, 106–9, 110, 111; *El auxiliar del misionero de Darién*, 106–7; Guna-language grammar by, 109

Berg, Ralph, 144
Bianchi, Raymond, 70, 72, 74
bilingualism, 16, 63, 75, 76–100
birth control, 135, 142
Bishop, Robert, 130
Bossi, Louis, 2
bracero program, 151
Braun, Sr. Mary, 126
Briskey, Anthony, 114, 116, 117–18, *117*, 120
Brown, Len, 143
Brownsville, Texas, 27
Brualla, Medardo, 46
Brummel, Mark, 135
Buena Vista, Panama, 105
Bulletin of the Province of the East, 135
Butler, Matthew, 23
Byrne, Thomas Sebastien, 45

Caal, Emilio Ich, 125
Caal, Felipe Ich, 125
Cabrini, Frances Xavier, 193n17
California, 2, 26, 29, 37, 55, 57, 63, 77–78, 90, 98–99, 102, 105, 164–66; Guna people in, 109–12; provincial office in, 87–88; seminaries in, 94. *See also specific locations*
California State University, Fresno, 167
"Call to Assist Latin America," 17, 113
Calles, Plutarco Elías, 60–61
campus ministry, 140–41, 156–57, 163
Canadian Vice Province, 162
Cardinal's Committee for the Spanish Speaking in Chicago, 141
Carranza, Venustiano, 37
Carulla, José, 30–31
Casaldáliga, Pedro, 195n54
Catalina, Anthony, 63, 89
Catalonia, 27, 78
catechism, 22, 40–41, 107, 116, 166
catechists, 119–20, 121, 124, 125, 140
Cathedral of Our Lady of Guadalupe (Dodge City, Kansas), 44
Catholic Americanization, 16; spaces of, 48–75
Catholic Extension Society, 31, 43, 58, 59, 81, 148
Catholic Instructional League, 59

Catholic Inter-American Cooperation Program (CICOP), 113, 136, 197n38
Catholic University, 82, 96, 135, 142
Catholic Youth Organization, 63
Católicos por La Raza, 151–52, 154
Caxlanpom, Guatemala, 125
CELAM (Bogotá-based *Consejo Episcopal Latinoamericano*), 120
celibacy, 135, 168
Central America, 93, 122; growth of province in, 128; missionary efforts in, 17, 103–29. *See also specific countries*
Centro de Capitación (Campo de Dios), 120–22, 123, 124–25
Centro Intercultural de Documentación (CIDOC), 198n55
charism, 7, 131, 135, 153, 157, 159, 164, 170
Chavarría, Eduardo, 126–27
Chavez, Cesar, 152, 155, 203n73
Che, Luis, 126
Chen, Ralph (Rafael), 95, 197n27
Chicago, Illinois, 1, 3, 16, 18, 78, 87, 113–14, 154, 157, 161, 164, 166; Archdiocese of, 83, 113, 151; catechetical centers in, 59; highway construction and, 149–50; Latino Catholics in, 40, 49, 57–65, 97, 98–99, 105; Mexican colonias in, 59; as "Rome of American Catholicism," 58. *See also specific locations*
Chicago Católico, 151, 202n61
Chicago Police Department, 89, 91–92, s. *See also* St. Jude Police League
Chicano movement, 17, 18, 100, 131, 132, 152–56, 157, 203n73
Chile, 2, 22, 65, 98
Chinnici, Joseph, OFM, 168
Christ the King parish (Baton Rouge, Louisiana), 142
Christian base communities (known as *comunidades eclesiales de base* or *CEB*), 120
Christian Family Movement, 73
Chupampa, Panama, 111
church fires, 30–31, 47
Church of the Assumption (Perth Amboy, New Jersey), 65, 67
CIA (Central Intelligence Agency), 114, 128

citizenship, 16, 80
Ciudad Juárez, Mexico, 167
Claret, Anthony Mary (Antonio Maria), 1–2, 38, 49, 87, 101, 164; biography of, 81; canonization of, 2–4, 14–15, 78, 99; Catalan heritage of, 27; charism of, 164; legacy of, 4–7, 165; life of, 4–7, 52, 81; making a name for, 8; mandate to give preference in apostolates to the poor, 154; missionary drive of, 16, 47, 101, 102, 159; showcased in stained glass, 64, 158, 159, 164–65; sites associated with, 4; statues of, 42, 165; use of printing press, 84–85, 135
Claret Center (Chicago, Illinois), 140, 166, 201n26
Claret Center (Perth Amboy, New Jersey), 73
Claretian House of Studies, Washington, DC, 82
Claretian Missionaries, 1, 2n, 3, 3, 22; absence of Spanish leadership in, 100; benefactors of, 82; changes to formation program, 100, 138; charism and, 135, 153; communities in US, 15; creating refugios in, 29–36; embrace of renewal, 132–41; English language and, 99; first steps in Texas, 27–29; foreign-born clergy among, 171–73; at height of membership in mid-1960s, 18; history of, 19, 100; identity of, 153; image problem and, 136; importance of having houses in US, 46; inclusive, assimilationist expectations, 94; junior seminaries, 55, 94, 110; killed in Spanish Civil War, 90; leadership of, 13; learning English and building networks, 79–83; legacies of, 18, 165; making a name for, 8–13; mission of, 17–18, 153, 162; personnel shortages, 136, 137, 138, 140, 148, 157; purpose of congregation in US, 13–14; rapid rise and expansion in US, 13; rebranding of, 82; recorded history of, 19; reimagined mission of, 17–18; shifting sense of mission, 162; from Spain, 13–14, 14n41, 22, 27, 33, 44, 74, 78, 81, 82, 90, 93–94, 102–3, 105–6, 150; telling their story today, 13; today, 162, 163–67; unexpected role as parish priests, 16, 47; US-born and -educated, 93; vocation crisis at, 136, 137, 138, 140

Claretian Publications, 133–35, 140, 200n10. See also specific publications
Claretian Social Development Fund, 140
Claretians in America, 13
Clarke, Maura, MM, 123
clergy sex abuse, 19, 167–69, 191n44, 204n12, 204n19
CMF Eastern Province Newsletter, 135
Cody, Michael, 98, 136, 141–42, 157
Cold War, 9, 17, 102
Colegio Hispano-Mexicano, 22
Colombia, 110, 120
Colón, Panama, 104
colorism, 94
communications apostolate, 4–5, 84–85, 135, 161
Communism, spread of, 102, 113
community life, emphasis on, 144, 167
confraternities, 104–5. See also lay societies; specific groups
Congregation of the Missionary Sons of the Immaculate Heart of Mary, rebranding of, 82
conscientization, 120, 122, 124
Considine, John, MM, 114
Cordi-Marian sisters, 3, 3, 61, 130, 164
Corpus Christi, Texas, 27–28
Correa, José, 111
Correa, Juan, 197n27
cotton economy, 30, 31–32, 34, 46, 47
Cotulla, Texas, 34
Cristero War: Cristeros, 162; impact of, 60–61; refugees from, 51, 61
crónicas, 19
Cuban Revolution, 113
Cuellar, Leonard, 63, 95–96
Culley, Brian, 159
Curran, Charles E., 142
cursillos, 119, 120, 125, 132, 141, 156

Daley, Richard J., 85
Dallas, Oregon, 145, 146, 148
Darién, Panama, 103, 104–5, 108; mission in, 127
Database of the Accused, 168
Daube, Albert, 98–100, 191n40
Davies, Ibelele Nikkitiginya, 197n27

Davies, Juan Jose, 197n27
Dayton, Oregon, 147–48
De Prada, Joaquin, 2, 4
deaf, ministry to, 22
Del Amo Junior Seminary, 95, 110. *See also* Dominguez Seminary
Del Amo Seminary, 94, 95, 98
Delgado, Leslie, 197n27
Derilus, Beauplan, 161, 170, 172
Desfile Hispano Americano (Perth Amboy, New Jersey), 71–72
Día de San Juan, 67
Díaz, Porfirio, 22–23
Dielmann, Leo M. J., 51
disappeared persons (*los desaparecidos*), 125
Dodge City, Kansas, 37, 42–45, 46; diocese of, 44; limits of integration in, 47
Dominguez Seminary, 63, 77, 82, 94, 95, 96, 98, 110; language study at, 98; Mexican Americans in, 97–98; Missions Fair, 1949, 102
Dominicanos, 71, 73, 166
Dominicans, 57
Dominiguez family (benefactors), 82
Don Quijote newspaper, 38
Doran, Brian, 118, 119
Dot, Aloysius, 90
Drossaerts, Arthur, 48, 51
Dunne, Irene, 1
DuPont Engineering Company, 45
Durango, Mexico, 36

East Los Angeles City College, 141
eastern province, 140, 162, 197n34, 200n4, 202n50; Chicano movement and, 153–54; first chapter meeting in 1968, 136; Latino Catholics and, 153–54
ecumenism, 140–48
Egan, Marie, 118, 122, 125, 126
Eighth Day Center for Justice, 140
El Estor, Guatemala, 118, 122, 123, 124, 125, 126, 127
El Paso, Texas, 28–29, 37, 96, 149, 164, 202n54
El Salvador, 123, 147
Elizondo, Matilde, 55
Ellacuria, Aloysius, 89

Elorz, Honorato, 41
Encuentros, 157
England, 2, 120
English language, 16, 44, 100; Claretian Missionaries and, 99; directives to use, 99; need for clergy proficient in, 80–81, 93, 99, 171; publications in, 97–98; study of, 27, 30, 78, 79–83
Equatorial Guinea, 22
Erice, Jesús, 109–10, 111
Estrada, Richard, 155
ethnic diversity, 29, 95, 97
ethnocentrism, 24–25, 106
ethno-racial subordination, 73, 77
eucharistic devotions, 157
Euro-American Catholics, 29, 44, 61, 62–63, 67, 84, 91, 93; decline of parishes for, 72; integration and, 145–46; privileges of, 95; racism and, 152–54; at seminaries, 95; at St. Jude Seminary, 93–94. *See also* Anglo Catholics

Fairfax, Virginia, 93, 154
farmworkers, 14, 18, 34, 36, 67, 145, 147, 165. *See also* United Farm Workers (UFW)
Fátima, Portugal, 4
Fatima League, 67
Fatima Social Center (Perth Amboy, New Jersey), 67
Feast of the Immaculate Heart of Mary, 91–92
Felipe de Jesús, San, 64
female religious, 119–20, 122, 140, 147. *See also specific groups*
Fichter, John SJ, 135
Figueroa, William, 197n27
Fitzpatrick-Behrens, Susan, 116
Flores, Gerardo, 127
Flores, Elena, 2
Flynn, James J., 72
For Heaven's Sake, 93
Ford, Ita, MM, 123
foreign missionary work, 96, 101–29, 140. *See also specific countries*
Forest, John, 28, 29, 50
formation program, changes to, 100, 138
Fort Worth, Texas, 164
Franciscan Missionary Sisters, 109

Franciscans, 102, 106, 124
Franco, Francisco, 4
Freire, Paulo, 120
Fresno, California, 165–66
Frison, Basil, 133, 200n6
Fuentes, Teodomiro "Theo," 172

Gamm, Joseph, 145, 146, 201n40, 201n43
García, Mario, 95, 151
García, Miguel, 57
Garífuna language, 197n45
genocide, 125
Georgia, 78, 167
Gete Nebreda, Antimio, 43, 44
global Claretian congregation, 36, 171
Gonzales, Henry B., 99
González, María Elena, RSM, 118
Govea, Pauline, 99
Grainer, Eugene, 78, 113–14, 116, 133, 135, 136, 141, 142, 153, 197n38
Gramaje, Art, 166
Granjon, Henry, 36–37, 79
Great Depression, 41, 53–54, 57, 63, 84, 85, 86, 93
Great White Fleet, 105
Greene, Bob, 134
Griffin, William, 65, 66
Grupo de Oración Carismático, 69
Guadalajara, Mexico, 96
Guanajuato, Mexico, 22, 23, 37, 49
Guardian Angel parish (El Paso, Texas), 96, 202n54
Guatemala, 18, 115, 127; building an equipo pastoral in, 118–22; future church for, 126–28; la Violencia in, 123–26; missions in, 17, 102, 112–18, 115, 117, 128–29, 136, 140, 141, 144, 154, 157, 197n41, 197n45, 202n50; pastoral teams in, 123; repression in, 123, 125–26
Guayanilla Social Club, 71
Guerrero, Mexico, 25
Guna language, 106, 107, 109
Guna people, 103–12, 128, 196n7; in California, 109–12; ordination of, 197n27
Guna Yala, 103–12

Hacienda del Lobo, 24
Handly, John, CSP, 43–44

Hebbronville, Texas, 27
Hennessy, John, 43
Herguth, Robert, 168–69
Hernández, Carmen, 1–2
Hernández, Hilario, 44
Herrera, Henry (Enrique), 95–97, 146–47, 148, 156, 156, 195n61
Herricks, Sister Ida, OSB, 118, 120, 125
Hijas de María, 31, 49, 52, 53, 73
Hijos de Altagracia, 73
Hinojosa, Gilberto, 29, 47
Hispanic Catholics. See Latino Catholics
Hispanic Ministry Resource Center, 163
Holy Family Catholic Church (Jerome, Arizona), 36–42
Holy Name Society, 60, 61, 65, 67, 71–72, 73, 156
homosexuality, 134, 155
Hotel Santa Lucia, 3
Humanae Vitae, 142
Hutchinson, Kansas, 44

icons, 73. See also specific icons
Illich, Ivan, 128, 198n55
Illinois, 26, 87–90, 93, 94, 98, 105, 166. See also specific locations
Immaculate Heart of Mary, 4, 12, 24, 25, 32, 38–39, 54, 64, 84, 91, 134, 159
Immaculate Heart of Mary Church (San Antonio, Texas), 31, 48, 49, 50–57, 55, 74, 95, 163–64, 167; highway construction and, 149; ushers of, 53–54, 55
Immaculate Heart of Mary Church (Martindale, Texas), 32–34, 32, 33, 164; re-dedication of, 33
Immaculate Heart of Mary Mission (Perth Amboy, New Jersey), 65–75
Immaculate Heart of Mary School (Martindale, Texas), 33
Immaculate Heart of Mary School (San Antonio, Texas), 48, 54
immigrants: undocumented, 14, 151. See also Mexican immigrants
Immigration and Naturalization Services (INS), 151
immigration policy, 18, 151

inculturation, 162, 167
India, 19, 113, 161, 171
indigenous people, 17, 24, 121; denigration of, 25, 106; ordination of, 127
influenza pandemic, 45
integration: avoidance of, 47; in rural parishes, 146; in seminaries, 93–98
intercultural province, nurturing, 169–73
International Eucharistic Congress, 60
International Institute, 38
Ireland, 155
Irish Catholics, 59, 71, 83, 97
IWW (Wobblies), 39
Izabal, Guatemala, 114, 116–19, 121, 123–24; Diocese of, 115; martyrs of, 125

Jacona, Michoacán, Mexico, 61
Japan, 101
Jerome, Arizona, 36–42; limits of integration in, 47; strikes in, 39
Jersey City, New Jersey, 167
Jesuits, 50, 59, 101, 102, 114
Jim Crow, 30
Jogues, Isaac, 102
John F. Kennedy Farming Co-op, 116
John the Evangelist, St., 159
John XXIII, Pope, 159
Johnson, Lyndon B., 34
Joliet, Illinois, Diocese, 88
Juan Diego, 41, 64, 165
Jude Thaddeus, St., 62–63, 84–85, 85, 133
The Judean, 90
Juventud Sanblaseña, 111

Kairouz, Amos Muzyad Yaqoob, 85. See also Thomas, Danny
Kane, William, 57
Kansas, 21, 42–45
Kazel, Dorothy, OSU, 123
Kennard, Francis, 201n40
Kenneally, Martin, 85
Kennedy, James (Ned), 120
Kennedy, John F., Jr., 71, 116
Kirk, Marty, 144
Knights of Columbus, 60, 62, 65–66
Kolb, Edward, 109
Kyle, Texas, 30, 31

La Asunción Church (Perth Amboy, New Jersey), 69. See also Church of the Assumption
La Esperanza magazine, 26, 97, 107
La Placita Church (Los Angeles, California), 11, 81, 105
La Providencia (Our Lady of Providence), 68, 73, 167
La Trinidad Methodist Church (San Antonio, Texas), 51
laity, 13–14, 126; lay catechists, 119–20, 121, 124, 125, 140; lay pilgrims, 3, 3, 4; lay societies, 39, 52–53, 62, 65, 69 (see also specific societies); lay volunteers, 63–64, 84, 118–19, 122, 123, 140; training of lay leaders, 119
language skills, 16, 80, 98, 154, 167. See also specific languages
Laredito, 48, 50–57
Laredo, Texas, 28
Larraona, Arcadio, 133, 200n6
Latin America, 19, 101, 103–29. See also specific countries
Latin American Bureau, 114
Latin American Center (Perth Amboy, New Jersey), 65
Latin American Heritage Banquet, 72
Latino Catholics, 13–14, 18, 49–50, 99, 145–48, 150, 159, 161–63; accompaniment of, 162; Chicano movement and, 151–56, 157; devotions among, 16; in ministry, 56–57, 56, 152–55; second-class status of, 152–54
Lawler, Louis, CM, 98
Leatham, Gerald, 120
Lenten observance, 24, 34
León, Mexico, 22
León, Modesto, 145, 146
Lepage, Rene, 196n2
Lettau, Edward, 117, 134
Leuver, Robert, 114, 133
liberation theology, 102, 118, 120, 124, 136, 141, 147
Liga Protectora Latina, 39
linguistic diversity, 19, 46–47, 73, 171
Livingston, Guatemala, 116, 123, 124, 197n45
Lockhart, Texas, 34
Loggins, Kenny, 96

Long Island, New York, 132, 154
Lopez, Severino, 2, 3, *3*, 64, 65, 76–79, 82–83, 84, 94–96, 153, 194n41
Los Angeles, California, 1, 18, 28, 61, 82, 84, 96, 98, 149, 151–52, 155, 164
Louisiana State University, 140–41, 142–43, 154, 156–57
Lourdes, France, 4
Luisilla, Mariano, 27–28, 79
LULAC (League of United Latin American Citizens), 55
Luna, Constantino, OFM, 114, 116

Maíztegui, Juan José, 98, 103
Mano Blanco, 123
Marian devotions, 157. *See also* Our Lady of Guadalupe; Immaculate Heart of Mary
Marrero, Linda, 72
Martens, John, 143
Martín, Inocencio, 33, *33*, 34, 46, 164
Martin, James SJ, 162
Martindale, Texas, *32*, *33*, 34, 46, 84, 163–64; church fire in, 30–31; new church built in, 31–32
Martínez, Richard, 152
Martínez, Rosana, 34
martyrs, 90, 102, 123-26
Maruzzo, Tulio, 124
Maryknoll Center, 116, 120
Maryknolls, 101, 114, 141, 197n41
Mass: attendance at, 38, 39; concelebrated, 143; livestreamed, 18; in Spanish, 161
Matin, Thomas, 66, 67–69, *68*, 72, 74, 97, 146, 192n52
Mayan people, 120
McCarthy, Malachy, 62
McDannell, Colleen, 131
McMahon, Franklin, 134
McPolin, Patrick, 3, 88, 93, 97, 153
Melkonyan, Kristen, 200n10
Methodists, 51
Mexican American Catholic College (MACC), 140, 153, 155
Mexican American Cultural Center, 140
Mexican Americans, 17, 30, 33, 47, 79, 105, 154, 163; as clergy, 56–57, *56*, 152–54; in seminaries, 94–96, 97–98. *See also* Mexican immigrants
Mexican Catholicism, 25–26, 31, 59
Mexican immigrants, 15–16, 49, 83, 145–48, 150, 152–54, 162–63, 164; accompaniment of, 21–47, 162; ethno-racial subordination and, 73, 77, 78; extralegal violence against, 30; migration *al norte*, 26; as minority in Chicago, 57–58; in Texas, 26, 27–29
Mexican independence celebration, 41
Mexican Revolution, 26, 49, 51
"Mexican Village," 42, 44, 45
mexicanismos, 25
Mexico, 13, 102, 119; anti-clerical movement in, 60–61, 83; Claretian Missionaries in, 22–26; farmworkers from, 18; missions in, 22–26; modernization in, 26; as mother province until 1922, 25; Porfiriato in, 22–23, 26, 47; refugees from, 57; rural areas of, 24–25. *See also specific locations*
Mexico City, Mexico, 22
Michoacán, Mexico, 37
Milwaukee, Wisconsin, 59
miners, 36–42; hardships of, 37–38; politics and, 39
mining industry, 36–42, 47
mini-parishes, 143
Mischke, Walter, 72, 88
mission, 17–18, 153, 162; embodiment of, 14; race and, 78; re-imagining in wake of Vatican II, 130–59
Mission Claret (Misión Claret), 145, 146–48
Missionary Oblates of Mary Immaculate, 47, 50, 163
Missionary Sons of the Immaculate Heart of Mary, 2. *See also* Claretian Missionaries
mission in reverse, 173
Missouri, 167
Momence, Illinois, 87–93, *88*, 97
Monasterio, León, 45–46
Montero, Laurencio, 110
Monterrey, Mexico, 22
Montoya, Michael, 96
Moran, Thomas ("Don"), 118, 126
Mucú, Felipe Caal, 124–25
Mucú, Mercedes, 125

Mundelein, George, 57, 58–59, 62, 84, 88, 193n17
Mundelein Seminary, 60, 87
Muñoz, Fortunato, 106
Muñoz Marín, Luis, 66

Narganá, Panama, 103–12
Nashville, Tennessee, 45–46
National Conference of Catholic Bishops, 155
National Shrine of St. Jude (Chicago, Illinois), 2, 85–87, 105, 140, 161
Navarro School, 48
"Negro Village," 45
Neruda, Pablo, 105
networks, building, 79–83, 172
New Jersey, 40, 154, 166, 167, 191n44
New Orleans, Archbishop of, 45
New York, New York, 67, 83
Newman, California, 81
Newman, Chris, 124, 125
Newman Centers, 136, 141, 167
Newman Club, 99
Nigeria, 140, 171, 183
Nixon, Richard, 123, 128
Nuestra Señora de Fatima parish. *See* Our Lady of Fatima (Perth Amboy, New Jersey)
Nuestra Señora de la Esperanza, 61

Oblates. *See* Missionary Oblates of Mary Immaculate
O'Gara, James, 135–36
The Old Hickory News, 45–46
Old Hickory Powder Plant, 45–46
Olivares, Damaso, 52, 53–55, 99
Olivares, Henry, 95, 99
Olivares, Louis (Luis), 95, 99, 138, 149, 151–52, 154–55, 157
Olivares family, 52
O'Malley, John, SJ, 131
Oregon, 18, 96, 140, 145, 146–48
Orengo, Nicholas, 70
Orsi, Robert, 84
Ospino, Hosffman, 203n5, 204n19
O'Toole, James, 13
Our Lady of Divine Providence, 162

Our Lady of Fatima Church (Perth Amboy, New Jersey), 18, 49, 65–75, 161, 166–67; CCD program, 73; dedication of, 72; highway construction and, 149
Our Lady of Guadalupe, 25–26, 30, 38–39, 41, 146, 156, 164, 167
Our Lady of Guadalupe Church (Chicago, Illinois), 49, 57–65, 76–78, 84, 85, 90, 112, 157, 161, 168–69
Our Lady of Guadalupe Church (Dodge City, Kansas), 44
Our Lady of Guadalupe parish (San Marcos, Texas), fire at, 30
Our Lady of Guadalupe School (Chicago, Illinois), 64
Our Lady of Solitude Church (Los Angeles, California), 146, 149, 152, 154, 155

PADRES (Padres Asociados para Derechos Religiosos, Educativos, y Sociales or "Priests Associated for Religious, Education, and Social Rights"), 152–53, 154
pamphlets, 76, 84, 134–35, 200n10
Panama, 17, 96, 98, 101, 102, 113; becomes independent province, 111; Claretian residences in, *103*; missions in, 17, 102, 103–12, 119, 128–29, 197n27; Preciado in, *104*; proposed seminary in, 110–11. *See also specific locations*
Panama City, Panama, 104
Panzós massacre, 123
parish service, devotion to, 149, 167
parishes: debates about administration of, 149–52; highway construction and, 18, 149–50; today, 162, 163–67; urban renewal and, 18. *See also specific parishes*
pastoral teams, 118–22, 123, 143, 147
Peace Corps, 134, 141
Peplansky, Joseph, 141, 157
Perales, Alonso, 55, 78, 99
personnel issues, 136, 138, 140, 148, 157
Perth Amboy, New Jersey, 16, 49–50, *68*, 113, 126, 149, 161, 166–67, 191n44, 192n52, 192n54; clashes between Puerto Ricans and police in, 69–70; Desfile Hispano Americano (Perth Amboy, New Jersey), 71–72; Hall Avenue riots in, 70, 192n55;

Latino community in, 65–75; pan-Latino parish in, 16, 65–75
Philippines, 13, 96, 101, 102, 140, 146, 147
Phoenix, Arizona, 77, 96–97, 105, 164, 188n49
Pius XII, Pope, 1–2, 201n22
Plancarte y Labastida, Antonio, 22
Poles, 65, 71, 72
Police Branch, 92, 194n46. *See also* St. Jude Police League
Pomés, Jerónimo, 24
Porfiriato, 22–23, 26, 47
Portland, Oregon, 148, 201n40
Portugal, 2, 4, 81
Portuguese, 65, 66, 81–82
Preciado, Joseph, 55, 89, 96, 103–4, *104*, 105, 111, 128
Prescott, Arizona, 36, 37, 39–40, 47, 59, 167
printing press, 84–85
processions, 24, 34, 41, 53, 54–55, 61–62, 85, 90, 102, 104–5, 147
protest movements, 141–42, 157
Protestants, 26, 29, 30, 31, 73, 107, 109, 190n8
the Provincial, 87
Provincial Bulletin, 11,19, 135, 181
Provincial Chapter, meeting of, *81*, 100
Provincial House, Los Angeles, 155
Provincial House, Oak Park, 18, 114, 135–36
Puebla, Mexico, 22, 25
Puerto Barrios, Guatemala, 119, 123
Puerto Rican nationalists, 66
Puerto Rican Community Council (Perth Amboy, New Jersey), 71
Puerto Ricans, 49–50, 66–69, 150, 154, 162–63, 166
Puerto Rico, 66, 114, 119
Puig, Manuel, 111, 112
Puigvi, Joseph, 89

Q'eqchi' speakers, 119, 121, 122, 126, 198n48
Québec, Canada, 167
Quebedeaux, Carl, 124, 143
Querétaro, Mexico, 24

Rabago Roberto, 37–38
race, 13–14; emergence of US province and, 76–100; mission and, 78; at St. Jude

Seminary (Momence, Illinois), 93–100; in United States, 78
racism, 25, 46, 77, 78, 152–53
railyards, 42–45, 59
Reardon, Patrick, 93, 97
recruitment, 16–17; advertisements for, 138, *139*; of Anglo Catholics, 97; of youth, 16–17
Redemptorists, 98, 101
refugios, 30; creating, 29–36; spaces of Catholic Americanization and, 48–75
relics, 2, 4, 11
Rementeria, José, 24
renewal, embrace of, 132–41
Resa, Andres, 28–29
Reyes, Francisco Javier, 163
Reynolds, Susan Bigelow, 169
Río Azúcar, Panama, 107
Ripero, Sebastián, 59
Rodríguez, Peter, 150–51, 152, 153, 157, 202n61
Rodríguez, Plácido, 97, 98, 162
Román, Antonio, 107–8
Rome, 1–3, 13; canonization of Claret in, 2–4
Romeo, Domingo, 37
Romero, Óscar, 123
rosary, 24, 27, 33, 34, 40, 42
Roy, Andrew, 66–67, 72, 168, 191n44, 192n48
Royko, Mike, 134
rural missions, 24–25, 31, 145–47
Ryan, Ed, 141–42
Rynne, Xavier, 135

Sacred Heart, devotion to, 52–53, 54, 61,162, 190n11
Sacred Heart Church (Dodge City, Kansas), 42–43, 44
Sacred Heart Church (Prescott, Arizona), 39
Salem, Oregon, 147
Sam Cabnal, Manuel de Jesús, 127
San Antonio, Texas, 1, 16, 18, 34, 46, *56*, 61, 105, 130, 143, 151, 166; Diocese of, 36; highway construction in, 149; Mexican immigrants in, 28, 29–30, 36, 37, 48–49, 50–57; PADRES meeting in, 153–54; Spanish-speaking parishes in, 28, 29–30, 36, 37, 48–49, 50–57, 95–96, 99
San Blas, Panama, 102, 103–12

San Fernando Cathedral (San Antonio, Texas), 29, 49, 50, 99

San Fernando Cemetery #2, 18

San Gabriel Mission High School, 96, 146

San Gabriel Mission (San Gabriel, California), 18, 81, 161, 166, 167, 171

San Juan Bautista mission (Lakehurst, New Jersey), 68

San Juan, Puerto Rico, 66

San Luis Gonzaga society ("Luises"), 52, 53

San Marcos, Texas, 30, 33, 34, 36, 80, 130–31, 157–59, *158*

San Miguelito, Panama, 113, 119

San Pedro church (Guatemala), 126-27

sanctuary movement, 151–52

Santa Cecilia Club, 41

Santiago de Xitumul, Andrea, 122

Santo Nombre, 55, 72,156. *See* Holy Name Society

Santo Tomás, Guatemala, 116, 120, 121, 123, 125, 126, *127*

Santuario de Nuestra Señora de Dolores de Soriano, 24

Sanz, Martin, 87

Scalibrinians, 80

Schedlo, Antona, FSPA, 147

schools, 22, 33, 38, 43, 48, 54, 64, 96, 109. *See also specific schools*

Second Vatican Council, 17–18, 72–73, 100, 112, 118, 120, 131, 136, 157; Claretians at, 133; Communication decree, 135; impact of, 143, 156–59, 200n6; re-imagining mission in wake of, 130–59; spirit of, 136

segregation, 30, 39, 40–41, 47, 78

Seguin, Texas, 34

self-sacrifice, 21, 23, 46, 78, 102, 114, 172

Selva del Campo. Spain, 90

seminaries, 79, 98; African Americans at, 97; closure of, 136, 138; colorism and, 94; directives to use English, 99; Euro-American Catholics at, 95; foreign missionary work and, 101; integration in, 93–98; junior seminaries, 55, 94, 110; language study at, 98; Mexican Americans at, 94–98; no-Spanish policy at, 94–95; racism at, 77; retention issues at, 94; Spanish language not emphasized in, 98; training after Vatican II, 132. *See also specific seminaries*

Serra, Junípero, 102

Serrano, Jesús, 108–9, 111

Serrano, Rafael, 42–43, 44

Simon, Sr. Miriam, 126

Slovak Catholics, 65, 191n45

social justice, 119, 126, 129, 132, 140, 141, 145, 150–51, 157

Soledad parish (Los Angeles). *See* Our Lady of Solitude Church (Los Angeles, California)

Solemnity of St. Anthony Mary Claret, 169

South America, 13, 106. *See also specific countries*

Spain, 13–14, 22, 27, 90, 105, 194n41

Spanish Caribbean, 50

Spanish Civil War, 90, 194n41

Spanish language, 14, 16, 17, 44, 49, 63, 99, 100; learning, 171–72; need for knowledge of, 46–47, 79, 146, 154, 171; not emphasized in seminaries, 98; Spanish-speaking ministry, 99; at St. Jude Seminary, 97. *See also* Spanish-speaking parishes

Spanish-speaking parishes, 65, 77–78, 79, 99, 141, 154, 159, 161, 163, 165–66, 167; in Chicago, Illinois, 57–65, 97; differences in dialect, 172; emergence of, 48–75; no-Spanish policy at seminaries and, 94–95; in Oregon, 145–48; in Perth Amboy, New Jersey, 67–75; in San Antonio, Texas, 50–57

Special Operations Research Office, 111–12

Springfield, Missouri, 167

St. Anne Catholic Church (Arvada, Colorado), 143–44

St. Anthony Claret mission (Lakewood, New Jersey), 68

St. Anthony Mary Claret Church (Fresno, California), 9, 165–66

St. Francis of Assisi Church (Chicago, Illinois), 49, 59–60, 90, 97, 112, 149–51

St. John the Evangelist Church (San Marcos, Texas), 130–31, 146, 157–59, *158*

St. Jude, 133. See also *The Voice of St. Jude*

St. Jude devotion, 16, 61, 62–63, 64, 83, 93, 113, 161; directives to use English, 99; promotion of, 83–87

St. Jude League, 65, 84–85, 92. *See also* St. Jude Police League

St. Jude Police League, 16, 77, 84–85, 88–91, 133, 194n46

St. Jude Seminary (Momence, Illinois), 83, 87–93, *88*, *91*, 98–99, 112, 114, 141, 194n46; 1969 assembly at, 136; advertisements for, 97–98; closure and sale of, 136, 140; ethnic diversity at, 97; falling enrollment at, 136; language study at, 98; Latinos enrolled at, 97–98; library of, 135; mothers' club, 91; race at, 93–100; Spanish language at, 97

St. Louis, Missouri, 83

St. Louis University, 138

St. Martin de Porres Church (Dayton, Oregon), 148

St. Mary of the Lake University, 169–70

St. Monica's mission (Cassville, New Jersey), 68

St. Peter Chapel Car, 43

St. Peter's Basilica, 1

St. Vincent DePaul Society, 62, 63

stained glass windows, 53, 64, *158*, 159, 164–65

Stations of the Cross, 31, 32, 164, 165

The Stepping Stone, 90, 97

Stone Mountain, Georgia, 167

Stritch, Samuel 86

Sugrañes, Eugenio, 80–81, *81*, 93, 187n26

surnames, anglicization of, 78, 80

Tejanos, 29, 30, 34, 51, 63, 146

Tennessee, 21, 45–46

Tentler, Leslie Woodcock, 157

Tepeyac, Mexico, 26

Texas, 2, 21, 25–28, 37, 43, 47, 78–80, 87, 90, 99, 105, 161, 164, 166; anti-Catholic attitudes in, 29–30, 31; anti-Mexican attitudes in, 29–30, 31; Claretian houses and mission churches in, 35; creating *refugios* in, 29–36; first steps in, 27–29. *See also specific locations*

Texas State University, 140–41

Therese de Lisieux, St., 84, 159

Thomas, Danny, 85–86, 133

Time magazine, 114

Todd, Richard, 78, 101, 102, 113, 119, 120, 121, 123, 126, 128, 198n55; "Claretians are Missionaries," 102; Guatemala and, 112, 118

Toluca, Mexico, 22

Torrente, Camilo, 24–25, 27–28, 37, 47, 79–80

Tort, James, 39–40, 48, 49, 64, 76, 80, 83, 86–87, 93, 98, 133, 193n21, 194n41; advocacy for Spanish speakers, 65–66, 73–74; Preciado and, 104–5; processions and, 61–62; scouting locations for seminary, 87–88; St. Jude League and, 92; unorthodox methods of church-building, 59; use of printing press, 84–85

Tracy, Robert, 141

traqueros, 42–45

Treviño, Richard, 96, 152

Tule Rebellion, 109

Turon, Luis, 73

Uhland, Texas, 30, 31

Ukrainian Catholics, 65, 67, 71

United Farm Workers (UFW), 140, 152, 155, 203n73

United Fruit Company, 105, 114

United Neighborhood Organization (UNO), 140

United States, 2; Claretian communities of, 15; emergence of province in, 76–100 (*see also* United States Province); imperialism of, 128–29; importance of having houses in, 46; as "mission country," 21; race in, 78; racial stratification in, 47

United States Agency for International Development (USAID), 121

United States Province, 162; becomes USA-Canada Province, 169–73; division of, 197n34, 200n4; eastern province, 136, 140, 153–54, 162, 197n34, 200n4, 202n50; emergence of, 76–100; as intercultural province, 169–73; western province, 138, 140, 143, 144–45, 153, 154, 155, 162, 197n34, 200n4

United Verde Mining Company, 36, 39, 188n57

University of Illinois, Chicago, 149

University of San Francisco (later Graduate Theological Union), 138
urban parishes, building of, 48–75
urban renewal, 149
urban uprisings, 69–70
Urrabazo, Rosendo, 130–31, *131*, 145–46, 148, 155, 159
US Army, 111–12
U.S. Catholic, 93, 112, 133–34, 136, 138, *139*, 161
US imperialism, 17, 101–29
USA-Canada Province: building connections across, 172; internationally diverse community of, 169–73

Valerio-Jiménez, Omar, 29
Vallvé, Arturo, 43
Vancouver, British Columbia, Canada, 167
Vatican, 21, 113, 125
Vatican II. *See* Second Vatican Council
Vattamattam, Mathew, 171
Velez, Chuito, 72
Veracruz, Mexico, 23
Verdaguer, Peter, 27, 186n15
Vietnam, 19, 134, 141, 161
Villanueva, Robert, 143, 144
Villareal, Manuela E., 52
Virgin Mary, 64. *See also specific devotions*
Virgin of Guadalupe, 32, 39, 40, 43, 61, 64, 73, 84, 159, 162, 163, 165; procession honoring, 54–55
vocation crisis, 136, *137*, 138
Vogt, Dan, 126
The Voice of St. Jude, 3, 85, 86, 97, 103, 104, 105, 133. See also *U.S. Catholic*

Waukegan, Illinois, 59
western province, 138, 140, 143, 144–45, 162, 197n34, 200n4; Anglo Catholics and, 155; Chicano movement and, 153, 154; culturally relevant change in, 155
White, Br. Richard, 118
white American Catholics, 14
Wichita, Kansas, 43, 46
Wilga, Br. Richard, 118
Willamette Valley, Oregon, 145
women, 31, 38, 40, 52–54, 57, 69, 84, 119, 121, 122, 141
worker-priests, 142
Workers' Rights Project, 140
"A World to Win," 101–2
World War I, 36–37, 39

Yat, Ricardo, 125
Young, Julia, 61
Young Catholic Workers (JOC), 150
Young Christian Students, 73
Young Men's Christian Association (YMCA), 45
Young Women's Christian Association (YWCA), 38, 45
youth, recruitment of, 16–17
Yuma, Arizona, 81, 98, 164, 188n49

Zacatecas, Mexico, 23, 24
Zalvídar, Domingo, 57, 80, 81–83, *81*, 93, 193n17
Zenith factories, 150–51
Zettler, F.X., 64
Zimmerman, Greg, 114, 116, 117–18, *117*, 120

ABOUT THE AUTHOR

DEBORAH E. KANTER is Professor Emeritus of History at Albion College. She is the author of *Chicago Católico: Making Catholic Parishes Mexican*, and *Hijos del Pueblo: Gender, Family, and Community in Rural Mexico, 1730–1850*.